BICYCLE
TOURING
IN
EUROPE

Pantheon Books
New York

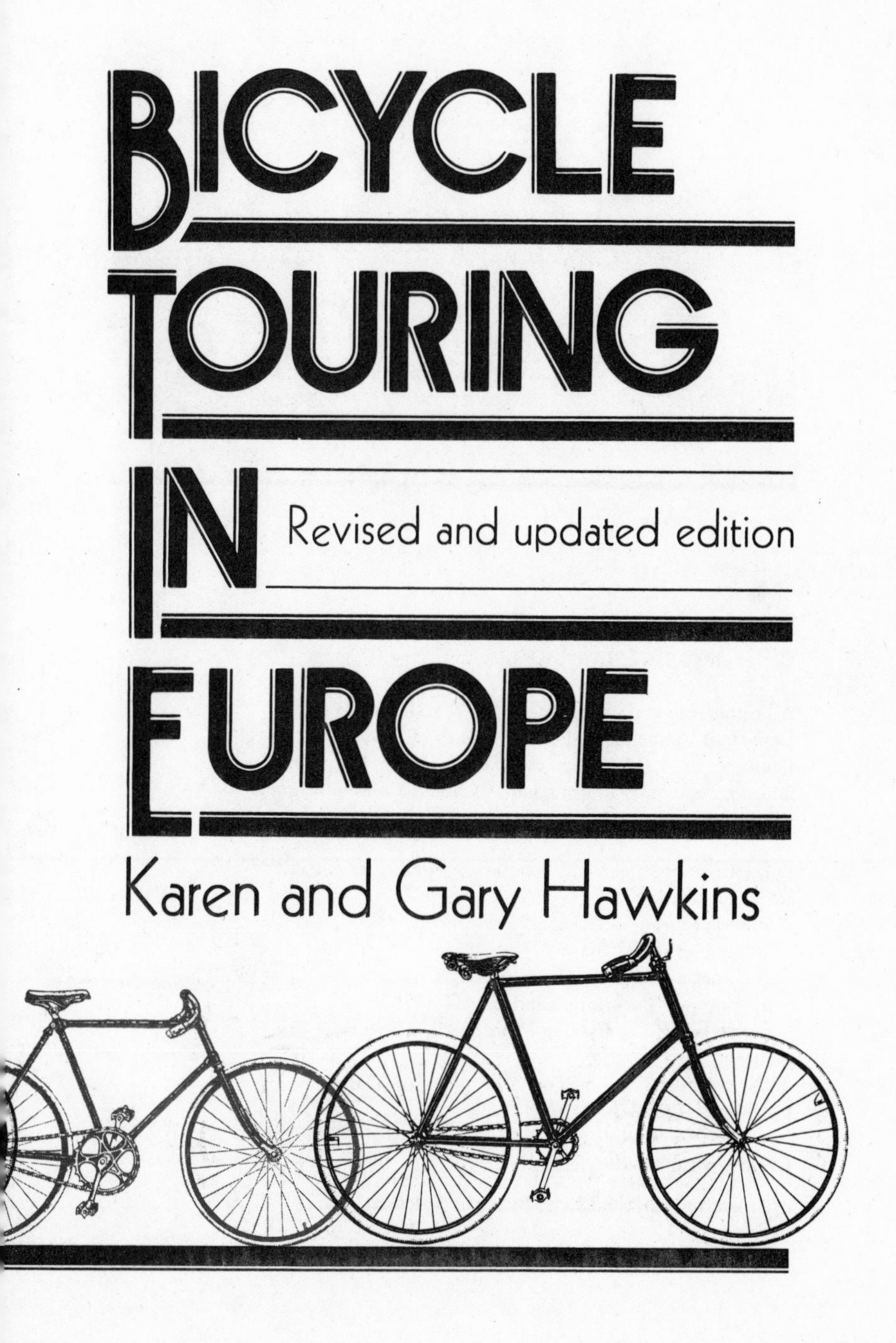

# BICYCLE TOURING IN EUROPE

Revised and updated edition

Karen and Gary Hawkins

For Benjamin

 Published in the United States by Pantheon Books, a division of Random House, Inc., New York, and simultaneously in Canada by Random House of Canada Limited, Toronto.

LIBRARY OF CONGRESS CATALOGING IN PUBLICATION DATA
Hawkins, Karen.
Bicycle touring in Europe.
Bibliography: p.
Includes index.
1. Europe—Description and travel—1971-
—Guide-books. 2. Cycling—Europe. I. Hawkins, Gary, joint author. II. Title.
D909.H394 1980 914'.04'55 79-3316
ISBN 0-394-73852-7

Design by Susan Mitchell

Manufactured in the United States of America
987654

# Contents

| | | |
|---|---|---|
| ONE | Another Europe | 3 |
| TWO | Touring styles plain and grand | 19 |
| THREE | Planning a European tour | 29 |
| FOUR | Where to go touring | 50 |
| | Austria | 51 |
| | Belgium | 53 |
| | British Isles | 54 |
| | France | 62 |
| | Germany (Federal Republic of Germany) | 65 |
| | Greece | 67 |
| | Holland | 69 |
| | Italy | 71 |
| | Portugal | 73 |
| | Scandinavia | 74 |
| | Spain | 79 |
| | Switzerland | 80 |
| | Yugoslavia | 82 |
| FIVE | Getting ready to go touring | 84 |
| SIX | Days of a bicycle tourist | 100 |
| SEVEN | Buying and equipping a touring bicycle | 127 |

EIGHT Your wardrobe, packs, roof, and bed 150

NINE Eating and touring 167

TEN Fourteen European tours 181

1 A Taste of Two Wines—The Burgundy and Alsace Regions of France 183
2 Southern England—A Quiet Visit to Britain's Past 188
3 The World of Wales 193
4 The Song and Art of Italy's North 197
5 Fields and Fortresses of Denmark 204
6 Lochs and Moors of the Scottish Highlands 208
7 Châteaux of the Loire 213
8 A Town-and-Country Tour of Holland 218
9 Germany's Black Forest 223
10 Faint Strains of Mozart—From Graz to Salzburg in Austria 228
11 The Charm and Magic of Brittany 234
12 Blue Water Pathway to Athens 241
13 The Spanish Pyrenees 247
14 The Grand Tour—London to Athens 255

APPENDICES 273

1 Estimated weight and expenses 273
2 Average temperature and precipitation in Europe 276
3 Guided tours and tour itineraries 281
4 National tourist offices 287
5 Bicycle touring organizations 290
6 Where to rent a bicycle 292
7 Mail order map sources 332
8 Bicycle equipment sources 336
9 Camping and hosteling information 338
10 Conversion charts 340

Bibliography 342

Index 345

BICYCLE
TOURING
IN
EUROPE

ONE

# Another Europe

Monsieur C. Beauvy runs the cycle shop on the Rue Brunel, a narrow street angling off the Avenue de la Grande Armée in Paris. His wife, a stout 45-year-old woman with a broad face, helps him and is there all day.

Yes, he had two bicycles our sizes, he said. We wanted them as soon as possible. In an effort to save money we had given up our Paris hotel room and were carting around two sleeping bags, a tent, cooking pots, a small butane stove, two rain capes, wool sweaters, underwear, and two sets of interlocking silverware. Paris was hot, and we wanted out.

We ordered some gear changes on the bicycles, and he said we could come and get them that evening at six. Mercifully he allowed us to store our equipment in his shop.

We returned at six. He greeted us with a sad look. His wife also came out, and said, "He'll have them ready tomorrow morning at nine. Is that all right?" We looked sadly back at her and said we guessed it had to be.

The next morning at nine Mme. Beauvy greeted us

again with the same sad smile, but the news was more hopeful.

"It'll be just a few minutes," she said.

The few minutes lingered on for some time. By ten o'clock we were fingering the riding shorts and gloves for sale on the shelf, and by ten-thirty we were lifting bicycles up and down trying to find the lightest frame. Finally M. Beauvy appeared and smiled broadly at us.

"It'll be just a few minutes," he said.

We'd heard that one before, but in the meantime he was exchanging with his wife some rapid French which we didn't understand. He then disappeared into a square hole in the floor, which apparently led down to his workshop.

"Would you like some coffee?" Mme. Beauvy asked us. We walked across the tiny street to a bistro. She shook hands with the barman, introduced us to him, and we in turn shook hands.

"They're going to bicycle through Europe," she told him.

"On *vélos*?" he asked and looked at Karen. (*Vélo* is the universal word used in France to denote bicycle.) Yes, on *vélos*, we assured him, the kind you pedal. He looked at Karen again. We drank our coffee, shook hands again, and left.

"*Bon voyage,*" he called out after us when we were on the street. From the tone of his voice, it sounded as if he thought we'd need all the help we could get.

By the time we returned, M. Beauvy was happier than we had seen him since we first walked into his shop. The bicycles were ready.

We strapped all our equipment to them, more or less attaching it to any place it looked likely to fit, and pedaled off up the tiny Rue Brunel, then down the large, crowded—and worst of all, cobbled—Avenue de la Grande Armée, and turned south through the Bois de Boulogne, which had fewer lanes of traffic than the avenue. The cars compensated for it by moving twice as fast.

Loading a bicycle correctly takes a good bit of experimentation, and with sleeping bags and tent, cooksets and collapsible knife, spoon, and fork sets hanging from ours, we were nowhere close to perfection. I tried desperately to keep my bicycle from wobbling from all the weight carried on the rear, and Karen, who had done a better job at packing than I, had her own problems. She was terrified by the traffic, and like a man stranded on a steel girder who refuses to move either backward or forward to save himself, she would consent only to ride in a straight line and would neither move her head or eyes from side to side nor reach down to shift gears.

"Your chain is rubbing on your derailleur," I screamed at her over the noise of the traffic.

Her answer was philosophical. "Who cares? I'm getting out of here."

Our escape was complicated by the fact that, with all our time spent fingering bicycle fenders and saddlebags in M. Beauvy's shop, we had failed to buy a detailed map of Paris. It seemed reasonable to me to compensate for this by sliding under the plastic map pocket of my handlebar pack a Paris *Métro* map someone had given us. While its main purpose was dedicated to showing where the subway went and where it stopped, to help orient the traveler some of Paris's main streets were sketched in light gray lines above the black grid of the *Métro* routes.

By consulting this frequently and relying in difficult situations upon my inspiration—remembering that Clark of Lewis and Clark could tell which river was a tributary and which the main stream simply by looking at it and dipping his fingers in it—we made progress. We threaded our way through the Bois de Boulogne, down the Seine, through one of the city's industrial quarters, cut across one parking lot, carried our bicycles over one footbridge, and finally came to rest at the end of an alley between two factories.

"I think we're lost," I announced. But by that time Karen had decided that things would go more smoothly if as little communication as possible passed between us, and said nothing. I turned my attention to the map. By calculating carefully I reckoned that we had covered a linear distance of about three miles from M. Beauvy's shop. I admitted that progress could have been faster, given that we had left there three hours ago. Well, at least we weren't lost any more, I offered. Responses were still limited.

Nevertheless, evening was coming on, the factories were letting out, we were blocking the alleyway, and we had to move on. A hill loomed from behind one of the factories, and we calculated that from the top of it we could get a view and perhaps orient ourselves. After all, if we sighted the Eiffel Tower and then headed south from there . . .

Fortunately the SNCF saved us. These are the initials for the French national railway system, and we've been in love with them ever since. Near the top of the hill a sign pointed down to one of its stations on the suburban line. The ticket man had difficulty understanding that we didn't care which city we went to, as long as it was the last stop on the line and as far from Paris as possible. But the French are quizzical about you only to a point, and with a shrug of his shoulders he sold us two tickets to Versailles. In twenty minutes we were on the train, our bicycles were in the luggage car, and we were speaking to one another again.

Thirteen months later we were in England, camped in the high grass just off to the side of a public footpath, one of the thousands that run along the borders of fields or beside fences throughout the English countryside. A large hardwood tree spread out above us and kept us reasonably dry from a light drizzle that was falling. A few miles away was Heathrow Airport, where we would go in a few days to catch our flight back home.

A man was coming down the path, which cut a depression between the high wet grass on either side. He wore a rubber raincoat, and the letters BOAC could be seen in faint stenciling on the chest. He walked by, a large man with balding head and sad basset eyes, said hello, then climbed the stile put up at the fence for walkers to pass over, and disappeared with his dog around a clump of bushes.

Later he made his way back over another route and this time paused at an old pine gate at the rear of our tent. The green of the neighboring field stretched off into the mist. A small creek separated us from the road, and from time to time the fluttering of doves could be heard from the trees there. He looked at us with his sad eyes, but neither of us spoke—afraid, we supposed, of invading the other's privacy. Finally we asked him if he thought it was going to clear up. He said that since his head was aching he thought it was going to hold on for a while.

He wanted to talk. We could tell by the way he climbed over the gray wooden gate, then alternately crouched and stood in his rubber raincoat near our tent as we assessed the weather.

Two people on bicycles, a yellow tent pitched in the high green grass of Surrey, and a light drizzle falling have a power of their own. People pause at the edges of it. We had experienced the same phenomenon elsewhere—on a pebbled beach beneath two cypress trees in Greece, when

Christos, whom we had known for fifteen minutes, offered us a house to live in rent free for five months, and five months later came to the pier and embraced us with tears in his eyes as we left. We had tasted it in the cool cherries given us by a timid old lady on a blistering Sunday in the middle of France, a lady who pressed them into our hands, then scurried shyly back up the stone path to her shop. Great things and small things, hundreds and hundreds of times in thirteen months. Sometimes they were pressed upon us because our belongings looked so sparse. Sometimes, we thought, because there seemed to be enough room on our rear carriers for a little bit of someone's life—a substitute voyage for those who could never go along. Les Wheeler, the BOAC man walking his Irish setter, fell into the latter category.

"My wife and I used to travel like this. We went all over the country on our tandem. Everyone used to ride then, not like now, when everyone drives a car and stays in bed-and-breakfast places. Those were the days, all right. No one could afford a car, and everyone toured on bicycles. You weren't allowed to stay in youth hostels unless you made it there under your own steam.

"I remember lying in a hostel in Devon and looking out to sea—the bunks were right next to the window—and I lay there and thought to myself, 'I got here all on my own. No one helped me.' You can't beat that feeling.

"But those days are gone now, and I travel by car and stay in hotels just like everyone else. I used to camp the way you're doing it, just in a field, and make my own way—but we don't do that now. I have two girls, grown and married. Neither of them took to riding. Perhaps if I'd had a boy he might have. Oh yes, those were the days."

He paused and looked out across the field, then turned and looked at us again.

"You know, I envy you."

"Oh?" we said.

"No, I really do. I envy you." For him it was an important confession. We looked up at him and smiled. He had risen to his feet again.

"Look, is there anything I can do for you?" he asked. No, we said, we're nearly ready to leave for home. We really have everything we need.

"What's your greatest need, your greatest hardship when you travel like this?" he pressed.

Water, we told him. Not rain, but the need for water each evening to cook with, to drink, and to wash ourselves with. We had that evening, in fact, ridden a mile back to a children's playground to fill our plastic container with about a gallon.

We went on to other things. We talked about noise pollution, air pollution, and the loss to the human spirit as mechanization advanced around the edges of our lives. We joked about our carton of milk, which was so sterilized that it would keep for weeks without refrigeration, but which no longer tasted of cows and the country.

We were ready to eat, and he left, leading his beautiful Irish setter with him.

It was dusk and turning to dark when we saw him coming down the path again, still dressed in his rubber BOAC raincoat, but this time carrying in one hand a bottle of fresh, genuine milk with cream jiggling on the top, and in the other a jerry can of clear water.

"I thought you might need these," he said.

The appearance of Les Wheeler out of the mists of Surrey was a symbolic ending to what was to be the first of many European bicycle trips for us. We had, in fact, gone on that first trip in order to find him, or find others like him.

Neither of us was new to Europe. Between the two of us, we had passed through most of its countries by tour bus, automobile, or train, seen the major cities, "done" the appropriate sites. But like many tourists, we felt a lingering sense of wanting more. Beyond the façades of an architectural monument, the statuary, the geometry of a rose window at Notre Dame or Chartres, there always seemed to be another land out there, eluding us.

This was the Europe of Europeans, of its peoples. We wanted to know them beyond the casual sentences passed between waiters and hotel clerks, to see more than just the glimpse through the sheen of a bus window. If possible, we wanted to vault over the barriers of language, history, and customs and—however briefly—touch this other entity.

Would bicycles help us bridge this gap? Our guess was that they would.

Never have we been showered with such an abundance of riches for taking those first small risks. For the relatively minor annoyances of rain, of difficult hills, of wondering if we would get to the next town in time to buy lunch before the shops closed, we have been repaid thousands of times. People have applauded us, smiled at us, joked with us in cafés. Men in Greece hailed us off the road to treat us to drinks in a sidewalk café. Some of those we met have become friends. Most remain just as memories, the blurred vision of a moment important, we suppose, only because it happened to us, yet indelible nonetheless—of gypsies in a makeshift campground inviting our child to play in a wading pool with their children, brown and white bodies tangling and untangling like dolphins; of a bocci ball court behind a café in Italy where we happened to pitch our tent, charmed by men making jokes that were centuries old; of the veined face of a peasant drinking a tumbler of chilled white wine on a blistering day in France, downing it in one gulp with only the comment afterwards, uttered to no one in particular, "It's hot outside."

These things happened to us most often because we were in villages and on roads unnoted for anything special at all, except that they were places and pathways worn by others for centuries, paths we happened across or noticed because we were traveling slowly, on bicycles.

The rest of this book discusses the practicalities of seeing this other Europe on a bicycle—how much it will cost, which countries are best for touring, how much energy and money (both are flexible and up to you) you'll have to spend to do it. There are sections on equipment—how much you'll need and what it will cost, how to take your bicycle with you on the plane free of charge, or how to buy or rent one abroad. One chapter gives information on how to find one of Europe's best-kept secrets, a maze of secondary roads that most tourists never see, where your greatest interruption is likely to be a passing farm tractor on its way to the fields. Another chapter helps you to sort out where and how to eat when you don't know the language, and introduces you to one of Europe's best assets—food that has not been processed and injected with chemicals before it reaches your plate. Finally, there is a selection of fourteen tours, with maps and itineraries, which we hope will get you on your way to a rendezvous with your own Les Wheeler, to a taste of water someone thought you might need, to a gift of fresh milk with cream jiggling on the top.

But before you pedal off down one of Europe's quiet back roads we are going to pause briefly to consider some of the things people worry about: that for all the advantages of seeing a kind of Europe most people miss, you will be seeing it from the seat of a bicycle that you must pedal with your legs, push uphill, one eye warily regarding a sky thickening with gathering clouds.

Frankly, what are the chances that you will either die of exhaustion, be caught in a three-week rainstorm, be run down by a mad Italian or French motorist, or perish of hunger because you can't remember that *fromage* means cheese in French and *queso* is what you have to say if you're in Spain?

Let's take a brief look at these reservations. They are important ones.

*How tired will I be?* There will inevitably be days when you get tired. If you aren't careful, there will be days when you will be *very* tired. This is particularly true if you try to go too far, especially at the beginning of a tour. If you don't bicycle at home, before leaving you should be willing to invest some time riding and building up muscles you are not used to using right now, much as if you were going on a skiing holiday. You should like the feeling of exercise and of being outdoors in the fresh air, of being active.

This question raises others. How well did you feel the last time you were confined in a car for twelve hours? Or on a train? Two things are certain: you will feel more alive after a day of bicycling than you did then, and you will feel that you have contributed something of yourself in getting there.

At no time should you go so far or over terrain so difficult that you feel exhausted. Neither is necessary. A bicycle tour does not have to be a day-to-day struggle to grind out miles. Some of our own best trips took us at a leisurely pace of 10 or 15 miles a day, with frequent stops for sightseeing, snacks, picture taking, and the rest.

In addition to short tours, many people combine biking

with other means of travel and use a bicycle only to get out in the country for an afternoon or a brief overnight trip. The great availability of rental bicycles throughout Europe makes such a tour easy to arrange. Hundreds of railway stations rent them, as do thousands of private establishments. While rental bicycles are usually not sleek ten-speeds, they are serviceable and do permit great flexibility in arranging tours with varying degrees of difficulty and duration. Some countries also have programs where bicycles may be rented at one shop, youth hostel, or railway station and returned to another, making a short linear (point-to-point) trip quite feasible—without the problem of disposing of the bicycle after you are finished with it. Rental possibilities are discussed in our country-by-country descriptions in Chapter 4, and a list of rental facilities in most European countries is included in Appendix 6.

*What do I do if it rains?* Rain is a factor in summer weather in Europe as it is in much of the United States. Most bicyclists will encounter it at least once in a tour of any length unless they stick to countries bordering the Mediterranean Sea; even here there is still the chance of an isolated summer shower.

On the other hand, most novice or uninitiated bicycle tourists overemphasize its importance. You encounter rain under one of two conditions: either it is raining (or threatening) when you get up in the morning, or it starts raining after you are on the road. In the first case, you simply stay where you are. You can use the day to sightsee, write letters, play cards, drink coffee in cafés, or just rest. If you have decent rain gear, you can walk around. In this case you are little different from any tourist caught in a rainy day. You would not be much better off if you were traveling by train, which is what you can do if you fall seriously behind schedule. In most of Europe it is quite easy and inexpensive to carry your bicycle on a train. It is a convenient way of making up lost time or seeking out a more temperate climate, if need be.

More annoying is being caught in the rain while riding. We offer a number of suggestions on how to deal with this in Chapter 5. But basically you can ride in a light rain with relatively little discomfort. With a decent windbreaker or other breathable rain gear, drizzle evaporates about as quickly as it accumulates. If it rains hard, you seek shelter. We have spent some enforced but charming hours in cafés, in covered markets, in people's homes, as well as some less exotic time in the country under the inevitable tree. While all of this cannot be described as thrilling, you usually find there are enough breaks in the weather for you to hopscotch to the next town or village and get more permanent shelter.

Because of this, most experienced bicyclists regard rain as more of an annoyance than a deterrent to a good vacation. Summer rains last days, not weeks, and the appearance of the first ray of sunshine has a wondrous ability to change your whole point of view.

*Will I be run over by a car?* We spend considerable time later on discussing how to find small, quiet roads in Europe. They exist in abundance in most, although not all, European countries. The secret to finding them is to buy detailed regional maps that show you where they are. They can be purchased here and in Europe, and later on we tell you how to buy them. For now, suffice it to say that if you choose your routes wisely, you probably cannot find a safer place to bicycle than in Europe. In our own cycling, which adds up to something well over 15,000 miles, we have never had a car-related accident. Of course we make a fetish of discovering small country roads and encourage you to do likewise. If you do this, what you'll encounter throughout the majority of Europe are well-paved, quiet farm roads where your most serious disruption is likely to be a herd of cows or sheep crossing from one pasture to another.

*Will I die of hunger?* Our axiom, long tested and found true, is that if you have money, you will eat. Chapter 10 gives you some tips on how to shop in a strange land. As for language barriers, memorizing a few simple words in another language such as "grams," "a little," or "that's enough" will get you by in most circumstances. And if you are stricken with timidity—as we are, frankly—you will be surprised how the pangs of hunger will give you the courage to become a linguist in the international language of pointing, shaking your head, or smiling, "Yes, that's what I want."

*Are you too old?* We once sat arguing with some English friends whether the road we were picnicking beside could be climbed by a cyclist. We were high on the Yorkshire moors, and the little Morris we had ridden up in was steaming by the time we stopped. A sign at the bottom of the hill indicated a tough 33 percent grade. Our host, a Yorkshire man, has the local accent.

"Y'd ne'r make it on a bicycle, lad," he was saying. We argued that it was possible, particularly if you were traveling without weight.

"Nah, it's a thirty-three percent grade, tha' one is."

We let the subject drop and looked out in the distance at the remains of an old brick ironworks standing out starkly from the peak of the next hill. A few moments passed and then we heard the sounds of heavy panting and breathing coming from the road below us, around the bend and out of sight. In a few seconds the front wheel, then the handlebars, then the rider of a bicycle appeared.

He worked his way up level with us and we got a closer look at him as he strained on the pedals—shirtless, perspiring heavily, bald-headed, and at least 60 years of age. The four of us watched in silence—you could even say amazed silence—as the man passed us, reached the rock fence at the top of the field above, then disappeared down the other side of the hill. He was carrying beneath his seat a large saddlebag which appeared to be full.

Obviously, you should plan a trip that suits your own personality, and this sometimes does vary with age. If you have a history of heart disease, you should consult your physician about bicycling. But age, any age, in itself will not prevent you from touring.

At the other end of the scale, we used to think that the minimal age for someone going on a bicycle tour was about 14. Over the years, this estimate kept getting whittled down as we saw younger and younger children touring, some as young as 8 or 9.

We ourselves may have pushed it to its ultimate limit.

In 1978, just two years after our son was born, we found ourselves free and once again possessed with a burning desire to go bicycle touring. Touring with a baby in diapers? Our friends and parents were skeptical—if not totally aghast at the idea. But spring and a sense of movement were in the air. We couldn't resist.

We had recalled an article in *Bicycling!* magazine that described a trailer with a specially designed seat for kids. It took some phoning to find a dealer who had one. Triumphantly we brought it home in the trunk of the car. We had left our bicycles in France and had no real way of trying it out. As a gambit, we took a mile walk down a nearby country road, pulling it behind us, while Benjamin squirmed unmercifully and repeatedly demanded to get out and walk.

With no real confidence at all we packed our bags and set out for a rendezvous with our bicycles. If we made it, fine, we told ourselves. If not, that was fine too. The last thing we were going to do was to drag him, screaming, across Europe.

In the early part of May, just after his second birthday, we tied a favorite toy on the trailer with a string, strapped him in with his safety belt, and pumped with some trepidation to gain the outskirts of Calais, in northern France. A bright orange flag flapped in the cold spring air above his trailer, as much a symbol of hope as it was a warning to motorists.

Some four months—and 4,200 miles—later, we pulled into a campground just within the city limits of Athens, Greece. Except for one ferry trip from the coast of Italy to the nearest Greek port at Patras, we had covered every inch of the way on our bicycles. This included two excursions into the Pyrenees and a circular tour of the French Alps.

Benjamin was now a seasoned traveler who knew the word for every conceivable means of transportation, usually in two or three languages. He was an encyclopedia on farm animals, and had learned to play with children across the breadth of the European continent. Whether because of the trip or from natural reasons, he was in the bloom of 2½-year-old health. Frankly, he had received so much attention and fawning over that it was embarrassing.

Hoping to stem the tide of impossible vanity, we reminded him frequently that he should share the plaudits with Papa, who had pulled him, and Mama, who had lugged food and diapers all along the route.

Secretly, we thanked him for turning a tremulously undertaken experiment into one of the richest experiences we have had together.

Someday we will tell him that, too.

For now, we let the statement stand which we made in an earlier version of this book, long before he came along, that given our experiences and those of others, anyone can bicycle tour if he or she really wants to.

We also believe that once the risk is taken, the jump made, you will be rewarded with your own particular memories of that other continent, a different Europe.

TWO

# Touring styles plain and grand

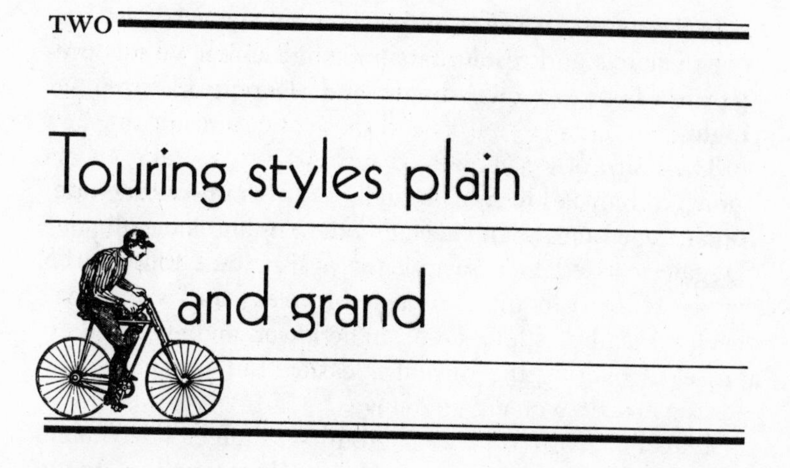

Planning a bicycle tour is not unlike planning any other vacation. The first question most people ask is "How much is it going to cost me?" A second thought, hovering in the minds of many, will undoubtedly be "How hard is it going to be?" In many ways, these questions are interrelated as far as bicycle touring is concerned, because—within limits—it can be as luxurious or as Spartan as you wish. Do you look forward to a hotel room, a drink, and a restaurant meal at the end of a touring day? If so, it will cost you more than some other ways of touring, but the physical side of it most likely will be easier. You won't need to carry as much gear on your bicycle. Later on, we show you how to pare your weight down to about 10 pounds of essentials if you are planning to stay in hotels during your tour. On the other hand, you can cut costs considerably by camping along the way. Your daily expenditures will nosedive, but bicycling will be harder because you have added tent, sleeping bag, sleeping pad, and usually a cookset to your gear. And most people will carry some basic food staples that also add weight.

Some people will stay in youth hostels for much of their

trip. This way strikes a middle ground between the luxury of hotels and restaurants and the camper who is preparing his or her own dinner and sleeping in a tent at night.

There are other choices to make. You can take an organized bicycle tour, complete with your own guide, prearranged meals, and accommodations and have all your luggage carried in a sag wagon, a van that follows the group to carry equipment and bicycles—and sometimes cyclists! Daily distances tend to be lower, and even if they are not, covering the terrain is easier. But you pay extra for the luxuries you are enjoying.

Traveling with your own group will affect how much you spend. Three or more people traveling together, doing common shopping, sharing the same campsite or hotel room will spend less than the same number of persons doing this individually. Group travel often means a reduction in the amount of weight each must carry.

You may decide that you will cover the long distances of your tour on the train, either taking your bicycle as baggage or renting a bicycle at your various stopping points. If so, your costs will go up as a result of your additional transportation fees. But by taking the train over difficult sections or just by using a bicycle as a pleasant accompaniment to what amounts to a rail trip, the amount of physical energy you have to expend will go down.

In brief, how much you spend depends in large part on what style you choose to travel in. To give you a clearer idea of this relationship between style and costs, we have divided modes of bicycle travel into four separate categories:

1. The Lightweight Tourist—using hotels and restaurants and eating breakfast and dinner out. You normally

shop for your own lunch, with the added benefit of an incredibly extensive array of cheeses, meats, fruits, and breads available en route: You carry minimal weight on the bicycle. Costs will reflect the relative luxury of a good, clean bed and having someone else doing the cooking for you.

2. The Camper Tourist—carrying your own bed and roof, and preparing your own food. Usually the cheapest way of all to travel.

3. The Hosteler Tourist—a combination of the other two, where you stay at night in youth hostels and usually prepare two or more meals a day yourself. You may carry a tarp and lightweight sleeping bag for fair-weather camping. Costs will be somewhere between those for the Lightweight and the Camper tourists.

4. The Organized Tour—this may fall into any one of the three foregoing categories in terms of nightly accommodations, but you have the advantages of predetermined costs, a guide or leader, a set itinerary, oftentimes a sag wagon to carry your luggage, and usually at least part of your eating in restaurants or youth hostels. Costs will vary depending on the extent of these amenities and the countries chosen for travel.

What would a typical tourist traveling in any one of these modes be taking along, how much will it weigh, and most importantly, how much will it cost? Since "average" costs of things can be deceptive with the wide range of restaurant, hotel, and food prices prevalent in western Europe, we have included what are reasonable minimum and maximum costs based on our experiences and data we have gathered from others. You may experience a slight increase in all prices, as the value of the dollar is uncertain and inflation a fact of life everywhere. Of course costs vary depending on other factors such as your ability to say no if a hotel room seems too expensive or your preference for simpler food than we have at times eaten. In terms of clothing and equipment taken along—which in many ways determine the difficulty of your cycling—we have estimated it on the basis of minimal but not hermitlike standards, and have allowed 3 pounds for miscellaneous items such as cameras, paperback books, and guides. These will also vary from person to person.

*Lightweight tourist.* This traveler stays in hotels and youth hostels and eats at least his main meal each day in restaurants. For your other meals we recommend that you shop in grocery stores offering the fresh fruit, cheeses, breads, yogurts, and pastries special in each region. Eliminating a midday meal in a restaurant reduces costs considerably. Carrying only the clothing and personal effects you need, you are unencumbered by heavy gear. One great blessing is that you have few worries about finding places to stay or adjusting the distance of your planned day's ride because inexpensive small hotels are plentiful throughout Europe. Only in some of the poorer countries do you have to exercise some care in planning where you will stop for the night. Your hotels will usually be in smaller towns well off the beaten tourist paths, and this means mingling with other Europeans and living on the same level as they do when traveling. Because you come on a bicycle you have a topic of conversation to share with others, if only in the language of gestures. You can show where you have been on the map, and if you have any grasp at all of the language you will be given countless travel tips. Most surprisingly, you begin to receive "visitor" and not "tourist" treatment. This subtle distinction can wind up giving your trip an entirely different feeling.

Based on our experiences and those of others we have known, a Lightweight tourist will spend from a little over

$13 a day to $28 for a moderate but not luxurious hotel room, breakfast and dinner out, and buying lunch on the road. If diligence is used in seeking out hotels, or if youth hostels or rooms in private homes are substituted occasionally, costs will drop considerably. How much more you *could* spend depends on personal factors that are impossible to estimate. But you can eat well and sleep soundly within the ranges we have indicated. Keep in mind that one of your greatest expenses is eliminated—that of other means of transportation. Even hitchhikers will usually end up spending more than Lightweight tourists; they are often not where they want to be at day's end, and an expensive accommodation may be the result.

The Lightweight tourist should be carrying about 10 pounds of weight. After a day or so this will not feel much different from when you were riding without any weight on your bicycle. A detailed breakdown of costs and a checklist of clothing is given in Appendix 1.

*Camper tourist.* This tourist has the ultimate in personal freedom and independence, and it is the style of travel we personally enjoy the most. You are self-contained, carrying your bed, roof, and kitchen with you in the form of sleeping bag and pad, lightweight tent or tarp, small stove and cookset. You also travel the most economically, since you pay only a minimal camping fee each night or nothing at all if you get permission to sleep in someone's orchard or field. Both camping and free-lancing on someone's land have their own rewards. Of all the times we asked for permission to stay on private land no one ever refused, and only one person asked to be paid—a wrinkled old woman who managed an inn in Kent, England, who asked in a quavering voice if we thought 10 pence too much. At 12¢ each, we thought we could afford it.

The whole concept of a campground is quite different in Europe from what you may be used to at home. In Europe there is no façade of returning to nature. Europeans camp because it is the least expensive way to take a family vacation. Yet they still insist on luxuries many American tent campers would never think of. Their tents are usually large—many with two or more rooms. Some Europeans set up their tents for the entire summer, and equip them with ranges, ovens, refrigerators, and even flower gardens at the borders of the site. If you are used to wilderness-type camping these refinements may come as a surprise. But once accustomed to the style and personality of the European camper, you will find it one of the best ways to bring yourself into contact with the widest variety of people. Young and old surround you. People will be interested in the fact that you are cycling. Occasionally you will meet other cyclists with whom you can swap experiences and information.

If you plan to do much camping, a helpful and at times essential addition to your documents will be an International Camping Carnet (see Chapter 3).

Campground costs vary from 50¢ to $2.50 per person per night, with something of a reversal of normal economic trends. In some of the more expensive countries to travel in, such as England and France, campgrounds are relatively cheap. In some of the countries where everything else is cheaper, including Spain and Greece, campgrounds tend to be more expensive.

More expensive campgrounds usually provide hot showers, and some have laundromats; almost all will have washtubs for doing laundry. For the most part you pay a set of separate fees, one for the tent, one for each person, and in some cases one for your bicycle. Our most luxurious campground was on the Riviera before the high summer season got under way. We had a secluded campsite in the pines, free hot water and showers, a small store and restaurant within the campground, and a large game room where we could sit in solitude during the day or come to in the evenings to watch television with the other campers. The sea was a two-minute bicycle ride from our tent. Cost per person was $1.50 each day for the site.

These factors of economy and a chance to mix with other European campers more than offset the 10 or so extra pounds we carry over the Lightweight tourist. Including both food and camping, your per-person costs should run from $4 to $9.50 per day, depending on which country you happen to be touring. A complete breakdown of daily expenses is given in Appendix 1.

*The Hosteler.* This is a compromise, in cost and needed equipment, between the other two. As the name implies, its chief feature is that you stay in youth hostels—large supervised dormitories, usually segregated by sex, operated on a noncommercial basis, and found throughout Europe, in cities and towns, as well as in scenic out-of-the-way places. While most have a minimum age of about 6 years old for guests, there is no maximum age for hostels except in the Bavarian section of Germany. A few, such as those in Switzerland, do give priority to people under 30. While this makes the population of most hostels youthful, the age range commonly stretches well up into the senior years.

The quality of hostels varies as much as their per-night charges, which run from about $1 to about $4 per person per night. Almost all of them have kitchen facilities, and some serve meals for a nominal charge. Usually there is a set time by which you must be registered and another in the morning by which you must be out. Often you are asked to do a simple housekeeping chore in the morning.

The hostel usually furnishes blankets and will rent a required sleep sheet if you do not have your own. If you are going to use hostels extensively, you should carry your own sleep sheet. They can be purchased through the American Youth Hostel headquarters (see Appendix 3). You must join the American Youth Hostel Association to use the hostels; membership is $11 for persons 18 and over, $5 for those under 18.

It could well be that the Hosteler has the best of all three worlds. By avoiding hotels you shear expenses from 40 to 60 percent, yet you add only about 4 pounds over the Lightweight tourist in the form of a light sleeping bag, sleep sheet, and cookset. A simple tarp may be added for fair-weather camping, if you wish. Your total weight in clothing and equipment will be around 15 pounds, and you should be spending from between $4.50 to $11.50 per day on basics (see Appendix 1 for further details).

*The organized tour.* If your circle of acquaintances does not include someone with whom to tour, or if you prefer to have details of routes and stopping places arranged for you, there are numerous organized bicycle tours available which relieve you of some or all the details of route finding, hotel hunting, and cooking your own meals. Such tours are offered by a number of organizations both here and in Europe, most by nonprofit groups, some by travel-oriented businesses. In each case you get a guide who arranges hotel or hostel accommodations; most meals are prepared for you; and you receive a tour itinerary, usually accompanied by maps. Often a sag wagon carries your luggage for you—or carries you if it has to. Details of other means of land travel—such as train or bus connections—are arranged for you and are often included in the tour price. Some tours even include the cost of a rental ten-speed bicycle so you don't have to take your own or buy one abroad.

Given the wide divergence of services offered, tour costs vary. In most cases you may save on air fare that is included in the tour price, as tour operators usually take advantage of group or charter rates. On the other hand, a tour will usually cost you more than it would if you traveled in the same style on your own (assuming you can hold to a budget and plan carefully). You are in effect paying for such amenities as a sag wagon or the costs of the guide or leader. From the range of tours currently being offered, costs run from $28 to $42 per person per day, exclusive of air fare. A more complete discussion of tours and their costs is given in Chapter 3.

## A QUICK GLANCE

Here's a summary of the various means of travel just discussed and their respective costs:

*Lightweight Tourist*

WEIGHT: 10.5 pounds
COSTS: $13 to $28 per day

*Camper Tourist*

WEIGHT: 20.5 pounds
COSTS: $4 to $9.50 per day

*Hosteler Tourist*

WEIGHT: 15.5 pounds
COSTS: $4.50 to $11.50 per day

*Organized Tours*

WEIGHT: 0 to 15.5 pounds
COSTS: $28 to $42 per day

Are there cheaper ways of seeing Europe? Probably. There are undoubtedly bicyclists who travel even less expensively than these figures suggest. We tend to spend a great deal of our budget on food, as we like to spoil ourselves in the evening after a day's ride. Some people, of course, will spend more.

But in the final analysis, within any mode of travel, we are certain that you would be hard pressed to find a less expensive way of seeing Europe than on a bicycle. And of course this does not even begin to take into consideration the difference between how you are treated as compared to the hitchhiker standing forlornly along a busy route or the tour bus disgorging its tired charges after a day of organized learning. You earn the distinction of someone making it on his or her own.

THREE

# Planning a European tour

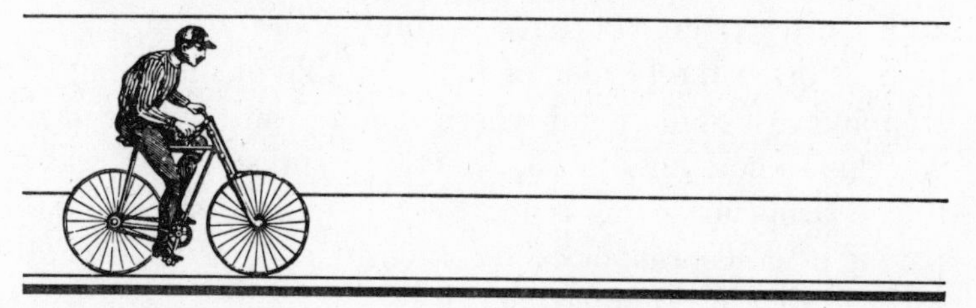

More than anyone, bicyclists need to spend some time on pre-trip calculations. Amost all of us approach planning a trip in a kind of dreamlike state—which is as it should be. Part of the joy of traveling is imagining what you will see and experience once you get there. But along with these pleasant conjectures come more practical decisions as to how much money you can afford to spend, how far you will travel in an average day, and what countries you want to tour. For the bicyclist, all these decisions are made from a special point of view. Let's begin with the last item first.

*Where and when to go touring.* From your own reading, from past European experiences, family history, or just inclination, there will probably be certain European countries you are interested in seeing. There undoubtedly will be specific sites you are curious about—a particular cathedral, a region known for its scenic beauty, the unusual characteristics of its inhabitants, the charm of its capitol.

Before you definitely fix your plans for seeing such places, you should become familiar with some of the limitations as well as some of the freedoms involved in bicycle touring. One of the primary freedoms is that you are off on your own, often in uncrowded areas where other tourists are rare, and where your reception will be qualitatively different. But there are some limitations.

First of all, bicycles and large cities do not mix well. In addition to traffic, you have to think about getting tired; there is often the burden of being unable or unwilling to stop and rest; finding out where you are can be difficult if you don't know how to ask directions; and so on. In addition, European towns tend to have narrow streets and paving often is brick or even cobblestone—not the kind of surfaces that lead to relaxing rides.

For the very largest cities—including all capitols with the exception of Amsterdam and Copenhagen—we recommend you see them without your bicycle. You may either check it at a suburban station and take the train in, or if you are arriving by train and your bicycle is with you, check it at the main train station until you are ready to leave. When that time comes, put yourself and your bicycle on a local, and take it to a quiet suburb to begin riding.

All major train stations in Europe have facilities for checking your bicycle. Fees range from 50¢ to $1.25 per day. Remove all valuables such as passport, money, and camera. Items such as panniers and handlebar packs may be left on if you wish. If you are checking your bicycle for a long period of time, prudence would indicate that you should take anything with you that you need or feel you can't do without, such as a good sleeping bag or tent. We have left our bicycles in train stations all over Europe, at times for a week or longer, with no problems whatsoever.

The second factor you should keep in mind is the condition of roads and traffic in the various European countries. This is probably the single most crucial factor in determining the character of a tour. In countries such as Great Britain, France, Holland, Belgium, Denmark, and Ireland you can tour just about anywhere outside the major cities and find an abundance of quiet roads. In other countries you must be more selective as to regions. With careful planning and map scrutiny, which we come to shortly, you will be able to tell where these regions are.

Third, you should consider the general nature of a country's geography and climate. Hills and mountains will affect the kind of tour you have. We go into considerable detail in Chapter 5 on how to handle hills on a bicycle and how to avoid them if you wish. Since in the minds of many, hills represent the most single trying feature of bicycle touring, we wish only to make the point here that you should not dismiss any country out of hand because it is hilly or mountainous. Even countries known for their mountains—such as Switzerland and Austria—have numerous valleys and plains where cycling is less strenuous. Moreover, there are some cyclists—ourselves included—who thrive on mountain travel, either as a steady diet or as a relief from flatland bicycling. After a little experience you might be surprised to learn that you are in that camp also.

Finally, you should consider climate. Europe has about the same climatic range as that found within the United States in summer. Parts of Sweden resemble Minnesota in climate and terrain. Much but not all of Spain has a climate similar to Southern California. Ireland has a climate somewhat resembling that of the Pacific Northwest, gray and sometimes rainy. In all of these you will find people out on bicycles or bicycle touring. Where you choose to tour depends upon your own temperament.

The particular season you intend to go to Europe may also determine where you go. Generally speaking, bicycle touring is reserved for the period between May and October through most of Europe, from April through mid-November in the warmer regions of Spain, Portugal, and Greece. You can tour in the winter months in the latter three countries, but weather will often be cold, rainy, or both, and such adventures are for the hardy only. The temperature and rain charts we give you in Appendix 2 will help you plan your tour during the summer months.

Camper or Hosteler tourists should pay particular attention to the opening dates of hostels and campgrounds. The *International Youth Hostel Handbook, Volume 1* (see Bibliography), gives opening dates for hostels throughout Europe. Campgrounds open at various times, depending upon the country and the location of the camp. For most countries it is safe to assume that the majority of the campgrounds will be open only during June, July, and August, although campgrounds in resort areas and in large cities often are open year-round. Detailed information is generally available in camping literature supplied by the national tourist boards of the respective countries or from some of the camping sources listed in the Bibliography at the end of this book.

With these general factors of road conditions, geography, and climate in mind, you are ready to begin your tour planning in closer detail.

*Number of countries or how much of one country you are going to see.* There is no formula for this one, but try to be realistic. If you are on a two-week vacation, don't count on a grand tour of Europe—at least not by bicycle. Two- and three-week tours lend themselves best to one or possibly two countries. Seeing even three small countries within that time is stretching it, if you include time for jet lag, sightseeing in the capitols, and getting ready to go back home again. If you are limited to two or three weeks and determined to see more than just two or three countries, you might consider doing your major traveling by train and renting bicycles for short excursions. There are thousands of places to rent bicycles in Europe, including a good many train stations. We list most of them in Appendix 6. You can also take your own bicycle on the train with you and take short trips on it, either radiating out from a single locale, or leapfrogging along in a train/bicycle sequence. But whatever the case, don't run yourself ragged trying to do everything in one tour.

*General route planning.* Once you have settled on the countries or regions that interest you, you are ready to begin the process of plotting your tour. For this you need a good map of the country, either one of the ones supplied by the national tourist agencies or one available from a bookstore or map dealer. (See Appendix 7 on map ordering.) Use these maps to pick out the regions you intend to tour, determine which places most interest you, get a good idea of how much mileage this means totally, and most important, what you will have to average per day to cover it. This last factor can be a bothersome subject for some people. If you have never cycled before, the distance you can cover easily in a day may seem rather high to you. Our normal touring range is about 50 to 60 miles a day. This includes our more recent excursions with our son in his bicycle trailer and a full complement of camping gear. This is enough to make us feel we have done something, yet it is not so great a distance as to leave us exhausted. Of course, in serious headwinds or in rugged cycling country we do less than this. We have friends who think that 10 or 15 miles a day is quite enough. And then there are some persons traveling with a sag wagon or who are strong cyclists who often knock off up to 100 miles a day on a regular basis with no ill effects. This is too strenuous for most tourists, including us.

In our own planning, we calculate an average of 50 miles a day, then add one and a half to two days a week for contingencies such as rain, rest, an unexpectedly enjoyable town or campground, or an invitation to stay over. This happens on a surprisingly regular, if not frequent, basis.

This kind of scheduling, where we take our normal minimum average then add contingency days to it, gives us enough "elastic" in our itinerary so that in practice we often find ourselves ahead of schedule. We then use this extra time for a side trip or to extend our general tour by one day. Sometimes we use it to just loll around.

From your own training and riding experience you will know how much daily distance is right for you. Your personality will also have a lot to do with how you cover this distance. If you want to loiter along taking pictures, talking to farmers, or getting free language lessons by showing children your bicycle, you will obviously cover less distance than the person who is more comfortable setting a pace and holding it for an hour. If when you actually begin touring you find yourself falling behind your intended schedule, don't start pushing yourself too hard to catch up. In most instances you can put your bicycle on a train and make up the distance. Once, we made one short but important 10-mile hop on a bus for about $1 each. It took us from a large lake in the foothills of the Vosges Mountains in France to the top of a high pass. We got off and coasted 12 miles down the other side before we stopped. It saved us the better part of a morning spent laboring up a pass.

*Specific route planning.* After you have completed your

general planning of regions, towns to be seen, and distance per day, you are ready to begin planning specific details of which roads to take and where to stop for the night. You may do this either before you leave home, or if you feel comfortable about it, on a day-to-day basis once you are in Europe. Whatever the case, probably the greatest factor affecting the success of a bicycle tour is the care you take in choosing your specific route. Not only does this determine what you will see, it will also determine how you see it.

Roads in Europe tend to fall into three categories: the toll roads and autoroutes which are off-limits to cyclists, the major highways (primary roads) that carry much of the day-to-day traffic within a country, and the small back roads (secondary roads) that normally connect villages and hamlets. The most typical mistake for an inexperienced bicycle tourist is to get hold of a general highway map, then make a beeline down the major highways that connect important cities. Most of these roads are heavily traveled. Some are dangerous to ride on. Moreover, you miss the most enchanting part of European cycling, an almost endless panorama worn by centuries of living. Of course there may be times when travel on major roads is necessary, and we confess to our share of using them. But throughout Europe there are thousands upon thousands of miles of paved secondary roads. They are quiet, scenic, and sometimes unknown even to the local populace. The key to finding them is in using detailed regional maps.

## MAP SCALES

Map makers use a scaling system to describe how much space on the map represents that much space in reality. This is usually expressed in terms of a ratio where one map unit (centimeter or inch) equals one unit of the real world (kilometer or mile). Without going into the technicalities of this, a map scale which reads, for instance, 1:200,000 means that for each unit on the map (centimeter in this case) there are two kilometers of real road out there (200,000 centimeters equals exactly two kilometers). The smaller the second number of the ratio is, the more detail the map will show. For instance, a map scale of 1:100,000 means that each centimeter of map represents one kilometer of real road (100,000 centimeters equals one kilometer).

In practical terms, this means if you see a map whose scale is 1:5,000,000, you will know that a large area of the real world is represented by a very small area on the map. Thus the map will have little detail, and will not show side roads, the existence of small villages, hills, or the score of things a bicyclist should know when planning a route.

We feel that for good bicycle touring, you must use a map that has a scale of at least 1:400,000. Any map with a scale where the second number is less than 400,000 is all the better. Most maps that we recommend for day-to-day touring have a scale of 1:200,000.

## GETTING REGIONAL MAPS

If you plan far enough ahead of time, you can secure detailed regional maps (scale of 1:400,000 or better) for much of Europe from outlets within the United States. Largely because we have had more experience with them, we prefer the Michelin and Bartholomew maps. Michelin is a French tire manufacturing company that has an extensive publishing arm. Bartholomew is a Scottish firm that has long set the standard for touring maps within the British Isles.

In addition to its well-known 1:200,000 series for all of France, Michelin markets detailed regional maps of Great Britain, the Netherlands, Belgium, much of Germany, Austria, Switzerland, Luxembourg, the Spanish Pyrenees, and northern Italy. Their map of Portugal, although not quite as detailed, is nonetheless excellent.

For Great Britain (England, Scotland, Wales) and Ireland, the Bartholomew maps are superb. Both the GT Series (1:253,440) and the National Series (1:100,000) are good for the cycle tourist.

Maps from both companies show topographical features in color, distances over even the smallest back roads, relevant elevation markings, small streams (crossing small streams usually means you're going up and down), and in the case of Michelin, the degree of slope on all roads above a 5 percent grade.

You can get Michelin maps from a number of mail order outlets in the United States, the addresses of which are in Appendix 7. Allow at least a month for your order to be processed. Bartholomew maps may be ordered from Europe.

If your city or town has a good foreign language bookstore, you can often find these or other detailed regional maps there.

Once in Europe, you can often find maps in larger bookstores in the capitols. If you land in London, there are several bookstores with extensive map collections not only for Great Britain but for much of the Continent as well.

These regional maps, incidentally, are relatively expensive, ranging in price from 75¢ a sheet up to $4 or even $5 if the map covers an extensive area. Many are handsomely bound in stiff covers which we, with great regret, tear off, since they will not fit the map pockets of our front packs.

## PLOTTING YOUR ROUTE

Once you have your regional maps, begin plotting your route. It is better to have your detailed maps before you leave home, so that you can familiarize yourself with them and do as much specific planning as possible. If you haven't left enough time to get them or the supply company doesn't have the maps you need, take the time to buy them when you land in the country you'll be touring, as large cities are more likely to have bookstores that stock them.

Whichever way it happens with you, you should leave some leeway in your planning, as there are a number of factors that might affect it once you are on the road. Often there are two or three back-road routes you can take to get from main point to main point. Many times, the one you thought you would use turns out to be poorly paved, or may perhaps have short, steep grades that, while they are not high enough to show up on a map, may in fact be difficult to bicycle over. An adjacent route might follow a small stream you didn't notice before. Local inhabitants may tell you of an interesting mill, or church, just off the route in a village you hadn't intended to cross. Or you get rained in and find that the interesting loop you had planned to take just won't fit your plans. You can even just get tired of a region and decide to move on to something else without finishing your intended route.

In our own touring experience, we most often leave specific details of route finding until we are on the road, whether we have the maps before we leave or not. We do know ahead of time what we want to see, and we map out generally the route we'll take. Once on the road, we have developed the habit of spending some time each evening, usually after supper, looking at the next day's ride. We figure alternatives, anticipate stopping points, calculate the total distance, and often set a goal short of that in case of rain, in case the cycling is rougher than we thought, or just in case we don't feel like going as far as we thought we would. If it is feasible, we also pick a goal just a bit beyond our expected one, in case we feel peppy that day or get in a very fast ride before lunch (we encourage you to do most of your riding before noon, as we discuss in Chapter 5).

These evening seminars, whether they take only a few minutes or an hour to hash things out, have become something of a joyful passion. Like many cyclists, we become fascinated with the problems presented in getting from point A to point B, and solving those problems provides one of our quieter satisfactions. There have even been times when we've bought two maps so that *each* of us could have our own to study and mull over as much as we pleased!

Whether you become so afflicted is a matter of choice. But the point we wish to emphasize is that whether you do it at home or while on the road, the importance of map reading and route finding to your European tour cannot be overestimated.

When you have finished with a map, stick it in an envelope and mail it home. If you are not in a hurry, send it printed-matter rate, which is inexpensive even in Europe. Your used map will provide an invaluable memory of your trip, calling to mind exact details you had no idea you had stored away. Maps, accompanied by our day-to day diary of distances traveled, weather, special events, or just moods, have been a storehouse of material which we pore over periodically with the greatest satisfaction. And your collection of maps can be the beginning of your next European tour.

As we've said, how much pre-trip planning you wish to do in addition to the basic suggestions above is up to you. Generally speaking, the more you know about a country, its customs, geography, history, architecture, and language, the more you will be open to appreciating it. Most European countries have national tourist offices located within the United States that will send you a wealth of free material, including general descriptions, festivals, and discussions of various regions; campground and youth hostel information; and very frequently information specifically relevant to the bicyclist. Be certain to specify that you intend to bicycle when requesting information.

Beyond this there are scores of guides that cover details of various European countries. Of considerable use to the cycle tourist are *Fodors* guides, the *Michelin Green Guides*, and for the budget minded, *Let's Go: Europe*. These and other aids are given in the Bibliography at the end of this book.

Depending upon your style of travel you may want two additional items. The first is the *International Youth Hostel Handbook*. Volume 1 covers western Europe. It covers the rules and customs governing the youth hostels in each country, addresses of hostels by city, and a map showing locations. Cost is about $5.

The second item is really a document, but a useful one if you are camping. That is the *International Camping Carnet*. It serves as a substitute for a passport in many campgrounds where the attendant may wish to hold some document as security until you depart. In other campgrounds, it can mean a reduction in daily fees. In certain countries, such as Denmark, you are officially required to have a camping carnet in order to use the grounds. In most countries it is a convenience. You can secure it by joining the National Campers and Hikers Association (see Appendix 9 for address). Cost is $14 per year.

## PREPARED BICYCLING ITINERARIES

If you want to cut short the business of plotting your tour, or if you want to take advantage of the experiences of other bicycle tourists, there are a wealth of prepared bicycling itineraries at your disposal. We offer sixteen such itineraries at the end of this book, all of which take you through excellent bicycling country across different parts of Europe.

You can get touring itineraries from a number of other sources. The amount of detail included varies. Usually the itinerary will pinpoint major towns or sights that you can travel to. Most will indicate distances you must cover. Some will give details of the terrain or an estimate of the tour's difficulty. Some will list accommodations and give you mile-by-mile (or more frequently kilometer-by-kilometer) sketches of what to see.

You should leave at least two months to request any special materials such as maps and preprinted tours from any foreign country. For specially designed itineraries, longer time is required.

Here are some of the sources at your disposal for getting detailed cycling itineraries:

The *Cyclists Touring Club* is an English-based organization dedicated, as its name implies, to the bicycle tourist. It is undoubtedly the most organized of all clubs of its kind. The CTC provides a number of services to members, including plotting a personalized tour for you if you give them enough time. But in addition to this, they have a number of stock tours available that cover all parts of the British Isles as well as the Continent. Tours list things to see, are fairly specific as to route, and give you mileage or kilometerage running both ways along the tour. You must join the CTC in order to make use of their facilities, and there is a nominal sum for the tour itself. Information on joining the CTC is given in Appendix 5.

The *British Cycling Federation* is the internationally recognized body for road racing in the United Kingdom but nevertheless has an excellent touring service situated in a separate bureau. The BCF has over a hundred stock tours available covering the British Isles and most of Europe, together with a *Handbook* which lists recommended accommodations for cyclists as well as an extensive list of repair shops in Great Britain. In addition, the BCF will plan individual itineraries for its members in Great Britain and through many parts of Europe. Maps that accompany the tours are also available. Americans may join as "Private Members" for £7.25. Check your newspaper for current exchange rates, and in all cases when sending money abroad, send it by International Money Order or on a draft drawn on a bank that has an office in the country you are dealing with.

The *American Youth Hostel Association* will help groups of six or more arrange tours in Europe. Hostel reservations, flights, and routes will be supplied to groups that qualify. For further information, contact the AYH Association.

*National tourist offices* of many European countries have cycling itineraries. These range from tours of only a few hours to trips of some weeks in length, and their quality varies from office to office. Most choose quiet roads and take you to scenic spots. Some are rather short on detail, and are most valuable as side trips from a given town or locality.

*Cycling clubs within Europe* provide a number of touring itineraries, usually to members, but often to nonmembers as well. The Dutch cycling club, Strichting Fiets! is exceptional in this regard, providing tours and maps of Holland's many bicycle paths. Cycle touring clubs in other countries are not as elaborately prepared as the Dutch, but if addressed in person can be of considerable help in providing tour or short trip itineraries. These are discussed in more detail in the country-by-country descriptions in Chapter 4, and their addresses are given in Appendix 5.

A good *travel agent* can be of help in booking you into moderate- or higher-priced hotels, although many do not have experience in making bookings in small-town hotels where you often end up. But if you are fortunate enough to have in your town or city a dedicated and knowledgeable agent, he can handle many details for you, from hotel bookings to train and ferry tickets to things to see along the way.

## GUIDED TOURS

If you do not wish to plan your own itinerary or take advantage of some of those planned for you, you may find any one of a number of organized tours just the thing for you. You will know well before you leave exactly how much things are going to cost; most tour organizers will send you detailed itineraries so that you can begin reading about some of the things you will see; and you will have the feeling of confidence that you are not venturing out into the unknown, never to return again. You may also have a son or daughter who wishes to tour but who you feel is too young to do it all on his or her own. Whatever the case, here is a list of tour organizers who have longstanding reputations for reliability in planning and executing European bicycle tours. All addresses are given in Appendix 3.

*American Youth Hostel Tours.* American Youth Hostels, Inc., is among the oldest hands at leading quality European tours. In 1979, ten different cycling tours were offered by the AYH in a host of European countries. Tours ranged from three weeks to up to forty-four days in length. Travel is primarily by bicycle, although trains, ferries, and hiking are included as features on some tours.

You must be at least 16 years old to join an AYH tour abroad; if younger, you must have participated successfully in one of their domestic tours. Membership in the AYH Association is required.

There is no maximum age for joining a tour, and the Youth Hostel Association reports an increasing number of senior citizens who go along on their bicycle tours. When this happens, it adds a balance and richness to the trip which is rewarding for everyone.

Your guide on an AYH trip functions more as a group leader, although most are familiar with the country and are happy to point out things to see. You bring your own bicycle, although AYH helps with arrangements for getting it ready for the flight over. Once on tour, you normally go from 30 to 50 miles per day, with averages in the 30s and 40s. You stay in youth hostels and take your meals there. In some hostels the meals are prepared for you; in others you cooperate with other group members and take turns being chef. You carry your own gear, including the required sleep sheet.

Trip costs vary, depending upon length, and all include air fare, hostel costs, food, accident and health insurance, and leadership expenses. In addition, there is a $50 emergency fund fee, the excess of which is refunded after the tour. Fees do not include your transportation to the starting point (Washington, D.C., or New York), nor your incidental expenses. Here is a sampling of AYH tours offered currently:

"English Countryside"—Three weeks starting and ending in London. You bicycle to Stratford-on-Avon, go through the Cotswolds, Bath, see Stonehenge, visit famous Winchester (the hostel in Winchester is a centuries-old mill where you can still see the millraces in the "basement"). Cost of the tour is $935, based on APEX air fare from the East Coast.

"Saddlebag Special"—Thirty-one days in England, France, Belgium, and the Netherlands, including Stratford-on-Avon, a Shakespearean play, Stonehenge, across the channel to Normandy in France, then down to the Loire valley with its fabled châteaux, up through Belgium, and then to Amsterdam. Cost $1,235, based on APEX air fare.

"European Explorer"—Forty-four days in Luxembourg, France, Switzerland, Austria, Germany, and Belgium. This includes the Swiss Alps and six days of "finding your own place," during which you stay together as a group but explore on your own, finding accommodations and meals where you please. Cost: $1,275, based on APEX air fare.

*International Bicycle Touring Society* tours. The International Bicycle Touring Society is a nonprofit, California-based organization that offers a number of tours both within the U.S. and abroad. The organization is led by Dr. Clifford Graves, who has done as much as any American over the years to sponsor serious bicycle travel both here and in Europe. The IBTS regularly schedules tours to England, France, Austria, and Greece. Tours are about two weeks in length. The distinctive feature of the IBTS's tours is their humane approach to the whole subject. The average age of tour members runs somewhere between 30 and 60. While no bones are made about your being able to spend a day on a bicycle, the emphasis is still on companionship, comfortable but not luxurious accommodations, and reasonable distances per day. Luggage is carried on a sag wagon, and hotels and meals are arranged and included in the cost of the tour. Accommodation is in moderately priced hotels, often in smaller towns and villages along the route.

If you want to go on a tour with the IBTS you must join first. Dues are $10 a year, individual or couple. Daily tour expenses abroad average about $35 per day. This does not include your travel to and from the tour starting and finishing points. You are on your own for lunch. IBTS tours are well organized and routes are carefully studied.

In addition to the AYH and the IBTS, there are a number of organizations which offer one or two guided tours a year in different parts of Europe. Style of travel and cost vary.

The *Biking Expedition* is a bicycle travel program for young people between the ages of 13 and 17. Founded by Susan and Tom Heavey in 1973, the Biking Expedition offers tours of England, Scotland, and Ireland, and will add a tour of France for the 1980 season. Two adult leaders accompany each coeducational group. Accommodation is in hostels, and young people cooperate in preparing their own meals. A good deal of emphasis is placed on cooperative living within the group, and tour leaders are carefully screened with this quality in mind.

Tours cover from 25 to 45 miles a day. You bring your own bicycle. Tour costs include air transportation from Boston to the tour starting/finishing point, food, and health insurance. Tours offered in 1979 included:

England and Scotland—Thirty-six days. Starting at London, cyclists follow the Thames to Oxford, wind through the Cotswolds, then head north toward England's Lake District and into Scotland. Cost is about $1,500, including air fare. The latter fluctuates depending upon a number of factors outside the control of tour operators.

Ireland—A thirty-three-day trip through the lovely southwest part of Ireland, including Limerick, the Ring of Kerry, Killarney's lakes, then on to Tipperary and County Clare. Cost is $1,335, with some margin left for air fare fluctuations.

*Club Tamuré* is a California-based travel organization offering two four-week tours of England, Switzerland, Germany, and France during the summer season. Daily distances range from 30 to 54 miles, the averages in the low 30s. You take your own bicycle with you. The Tamuré tours blend bicycle and train travel and, when necessary, use ferries. Accommodations are in moderate-priced hotels, with a few nights spent in youth hostels. The four-week tour price of $1,275 includes all accommodation costs, breakfast and dinner, guide services, a sag wagon, train and ferry travel. Not included are lunch expenses and air fare to and from London. You may, however, book passage through Club Tamuré from Oakland, California, via Laker Airways. Fares are at competitive charter rates.

*Euro-Bike Tours*, based in DeKalb, Illinois, offers four European tours from sixteen to twenty-three days in length. Riders stay in hotels, use high-quality rented ten-speeds (at reduction in tour price if you use your own), and travel via bus through regions not particularly suited to bicycling, or to cover long distances when necessary.

Some tours cover only a single country, such as the "Heart of England Tour," which begins in London, winds through the Cotswolds, leaves a day open for an optional train trip to Oxford, then circles south to pick up the cities of Salisbury, Winchester, Chichester, and return to London. A visit to Stonehenge is also included.

Other tours take in more, such as the "Heritage" tour through England, Germany, France, Luxembourg, and Holland. This takes twenty-three days, and considerable portions of it are covered in a bus.

There is a tour of France's Loire valley and Brittany, and a sixteen-day tour that covers eastern France in the Alsace region, takes in the area north of Zurich in Switzerland, a portion of the Black Forest, and a stint through Upper Swabia in Germany.

Accommodations are in modest hotels. Breakfast is included in the tour price, along with a few other meals during the tour, including arrival and farewell dinners. Tour participants pay for other meals out of their own funds.

You must be at least 18 years old to go on a Euro-Bike tour, unless you are accompanied by parent or guardian. All luggage is carried in a sag wagon, which is also on hand to pick you up if you have a breakdown. Distances covered on bicycles are in the 30- to 40-mile range. All the tours take in easy or moderately difficult cycling country only. Prices range from $628 for a sixteen-day tour of England to $878 for a more extensive "Heritage" tour. Air fare is not included in the tour price.

*Out Spokin'* is an Indiana-based group that offers an unusual European Mennonite history bicycle tour. The orientation of the trip is on Mennonite Anabaptist history, and includes a good many stopping points in Holland and Switzerland illustrative of this branch of Christianity. Accommodations are primarily in inexpensive hotels and hostels. You take your own bicycle with you. The trip is three weeks long, and costs include air fare, hostel, food expenses, and services of the tour leaders. Projected costs for 1980 are $1,700.

*Bike Tour France* is the obsession of a confessed Francophile, Jerry Simpson, Jr., who has lived there and knows the country well. Bike Tour France offers a single tour each year, beginning and ending in Versailles (just outside Paris). The tour winds down from Versailles to the Loire valley, scallops along the château country, then back to its starting point. It takes about three weeks, covers some 600 miles, and you average 46 miles a day. Accommodation is in small hotels, and both breakfast and dinner are included in the tour price. You are on your own for lunch. Also included: air fare from New York to Paris and back, all entry fees into the châteaux, maps, tips, and last but not least, rental of a quality ten-speed bicycle for use during the tour. The cost of the trip is about $1,200. Tours fill early, so inquire well in advance.

*The Cyclists Touring Club* of England offers organized tours somewhere between a guided tour and a complete do-it-yourself affair. As you might expect, you tour primarily with English people, and you will go far to find a group more knowledgeable about touring both in their own country and outside it. Accommodation is in hostels or guest houses, and tours range from one-week trips in England to two-week tours of places such as the French Alps, Corsica, Sweden, and Czechoslovakia. The CTC offers about twenty such tours each year.

FOUR

# Where to go touring

Some tourists go to Europe and rush from city to city in planes. Others get on a train and do about the same thing. Still others buy cars and drive madly through nine countries in three weeks. Your world as a bicyclist is a quiet contrast. You may spend a week exploring an area others pass through in a day or an afternoon. You find out that the personality of a Basque in the Pyrenees is different from the Catalan around Barcelona, that the Yorkshire man stands apart from his countryman to the south. But because your world is small the number of places in Europe to tour is nearly infinite. And while some countries may have better cycling features—a good climate and an abundance of small well-paved roads—no country is really barred to you. In addition to England and France, two favorite cycle touring countries, tourists annually pedal through Yugoslavia, the Pyrenees in Spain, the fjords of Norway, the bulb fields of Holland, the Black Forest in Germany, the valley of the Danube in Austria, the Peloponnese in Greece, or cross the Alps in Switzerland. The question of where to go is really more one of where you want to go.

## SOME TOURING POSSIBILITIES

If you are not now an old European hand, you may want a bit of specific information on what the touring possibilities are in the different European countries. We'll begin by looking at general bicycle touring conditions in fifteen countries of western Europe. This alphabetical list includes some facts about geography—where it is level and where you can expect hills—what the roads are like, the climate, what types of accommodations are available, where the better touring areas within the country are located, and how to get to and from the country.

Also included is information regarding organized tours within each country, as well as possibilities for securing itineraries you may follow on your own. If the country has extensive rental possibilities, we indicate their nature and cost. Finally, we suggest sources for detailed regional maps that show small back roads, an essential requirement for trip planning.

### AUSTRIA

*Geography and roads.* About two-thirds of Austria is very mountainous and provides excellent alpine cycling. The Tyrol around Innsbruck and the Alps south of Salzburg are two favorites. In each, you will have to stick pretty much to the major traffic thoroughfares since secondary roads are rare. Less strenuous touring is available in the northeast section of the country, particularly down the

Danube valley. Except for the area around Linz, which is industrial, the entire valley down to Vienna is picturesque and interesting cycling.

If you wish to see the Austrian Alps and not cycle over them, you can train to some of the more spectacular spots such as Innsbruck or Kitzbühel and cycle around there. Another touring possibility is to begin at Salzburg, cycle through the lakes of the Salzkammergut region, then intersect the Danube at Linz and proceed downstream to Vienna.

The tour of Austria we have included at the end of the book takes you through some of the most scenic yet less strenuous parts of the country. The itinerary and route choice was generously provided by Dr. Clifford Graves of the International Bicycle Touring Society. Dr. Graves terms the tour "a distillation of three previous tours in the same general area. Honed to a fine degree, it shows you the country in its best possible aspect. Practically all the cycling is on side roads rather than main roads." The tour starts in Graz, then winds through scenic farmland and mountain scenery to Salzburg.

Day tours and scenic itineraries are possible from a number of cities in Austria. The Bicycling Section of the Austrian Automobile and Motorcycle Touring Club, Schubertring 3, 1010 Wien, Austria, has a number of such itineraries.

*Bicycle rental.* Bicycles may be rented at thirty-seven railroad stations scattered throughout the country. Rentals are by the day, but can be extended for longer periods. Costs are about $3.50 per day, but only half that if you hold a valid ticket on the national railway. A list of stations renting bicycles is given in Appendix 6.

*Maps.* Michelin map no. 426 (1:400,000) covers all Austria. It can be ordered by mail (see Appendix 7).

More detailed regional maps are available within Austria.

*Accommodations.* Hotels are found throughout the country. Hostels are located mostly in the area southeast of Salzburg, along the lakes in Carinthia, and in the east just south of Vienna. Campgrounds are numerous throughout the Alps from Lake Constance (Boden See) to Salzburg and in the lake district of Carinthia, but less common elsewhere.

*Climate.* Warm summer temperatures in Vienna and in Carinthia, cool nights in the high mountains. Less rain throughout the country than in much of northern Europe.

*Access.* Good rail service from all neighboring countries. Good connecting pass roads to Switzerland, Italy, and Germany.

## BELGIUM

*Geography and roads.* This small country is surely one of the most amazing in Europe. Heavily damaged in two world wars, suffering years of enemy occupation in both, it recovered to become one of the most prosperous countries in Europe. Partly because of this the western portions of the country are heavily populated and industrialized and not particularly suited to the bicycle tourist. Brussels, Antwerp, and Ghent are all worth a visit, but it is better to leave your bicycle at a train station somewhere and explore them by other means.

The forests of the Ardennes in the east are another matter. Although the country is steeply hilly and calls for energetic cycling, the forests themselves are interesting, and this part of the country can make an excellent connecting route into France. There is a fair system of secondary roads in the area.

*Bicycle rental.* Bicycles may be rented from twenty-two

railroad stations throughout Belgium and returned to some seventy other stations that serve as drop-off points. The bicycles are single-speeds and rent for 115 francs per day for the first two days, and 100 francs a day thereafter. If you purchase a railway passenger ticket, rental prices drop to 85 francs per day for the first two days, then 75 francs a day thereafter. The list of rental stations is given in Appendix 6.

*Maps.* Michelin map no. 409 (1:300,000) covers all Belgium. Michelin maps 1, 2, and 4 (1:200,000) give more detail. All may be mail-ordered (see Appendix 7).

*Accommodations.* Hostels and campgrounds are common throughout the country, and are quite numerous in the Ardennes. You will find moderately priced hotels everywhere.

*Climate.* Cool, tending to be cloudy and sometimes showery in the summer. Take a sweater for evenings.

*Access.* By ferry (frequent daily service) from England and good train service from other parts of the Continent.

## BRITISH ISLES

### ENGLAND

*Geography and roads.* Because of the similarity in language and the cultural ties that bind us, England is one of the most popular tourist spots for the American traveler. For the cyclist this lure is increased by the promise of small roads and very friendly people. Where is the best place to cycle in England? Almost anywhere, with the exception of the industrial sections around Manchester, Liverpool, and Birmingham. The southeastern counties of Kent and Sussex are known as the Garden of England. This is a fertile, low, rolling area with many seaside resorts and historical sites, the most popular being Canterbury Cathedral.

The southwest counties of Somerset, Dorset, Devon, and Cornwall are known as the West Country. This area stretches from the wooded Salisbury Plain, where Stonehenge is located, to the dairy and fishing country on the Cornwall peninsula. This area is pocketed with fishing villages and seaside resorts. The land tends to be rolling along the coast, with a more hilly central core.

The central section of England is known as Shakespeare Country for it is here that the famous town of Stratford-on-Avon is located. This area is very picturesque and full of old Tudor houses tucked away in the woods.

The northwest counties are where to find the famous Lake District, a favorite with English cycle tourists. Within a relatively small area you get the full benefit of beautiful mountain lake scenery.

The northeast is the land of moors and ancient abbeys. The seacoast attracts a lot of English "holidaymakers," and the history attracts a lot of visitors. Whitby Abbey and the beautiful city of York are the most noted of the historic sites. The cyclist can also take full advantage of the solitude of the moors that stretch all the way to Scotland.

East Anglia is the name given to the southeast. It used to be an old Saxon kingdom, some good remains of which can still be seen. The area is flatter than the rest of England and has remained relatively unchanged by modern tourist influence.

Throughout England there is an intricate system of secondary and tributary roads. The roads are usually unnumbered, and you must learn to navigate between small towns. The side-trip possibilities are endless. We once met a man who prided himself on getting from his home in

Brighton, in the south, to the north of Scotland without traveling over a main road.

A number of organizations offer guided tours of England, Scotland, and Wales; they are listed in Appendix 3.

The British Tourist Authority (see Appendix 4 for address) offers a very informative pamphlet for bicyclists, "Britain on Two Wheels." It gives a number of itineraries and general hints on bicycling in Great Britain, and has a list of rental establishments in case you don't bring your own bicycle.

The Cyclists' Touring Club (see Appendix 5 for address) will assist members in planning tours. They also have a number of group tours each year as well as a good assortment of printed tours you can take on your own.

The Touring Bureau of the British Cycling Federation also offers preplanned tours for members. You must join first. Fees and addresses are given in Appendix 3.

*Bicycle rental.* There are some two hundred rental shops throughout Great Britain listed in Appendix 6. Kind and quality of bicycle varies. For long-term rentals you are advised to inquire well ahead of time, and send a deposit with your order. Rates for rentals vary, running from £2 per day for a quality ten-speed, less for five- and three-speeds. Long-term rentals run about £14 per week.

*Maps.* The Bartholomew National Series (1:100,000) covers all of Great Britain in sixty-two sheets. They are excellent and the best for thorough exploration of a given area. Less detailed but also excellent for the bicycle tourist is the Bartholomew GT Series (1:253,440). They cover the British Isles in ten sheets. Both may be mail-ordered (see Appendix 7). The Michelin Map Company also has maps that are adequate for the cycle tourist not much concerned with nuances of the route. Michelin maps 403 and 404 (1:400,000) cover Great Britain. See Appendix 7 for mail-order addresses.

*Accommodations.* It is easy to find good accommodations everywhere. Youth hostels are very numerous, and it is easy to plan a tour around them. Most hostels serve meals, and all have cooking facilities. Campgrounds are plentiful along the coastal area of Cornwall but tend to be scarce otherwise. It's a simple matter and quite acceptable to ask permission to camp in a farmer's field or behind a country inn. Usually no payment will be asked of you. Hotels and guesthouses are found everywhere—both along the road and in the smallest villages. Breakfast is always included in the tariff.

*Climate.* The summer weather is usually mild, frequently cloudy or overcast, but not excessively rainy. It is fine for cycle touring as long as you accept ahead of time that you aren't going to come away with a suntan. You will usually need a sweater in the evenings, and a rain-repellent cover is not a bad idea either. The weather never daunts the English cyclist, and if you want to take advantage of all the wonders of the English countryside you will have to remain undaunted too.

*Access.* There is very easy access by ferry from Holland, Belgium, and France to the seacoast towns of Dover, Folkstone, and Ramsgate. Regular boat-train services between London and Paris are also available. Make seat reservations for these. There are also numerous student charter flights to and from all the major capitals of Europe.

## WALES

*Geography and roads.* Three centuries ago, after a long and bitter struggle, Wales became a political part of England. Yet even today you can sense that this is merely a technicality, for the Welsh personality is still very much alive and intact, and quite different from its neighbor to the east. In many ways the diverse, elusive personality of the Welshman is reflected in his small but varied country.

The southeastern peninsula, in and around Pembroke, is an area of coal fields and valleys lined with the terraced homes of the coal miners. It's not a very scenic place for the cycle tourist as the countryside has been cluttered with the remains of the mining operations and the towns tend to adopt the bleak atmosphere of their surroundings.

The northern and western sections of the country offer many more scenic and historic possibilities.

In the north the coastal area rises from a narrow plain to a hard core of mountains. As these mountains move east they slowly change into rounded, gray moors cut by narrow river valleys. It is in these moors that the three major rivers of central Wales—the Usk, Wye, and Severn—have their source. As these rivers start their journey eastward to the Midlands of England, the valleys they form become broader and more gentle. In the last chapter we offer a tour of Wales that takes in a sampling of the different faces of the countryside.

There are paved roads throughout the country. Secondary roads exist but can be questionable for cycling as they are usually ungraded and often unpaved. Main roads are adequate for cycling.

*Rentals and maps.* See England.

*Accommodations.* There are hostels throughout Wales but they tend to be more highly concentrated in the northern section. All hostels have cooking facilities and many serve meals. Campgrounds can be found in the more popular areas of the north but are nonexistent elsewhere. Hotels and guesthouses are found in almost all towns, and greater numbers of them are located along the coast.

*Climate.* The Welsh weather is like that of England, but the evenings tend to be damper and cooler.

*Access.* Wales is accessible via train from all the principal cities of England.

NORTHERN IRELAND (ULSTER)

*Geography and roads.* The six counties that make up the Ulster countryside are full of glens, beautiful coastal areas, and rolling green hills. County Down with the Mourne Mountains running to the sea and the Antrim Coast road are especially worthy of investigation. There is a good network of primary roads that service most of the country. Secondary roads are also present but often are not well paved. The country is on the whole quite suitable for cycling, however, because of the distinct lack of automobile traffic.

*Rentals and maps.* See England.

*Accommodations.* Campgrounds and hostels are found primarily along the coast but only in moderate numbers. Hotels are located in all medium-sized towns and cities. Guesthouses are found frequently along the route.

*Climate.* Cool, inclined to be showery in summer.

*Access.* There are ferry services to Belfast from Glasgow in Scotland and Liverpool in England.

IRELAND (THE REPUBLIC OF IRELAND)

*Geography and roads.* Ireland is an outstanding place to cycle in from both a scenic standpoint and because of the lack of traffic on the tiny country roads. The soft green hills are alive with ghostly tales, old castles, monasteries, and friendly, forthright people.

The countryside is made up of a central rolling plain guarded by mountains on either end. The most scenic riding areas are the counties of Wicklow, just south of Dublin, Cork in the south, Kerry in the southwest, and Mayo and Galway in the northwest. All offer scenery that is a fine blend of wooded valleys and low mountains.

There is a good network of secondary roads throughout the country. They are usually well posted and easy to navigate. Automobile traffic is light, and the drivers you do see are generally very courteous to the cyclist.

The Irish Tourist Board and the Raleigh Company of Ireland have a collection of pamphlets detailing short tours that radiate outward from various regional centers. They cover Kerry and West Cork, Shannonside, Galway, Wexford and Waterford, Lake Land, Mayo, and the Midlands. They may be secured from the Irish Tourist Board (see Appendix 4).

*Bicycle rental.* The Raleigh Company has established over one hundred "Rent a Bike" centers in Ireland. All shops cooperating in the program offer three-speed bicycles and mini bicycles for rental. Rates range from £1.75 per day to £10 per week for a touring three-speed equipped with front and rear carrier and rear panniers. In some instances, bicycles can be rented from one shop and returned to another. A list of rental agencies in Ireland is included in Appendix 6.

*Maps.* The Bartholomew Irish Travel Map Series (1:253,440) covers Ireland and Ulster in five sheets. They may be ordered in this country from the Hammond Company (see Appendix 7).

*Accommodations.* Hotels are well located throughout the country, as are smaller bed-and-breakfast places. There are forty-five youth hostels in Ireland, most of them clustered on the coastal areas near Wicklow, Bantry, and Newry. None of the hostels serves meals but all are equipped with cooking facilities. Campgrounds exist throughout the country, but on the whole organized camping is a rarity. It is much more common to ask permission to camp on someone's land.

*Climate.* The weather is cool and often showery in the summer.

*Access.* There are regular ferry services from Liverpool and Fishguard in England to Dublin and Rosslare in Ireland. There is also a boat-train service from Paddington Station in London.

## SCOTLAND

*Geography and roads.* Scotland is an intricate labyrinth of small lakes, expansive moors, steep mountains, and steel-gray lochs. The central and northern sections are hilly or mountainous. The eastern coast is hilly but not as severe. The road system tends to be composed of primary roads or unmaintained secondary roads. The Scottish countryside and economy do not allow for much else. Throughout Scotland, Sunday is considered a day of rest, and very few establishments are open. This is especially true the further north you go. Plan accordingly.

Our own tour of Scotland will allow you to experience most of its mysteries.

*Rentals and maps.* See England.

*Accommodations.* There are many hostels in Scotland, well distributed geographically. Most of them have cooking facilities but do not serve prepared meals. Campgrounds are rare. There are some along the coast but almost nothing inland. It is possible to camp on private land, with permission of course. Hotels and guesthouses, with varying tariffs, are found in all cities and towns.

*Climate.* Cool in the summer, inclined to be showery. Take a thick sweater for evenings and a rain cape for cycling.

*Access.* By train from London and all principal cities in northern England.

## FRANCE

*Geography and roads.* France is a land of quiet roads, small villages, and a variety of climates and terrains stretching from cool thick forests in the north to the brilliantly warm limestone mountains of the south. There is hardly any place in the country that is *not* attractive to the bicycle tourist. You will find more paved secondary roads there than in any other European country, and for the most part it is a matter of picking which particular mixture of climate, culture, and terrain is most enjoyable to you. We suggest three tours in the last chapter which take you through four distinct regions—the level, château-studded Loire valley south of Paris; Burgundy in the east, a rolling, picturesque country noted for its outstanding wines plus Alsace in the northeast, a delightful mixture of Germanic and Gallic influences; and Brittany in the northwest.

But this is only the beginning. To get a better idea of the alternatives let's look briefly at the geography of the country. Except in the north and along the Atlantic Seaboard to the border of northern Spain, France is ringed by various mountain ranges. Yet only the Alps in the southeast make for consistently energetic cycling. In the other ranges you can make your way up long valleys with only periodically energetic cycling, or you can scallop the lower parts of various ranges. The Pyrenees in the southwest and the Vosges in the east are good choices for this kind of riding. Another good ride which takes you near mountains but not through them is in the south, from Aix-en-Provence to Nice, on the Riviera. Again this is primarily moderate, not energetic, cycling.

What else is there to see? Quite a bit, and most of it is over terrain more gentle than that just described. In the east there are the rolling farmlands and valleys of Savoie and Burgundy. On the Atlantic Coast, Brittany is a favorite. It is a unique land with its own language and culture. The green hillsides tumble down to the coast, with stretches of rocky fingers reaching out into the sea. Farther south is Bordeaux, producer of a great variety of excellent wines. As in most wine-growing regions, there are rolling hills. The Mediterranean is a lovely coast, but the road directly bordering the sea is highly congested, particularly in summer. With some care you can thread a route just inland, then stop along the sea at night if you wish.

Some areas that are better traversed by train are the Rhône valley south of Lyon, which is subject to extremely strong winds, and the area directly east of Paris, which tends to be rather uninteresting, composed mostly of rolling wheat fields, with, apart from Reims Cathedral, little else to see.

There are a number of private and nonprofit organizations that offer tours through much of France. Appendix 3 gives a list of them.

If you inquire in person at the Federation Française de Cyclotourisme (see Appendix 5), they will provide you with a list of local cycle touring clubs and youth organizations within France that have tours of from one day to several weeks. To join such a tour you should speak at least minimal French and be willing to arrange details with the tour organizers, usually the presidents of regional cycling clubs. Normally, you would also have to join the club. This is for the adventurous, but there is scarcely a better way of experiencing France first-hand than with seasoned cycle tourists. The Federation Française de Cyclotourisme is an organization in Paris with limited staff and budget, and cannot answer mail inquiries. Nor did anyone speak English when we last visited their offices. There is a fee for joining the organization.

The Bicy-Club de France, located in Paris, has a number of preplanned tours. To participate you must join the organization first. The fee is 50 francs per year and a one-time initiation fee of 10 francs. They have tours in central France, Alsace, Normandy, and the Loire valley. Their staff is limited also, and inquiries are best made in person. See Appendix 5 for their address in Paris.

The French Government Tourist Office (see Appendix 4) has a few itineraries that combine bicycle and train travel through some of France's more scenic spots.

For the grand splash, there are even some firms that offer a barge and bicycle tour, complete with your own chef and guide, through three different regions of France. These barges ply France's numerous canals and you get your own minibike for cruising off on dry land. Cost is about $550 per person per week, and that includes the barge. Your travel agent can give you more details.

*Bicycle rental.* In addition to numerous private establishments found in Paris and popular resort areas, there are eighty-five railway stations that rent bicycles. Cost is 15 francs per day, plus a refundable 100-franc deposit. A list of both major private rental agencies and all railway stations renting bicycles is given in Appendix 6.

For one-day rides through Paris's famous Bois de Boulogne, there is a bicycle rental kiosk that operates on weekends from September to June, and all day long, every day, from July to September. One day's rental is 20 francs. The kiosk is located just behind the Hippodrome in the Bois de Boulogne.

*Maps.* Michelin 1:200,000 scale maps cover all of France in some forty-two sheets. They may be ordered by mail (see Appendix 7). Within France, the GPA maps (1:250,000) are available in bookstores and many tobacco shops. They are also excellent.

*Accommodations.* Hotels are common everywhere, and finding ones at moderate prices will be no problem. Youth hostels tend to be spread out rather thinly throughout the country. As elsewhere, advance reservations are advisable. Campgrounds are more numerous in France than in any other European country. No area is without them, and popular resort areas have plenty.

*Climate.* Varies greatly between north and south. The south from the Spanish to Italian borders is dry and warm (but not excessively hot) from May through September. North of Lyons, summer weather is cooler, but still warm, with occasional thunderstorms.

*Access.* There is an excellent rail system connecting France with all parts of the Continent, and daily ferry and hovercraft services to England from Calais and Boulogne. Hovercraft are the best bargain for the cyclist.

## GERMANY (FEDERAL REPUBLIC OF GERMANY)

*Geography and roads.* While the north of Germany is flat and easy cycling, the more interesting touring areas are in the rolling or moderately steep central and southern regions. Here you have a wide contrast of terrains and cultures: quiet valleys such as the Neckar and the Lech; Bavaria, with its green undulating forests punctuated occasionally by an ornate castle rising from a hilltop; the Black Forest farther west; and in the south, the lakes and lower Alps that form the border between Switzerland and Austria. Sprinkled throughout the region are historic cities such as Heidelberg, Munich, Nuremberg, Augsburg, and Freiburg. Later on we suggest a tour which takes you through a great deal of southern and central Germany. The cycle tourist would do well to avoid the Rhine Valley in the west, which, while quite attractive, has highly congested road traffic that makes it more pleasantly seen from one of the many Rhine ferries that ply upriver and down. Also to be avoided for the same reason are the industrial centers in the Ruhr and Saar basins, and the areas immediately around Stuttgart. This is true even on weekends, when all trucks are forbidden to use the autobahns and are forced onto the side roads.

Germany has an excellent system of primary roads, but they also tend to be crowded with traffic, making the search for good secondary roads well worth your while. There is a good system of these too, particularly in the central and southern regions.

A number of local tourist offices in different parts of Germany offer tour packages designed for the bicyclist. Tours usually include routes, maps, hotel accommodations, and at least one meal, and most include a rental bicycle. Tours offered include one- and two-week trips through Munsterland, Upper Swabia, Allgau, Siegerland, Sauerland, Wittgensteinderland, and Lipperland. The typical price for a seven-day tour is about 190 deutsche marks, which includes hotel, breakast, bicycle rental, maps, and luggage transport. A private firm, Rotalia, has a number of cycling tours of one and two weeks duration. Prices range from DM 498 for a seven-day tour in southern Germany to a thirteen-day tour that encompasses much of the country and costs DM 1,131. That includes hotel, breakfast and dinner, luggage transport, and even bus transportation if it rains. In addition, some private American organizations offer tours that include Germany within a larger itinerary. All are described in Appendix 3. Our own tour of the Black Forest is given in Chapter 11.

*Bicycle rental.* Some two hundred railway stations rent

basic bicycles during the summer season. These are located throughout Germany, but are most heavily clustered in the south. Cost is DM 8 per day, but holders of a railroad ticket on the German system get a 50 percent reduction. A list of these stations is given in Appendix 6.

*Maps.* Michelin nos. 202, 203, 204, 205, and 206 (1:200,000) cover the eastern half of the country. They may be ordered within the United States (see Appendix 7). Mairs maps may be ordered from the British Cycling Federation, Touring Bureau (see Appendix 7).

*Accommodations.* Youth hostels were invented in Germany, and the urge felt by most Germans to be outdoors has also led to the creation of a good many campgrounds. You will find hotels everywhere. Both hostels and campgrounds are plentiful in the center and south of the country, a bit less common in the north. Camping outside organized campgrounds is not encouraged, but on one occasion, lacking accommodations after a night over huge mugs of draft beer with a fat, singing Bavarian, we rode to one of the forests that seem to ring every small town, threw our sleeping bags on the ground, and flopped down for an undisturbed night's sleep. No one seemed to mind.

*Climate.* German summers can be damp and cool, so take along a thick sweater for evenings and a good lightweight windbreaker for riding.

*Access.* An excellent rail system connects Germany with all neighboring countries. Daily ferry service from Denmark is available throughout the summer. Reservations on the ferry are advisable.

## GREECE

*Geography and roads.* Greece has one of the problems shared by most poor countries—heavily traveled primary roads and few secondary roads to choose from. Except for areas on both sides of Salonica in the north, most of the country is hilly or mountainous.

Should you still try to bicycle tour there? Yes, and yes again. First of all, the climate is sunny about half the year. Although it is hot inland, anywhere along the sea, which includes most of the country, is cooler, and in most places you can park your bicycle along the road and make your way down to the sea for a swim to cool off. The water is probably the clearest in the world. Our own tour of Greece, offered in the last chapter of this book, gets you from Patras to Athens via the old national highway. A new toll road runs parallel to it, leaving the old highway to carry mostly local traffic. We have cycled it twice in the off season (September) with good success each time.

*Rentals and maps.* There are some rental facilities on the more popular Aegean islands such as Crete, Kos, and Rhodes. Good, detailed maps are difficult to obtain outside of Greece, but adequate maps are available once you arrive. Check a large bookstore at your arrival point.

*Accommodations.* While hotels and restaurants are common in all the major population or tourist centers, in some out-of-the-way areas amenities are usually simple or sometimes even absent, especially in the small villages. If you ever do get stuck, go to the tourist police and make your needs known as best you can to them. In most cases local arrangements will be made. Do not be surprised if you end up as guest of honor at someone's dinner table. Hostels are rare, but campgrounds are plentiful along major tourist routes.

*Climate.* Sunny, hot in the interior; the sea breezes keep the coastal areas cooler.

*Access.* Via train from Yugoslavia, but a preferable mode of travel is by ship. Frequent ferry service from Italian ports on the Adriatic to Corfu and Patras.

## HOLLAND

*Geography and roads.* Until recently the bicycle was used in Holland primarily as a means of puttering down to the store for some cheese or bread. In the past ten years the Dutch have discovered bicycle touring, and now no nation in Europe does as much for the touring cyclist. In addition to the blessing of nearly perfectly flat terrain—the highest thing you see in most of Holland is a bridge arching across a canal or a church spire or windmill rising in the distance—the Dutch have constructed an incredible network of bicycle paths. They parallel main roads, border canals, wind through woods, and run along the borders of fields. How do you find these paths? Why, with maps, of course, and these are supplied by the Dutch cycling club, Stichting Fiets! (see Appendix 5 for address). Branches of the Dutch Tourist Office, which are found in most towns throughout the country (look for the initials VVV), will also provide you with maps and cycling guides for their areas.

Where can you tour in Holland? Everywhere. Because of the abundance of fellow cyclists and bicycle paths, some of the general rules about avoiding heavily populated areas can be safely ignored. Favorite touring areas are on the western side of the country around Amsterdam, in the bulb fields near Haarlem, and to such historic cities as Utrecht, The Hague, and Leyden. Our own suggested tour in Chapter 10 covers most of these places.

The eastern regions of the country also have their own quiet charm, with small rolling hills and quiet forests. The Limberg region in the south is well located for connecting tours of Germany or Belgium.

A number of regional tourist offices also offer organized tours. Prices include the cost of a rental bicycle, hotel accommodations, usually one main meal, and frequently luggage transport. On many of them you can take your own bicycle and cut the tour price. Charges range from a three-day/two-night trip around Bergen for 90 D.Fl. to an all-expense-paid, seven-day tour around Friesland for 395 D.Fl. This includes bicycle rental.

*Bicycle rental.* In a land largely given over to the bicycle, it is not surprising that there are some one thousand places in Holland to rent them. A complete list of these shops can be secured from the Dutch cycling club, Stichting Fiets! (see Appendix 5). Most of the bicycles are single- or three-speeds, which is what most of the Netherlanders use for getting about and touring in their own country. The bicycles are heavy and cumbersome by some standards, but are quite acceptable for travel in this tabletop land. Rates are about 5 D.Fl. per day. Weekly rates are cheaper. In Overijssel and Gelderland some sixty-five firms cooperate in a rent-a-bike system, which allows you to rent from one place and return to another. Addresses of these places can be secured from local tourist agencies (VVVs) in either Overijssel or Gelderland.

*Maps.* Michelin maps nos. 1, 5, and 6 (1:200,000) cover Holland and may be ordered by mail (see Appendix 7).

*Accommodations.* Campgrounds and hostels are numerous throughout the country but more heavily clustered in the west. Moderately priced hotels are found in nearly all towns and in all cities.

*Climate.* Cool, inclined to be cloudy; sudden showers are common. Prepare accordingly. The wind in the western parts of the country along the coast will be quite strong. Ride in the mornings when possible.

*Access.* There is an excellent train service to all adjoining countries, frequent daily ferries to England, and two regular ferries to Norway. There are special trains within Holland that will carry your bicycle for you. Some persons using the regular train service to carry bicycles have experienced delays of a day or more in their bicycle reaching them. Check locally for details.

## ITALY

*Geography and roads.* The northern parts of Italy are the best suited to cycling since they have more plains and rolling areas than the south and also a more moderate summer temperature. We offer a tour of the Po valley that takes in some of the gentler touring areas of Italy's north. A more vigorous tour through the Dolomites north of Venice is also possible. The riding is hard, but the scenery is lovely. Anywhere along the "spine" of Italy that runs from north to south down the middle of the peninsula will take you through untouristed areas, some not well known even to Italians, but the cycling is difficult, and the weather in summer is torrid. The southeastern areas along the Adriatic are less crowded than the north, and the sea keeps the temperature lower than in the interior. By careful route-finding we have been able to snake our way down through this area without encountering much car traffic. If you are entering Italy from France, the stretch from Menton on the French side down to Pisa has a great deal of summer traffic with no special provision for bicycles. Covering this stretch by train is advisable, although we have bicycled over parts of it in September with no horrendous problems with traffic.

In much of Italy's north and west, the major highways have wide shoulders for the use of bicycles and mopeds. These shoulders reduce the danger of traffic, although not the annoyance of trucks and fast cars. A good many of the main roads skirt the centers of towns, which gets the bicyclist out of the thicket of city traffic.

The island of Sardinia off the coast of Italy is accessible by ferry from a number of mainland ports and provides less crowded bicycling conditions. Many Italians take their vacations there during August, and hotels and campgrounds are crowded. Beach camping at both organized and ad hoc sites is possible. Cycling is moderate to rugged, with heat a significant factor in the afternoon.

One aspect of touring that you must accustom yourself to in Italy is the constant horn-honking. A good bit of it is just habit, and you will find that some of it is nothing more than a mechanical "Bravo" shouted to you as cars pass by. Italians tend to use the horn as a natural extension of their hands and arms—which are constantly in motion when they talk to you.

The reputation of a few of Italy's larger cities as places where your clothes will be stolen off your back was never a concern for us anywhere we toured in Italy. In fact, we found an abundance of honesty and good will. One night in the south after a particularly long and tiring ride we pulled into a campground and were met by one of the most sinister-looking persons we have ever seen. He turned out to be an art historian who took the campground guard's job for the summer. In excellent English he gave a little lecture on Italian Renaissance art, then gave us a bungalow to sleep in for the night free of charge. The next day he held some money for us which we had carelessly left in his office until we remembered and came back for it.

*Maps.* Available in this country are the Michelin 1:200,000 series covering the area north of Milan (see Appendix 7). The Touring Club Italiano has an excellent series of 1:200,000 scale maps covering the entire country. These are available at the frontier post on the Italian-French border outside Menton and at larger bookstores within Italy.

*Accommodations.* Youth hostels are not common in Italy, but there is a fair distribution of them north of Rome. Campgrounds are heavily clustered along all the coastal areas, even in the less touristed south. There are nearly no campgrounds along the central mountainous portion of the country. Hotels are located in most medium-sized and in all large towns and cities.

*Climate.* Dry throughout the summer. Very hot in the south, but pleasant summer temperatures prevail in the north. September is often rainy in the north.

*Access.* Good train and plane services from all adjoining countries. Ferry service to France is available from ports on the west coast, and there is frequent ferry service to major Yugoslavian and Greek ports from Bari, Ancona, and Brindisi in the east.

## PORTUGAL

*Geography and roads.* Portugal is just now improving its primary road network and has no real network of quiet secondary roads at all. But its isolation on the western edge of the Iberian peninsula also makes it less prone to tourist traffic than its more popular neighbor, Spain. Its temperatures also tend to be lower.

The Atlantic coastal areas are moderate cycling—hilly but with no large mountain ranges. The Algarve, in the south, is an increasingly popular tourist area and also a good cycling possibility.

*Maps.* Michelin map no. 37 (1:500,000) is adequate for Portugal. See Appendix 7 to mail-order.

*Accommodations.* There are very few hostels in Portugal. The campground situation is considerably better. Campgrounds are strung out along the Atlantic Coast north of Lisbon and along the southern tip of the country on the Algarve Coast. Increasing numbers of tourists have made hotels common all along the coastal areas.

*Climate.* Sunny and warm.

*Access.* Rail connections from Spain are good.

## SCANDINAVIA

### SWEDEN

*Geography and roads.* Sweden rates as one of the most technologically advanced countries in the world. Costs of traveling there reflect this, some items costing far more than they would at home. But it also has the midnight sun, helpful, efficient service, and a population that largely speaks English. It also is a good country for bicycling, with a variety of touring terrains.

The east coast is an agricultural region of rolling hills. The central section is heavily forested and dotted with hundreds of small lakes. As you continue west toward Norway, the terrain becomes steeper.

Some touring possibilities that we have found interesting are the lake district west of Stockholm and the heavily forested region between Stockholm and Umeå in the north. The cyclist searching for a rugged yet beautiful experience should try the Norrland—the Swedish word for the entire northern region of the country. It covers about half of Sweden, yet accounts for less than 20 percent of the country's population. It is an area of vast spaces, timber, and of course, in summer, the midnight sun.

Due to the sparsity of population, vast distances, and

the severity of the Swedish winters, the general rule for the roadways is the farther north you travel the fewer the secondary roads. Those that do exist are often gravel. Southern Sweden and the area around Stockholm have a better-developed secondary road system.

The Cyclists' Touring Club of Sweden, in cooperation with regional tourist offices, has scheduled cycling tours in almost every region of the country. The length of the tours varies, some just a few Swedish miles (10 kilometers, or about six times longer than our mile), with others lasting up to a week. The tours are described in folders and may be obtained within Sweden or from the national cycling club, Cykel- & Mopedframjandet (see Appendix 5 for address). The Scandinavian Tourist Office (see Appendix 4) has a brochure that describes the regions in which tours are offered. For longer tours, costs include accommodations in hostels, breakfast, a picnic lunch, dinner, bicycle rental, maps, and route description.

*Bicycle rental.* It is possible to rent a bicycle in most towns of any size in Sweden and at most holiday centers. The local tourist information office (*Turistbyra*) can help you find a specific shop. Costs are about Sw.kr. 5 per day.

*Maps.* You can find good, detailed maps for bicycle touring in most large bookstores in Sweden. *Svenska fjällkartan* covers the country in sixteen sheets, scales at 1:100,000 and 1:200,000. Also available is the *Turist Karten* at a scale of 1:300,000.

*Accommodations.* Well equipped and maintained hotels are in all towns and cities, but the prices are comparable to what you might pay at home (a little less in outlying regions). Swedes get around this by camping and doing their own cooking. Also helping out is the Swedish Touring Club, which operates sixty club lodges. These lodges provide the traveler with beds, hot and cold running water in each bedroom, free showers, and access to a communal kitchen where you can cook your own meals—all for a reasonable price. They are open to any traveler in Sweden, but priority and a discount are given to those with youth hostel cards or to members of touring clubs affiliated with the Alliance Internationale du Tourisme. Over 170 youth hostels are scattered about the country, most of them in coastal areas. There are over 500 approved campsites, but you can camp anywhere in Sweden as long as it isn't too close to a private home or a military base.

*Climate.* Summers are warm but not hot. June tends to have better weather than July and August. Rain can be a factor anytime during the summer. Evenings are cool or even cold, particularly toward autumn.

*Access.* There are frequent ferry services from Lübeck in Germany, and from major port cities in Denmark.

### DENMARK

*Geography and roads.* The countryside of Denmark is tailored for bicycle touring. Most of it is farmland, and the land is flat or gently rolling. The Danes take advantage of these excellent cycling conditions and have made it easy and convenient for visitors to do so also. Some ten regional tourist offices have devised a total of twenty-three tours that last from three to nine days and cover virtually every region of the country. Usually the cyclist gets hotel or hostel accommodation, full or half board, bicycle rental, maps, tickets for ferry crossings if necessary, and even a return ticket for your bicycle (but not yourself) if the tour ends in a different place from where it started. Prices range from Dkr. 450 to Dkr. 1,500. The Scandinavian Tourist Office (see Appendix 4) has a list of tour locations and current costs. You book the tour directly with the regional tourist office involved. You may do this yourself or make arrangements through your travel agent.

*Bicycle rental.* Bicycles may be rented from private agents in most towns and cities throughout Denmark. Costs run about Dkr. 10–25 per day, and about Dkr. 50–105 per week. Sometimes you must pay a deposit of Dkr. 200 and display some proof of identity. Bicycles are normally returned to the shop from which you rented them. A list of towns with bicycle rental shops is given in Appendix 6.

*Maps.* Available froom bookstores in Denmark are a variety of detailed maps of the country either in atlas form or in individual sheets. These are published by the Geodaestisk Institut. Scale is 1:200,000.

*Accommodations.* There are some eighty youth hostels in Denmark. They are evenly spaced throughout the country and easily within a day of each other on a bicycle. Almost all provide meals and are equipped with cooking facilities. The government maintains over 500 campsites, located mainly along the coast and in the more popular tourist areas. An International Camping Carnet is compulsory at all government-rated campgrounds (see Chapter 3 for information on the camping carnet).

You will find hotels in all cities and towns. In the country, there is a network of inns that are less expensive than hotels. As elsewhere in Europe, small-town hotels are much less expensive than those in larger cities.

*Climate.* Like all Scandinavian countries, Denmark has a cool, but not cold, summer climate. July and August are the warmer months, but June has fewer rainy days.

*Access.* There are daily boat-train connections from all principal cities in Europe and an uninterrupted ferry service between Lübeck in Germany and Puttgarten (located on the island of Lolland in southern Denmark). Reservations for the latter are advisable. There are also daily boat services from Oslo and Stockholm.

## NORWAY

*Geography and roads.* Norway is famous for having the most dramatic scenery of all of the Scandinavian countries. It has a magnificent maze of fjords, lakes, woods, and mountains set off by old wooden houses and friendly, energetic people. There are endless possibilities open to cycle tourists—especially if they combine cycling with mountain hikes and boat trips down fjords, and make use of the connecting train services. The Scandinavian Tourist Office has a number of preplanned tours available upon inquiry, but it is also quite easy to plan your own tour of Norway, as there are youth hostels throughout the country.

If you want only a mild sampling of Norway, the area in and around Oslo has some lovely rides through wooded hillsides. These are nicely complemented by a boat trip down the Oslo fjord. For a more involving look at Norway, the Reindeer Road, which runs over the Hardanger Mountains between Oslo and Bergen, is outstanding in its scenery. It tends to be difficult in spots but never impossible. Other trips that take you along the dramatic fjords are also possible. Frequently the roads will be dirt or gravel, and clincher tires are necessary (see Chapter 7).

*Bicycle rental.* Bicycles may be rented from shops in Oslo and in Stavanger (see Appendix 6 for addresses).

*Maps.* Cappelin regional maps are available within Norway, or may be ordered from the British Cycling Federation if you are a member of that organization (see Appendix 7).

*Accommodations.* There are about 170 youth hostels throughout Norway, well distributed geographically. Organized campgrounds are most numerous along the coastal areas. The mountain campgrounds are usually set in scenic locations. Camping carnets are compulsory in all approved campgrounds. Hotels within moderate price ranges are found throughout the country.

*Climate.* Cool, frequently cold in the evenings. Rain can be a problem anytime during the summer.

*Access.* Ferry services are available from Copenhagen and Frederikshavn (Denmark) and from England, and there is regular train service from Stockholm.

## SPAIN

*Geography and roads.* Spain does not have a good network of well-maintained secondary roads, and in the summer the combination of heat and truck and tourist traffic can make cycling considerably less enjoyable than it should be. It is cooler in the summer along the Mediterranean and Atlantic coasts, but tourist traffic in these areas is among the heaviest in Europe.

A better alternative is to tour the interior in the springtime, from late March to mid-May, before it gets too hot. The best area is within an ellipse with Madrid at its peak and Jaén at its base. The country between these points is level or gently rolling. Madrid itself is one of Europe's loveliest capitals and the cities to the south—Toledo, Albacete, Linares, Úbeda, and Jaén—are worth visiting. The olive-growing slopes north of Jaén are good for springtime riding too.

One of our more recent excursions was into the northern Pyrenees, an area we were so taken with that we now suggest a tour that takes you through some of the less-frequented mountain regions in Europe (see Chapter 10). There is an abundance of superb rural and mountain scenery, with much of the farm labor still done by hand or with animals. While the mountains lack the grandeur of the more famous Alps, they make up for it with the human touch you see in every orchard and field.

Road surfaces throughout Spain are good to awful, but drivers are more cautious than in much of Europe. As long as you avoid the major truck routes, your riding is adequate to good. Spain is also one of the last true travel bargains in Europe, the dollar holding its own with the Spanish currency.

*Maps.* For the Pyrenees, the Michelin regional 1:400,000 maps are excellent (see Appendix 7 for mail-order details). For the rest of the country, good regional maps are difficult to locate in the United States but are generally available in good bookstores in Spain. The Shell regional maps are among those available within Spain. They are excellent.

*Accommodations.* Hostels and campgrounds are clustered along the Atlantic and Mediterranean coasts, and near Madrid. They are rare elsewhere. Hotels are well spaced along the main routes connecting towns, but can be rare elsewhere. Check ahead before setting out. Hotel and restaurant costs are very reasonable throughout the country.

## SWITZERLAND

*Geography and roads.* Switzerland has a unique beauty —an incredible blend of three cultures, unsurpassed mountain scenery, lakes, small villages, vigorous, helpful people, and beautiful, clean cities. Geographically, there are three major areas: the Jura Mountains, which form the western boundary; the Alps, which form the southern and eastern boundaries; and in between them a less mountainous region known as the Midlands, which is liberally sprinkled with large lakes. A total of three-fifths of the country is covered with mountains. From the cyclist's point of view this might spell the impossible, but it doesn't have to. If you don't feel like tackling the passes, work out a tour that utilizes train travel as well as cycling. There are many beautiful rides possible in and around the major cities. Most are set on large lakes and are surrounded by many points of natural and historic interest.

The secondary road network is sparse, as roads are expensive to build and maintain in the mountains. Main pass roads tend to be narrow and in summer see a great deal of automobile traffic. Many of the pass areas have tunnels, so be sure that your bicycle is equipped with a headlight and taillight, and keep a sweater handy.

The Swiss Touring Club has established six cycle centers from which tours of a few hours or a few days are possible. Routes are marked, and information on the various itineraries is available at the regional center. Centers are located in the cantons of Vaud, Berne, and the Jura; in the St. Gallen Rhine valley; in the Aegeri district; and in the area around Zurich. Addresses of these centers are in Appendix 3.

The Swiss Tourist Office also has a list of seven short tours of 8 to 35 miles through various regions of Switzerland (see Appendix 4 for address).

Both the German- and French-speaking cycling clubs in Switzerland have established a series of cycling itineraries through scenic or challenging regions of the country. These are short excursions, many of which are directed toward "collecting" mountain passes, or *cols*. The addresses of these clubs is given in Appendix 5. You should send International Postal Reply Coupons when requesting materials from these and other organizations, which exist largely on volunteer efforts and small budgets.

*Bicycle rental.* Three-speed bicycles may be rented from and returned to any station in the Swiss Federal

Railways and at most stations of private railway companies in the country. Prices are SFr. 8 per day.

*Maps.* Michelin maps 021, 023, and 024 (1:200,000) cover Switzerland. In addition, the Swiss National Tourist Office publishes an official road map (1:300,000), available from that office for $5.25. The address for ordering the Michelin maps is in Appendix 7. The Swiss Tourist Office address is in Appendix 4.

*Accommodations.* There are approximately one hundred hostels located throughout the country, but they are concentrated around the larger lakes and along rivers. Most of the hostels have cooking facilities available. In general, priority is given to hostelers under 25 years of age. Campgrounds tend to be concentrated in the lake districts of the north and in the southeast region near the Austrian border. Switzerland is justly proud of its hotels. They are always clean and efficiently run. Those found in smaller towns and villages often are the best bargains.

*Climate.* The climate in Switzerland offers a spectrum of all European climates. Aside from the mountain environment with its glaciers and cool evening temperatures, there is the mild climate of Geneva and the warm, dry Mediterranean climate of Lugano. The Zurich area is noted for its rain throughout the year.

*Access.* All major cities in Europe have connecting trains to Switzerland. Within the country the train service is excellent. The famous yellow postal buses provide good passenger service through most areas but do not carry bicycles.

## YUGOSLAVIA

*Geography and roads.* Most of Yugoslavia is not particularly inviting to the cycle tourist, being mountainous with few well-paved roads. But two areas frequently toured on cycle are the plains between Zagreb and Belgrade and the Dalmatian Coast, on the Adriatic opposite Italy. The coast road, the more popular for tourists, rises and falls in long stretches, running near the sea and then gaining 500 to 1,000 feet in elevation. Roadbeds throughout Yugoslavia tend to be rough, and this one is no exception, so carry extra spokes. Bicycle shops, by the way, are rare. If you tire of the energetic cycling required on the coastal road, you can take part of the trip via the inexpensive Yugoslavian ferries which run its entire length. The pass road leading from the Adriatic Coast into Greece should be attempted only by those in excellent physical condition.

*Maps.* Maps for Yugoslavia are best located in the larger bookstores in cities.

*Accommodations.* Hotels, youth hostels, and campgrounds are common all along the Adriatic Coast. Inland you will find hotels in the larger towns, but hostels and campgrounds are rare. There are also numerous guesthouses in all tourist areas where you can find very inexpensive accommodations.

*Climate.* Sunny and warm throughout the summer.

*Access.* By train from Italy, Austria, or Greece. By ferry from ports on the Adriatic Coast of Italy.

FIVE

# Getting ready to go touring

Riding through the country, meeting new people, having adventures and misadventures, experiencing new foods and life styles—it all sounds great. In fact, it is, but only if you are physically ready for it.

In Greece we met two girls who had given up bicycle touring and were taking the train instead. They had bought bicycles in London, packed their things on them, threaded their way through some of the heaviest traffic congestion on the face of the earth, ridden seventy miles, and at dusk collapsed in a youth hostel in agony and tears. Neither had been on a bicycle in ten years.

Though the necessity of prior training is self-evident, most people don't know how much and what kind of preparation you really need. To begin a bicycle tour, as these girls did, with none at all, and to cover a distance that taxes even the most experienced cycle tourist, will bring on equally unpleasant results. With adequate preparation, however, you will have none of them.

Obviously, the "training period" will vary depending on what shape you're in now. You should allow at least a month's preparation time; six, eight, or even ten weeks would be better. Less time is needed, of course, if you are now riding. Some days it will be tiring, but it should never be exhausting. The exact amount of time and effort required also depends on what kind of touring you intend to do. Since this can vary so widely from one person to the next, we don't offer a rigid "program" of training. We do, however, give you some basic guidelines and some well-tested suggestions based on our own experiences or on those of others we have known.

## ADJUSTING THE BICYCLE

Begin by making it as physically easy to pedal as possible. You do this by buying a bicycle the proper size and adjusting it to fit your body. Here are the basic considerations:

1. The saddle must be high enough to allow your leg to stretch properly when pedaling. Some people use a series of mathematical calculations to determine this "proper" height, but it is easier just to have someone balance the bicycle for you while you sit on it. *Rest your heel on the down pedal and align the pedal shaft at the same angle as the slanting tube running from your seat to the pedal assembly.* This puts the pedal slightly forward of a true up-and-down position. Adjust the seat pole so that *your leg is straight but not locked.* This will allow you to get good leg extension when riding but will prevent your knee from snapping and becoming sore.
2. Handlebar height is determined by two things: the height of the handlebars from the ground and the distance between the tip of your saddle and the bars.
   a. To make the first adjustment loosen the nut or hex

bolt on the top of the handlebar stem five or six turns and then rap it sharply with a hammer or block of wood. The handlebar pole will then slide freely up and down. When the handlebars are the proper height they should be just even with the level of the seat.

b. To make the second adjustment place your forearm between the saddle and the handlebars. Your elbow should touch the front of the saddle and your fingertips just touch the handlebars. If the area is too large or

small move your seat back and forth to fill in the gap. If this still isn't enough you can buy a longer or shorter handlebar stem from your dealer.

## STARTING THE REGIME

Now that the bicycle is properly fitted you can start riding. If you are not now bicycling, start off slowly. The ten-geared bicycle takes some getting used to. For the first few days short stints of ten or fifteen minutes are enough. If, after two or three days, you can get in two such rides in a day, one in the morning and one at night, or before and after dinner, so much the better. During these first few days concentrate only on these things:

1. Always ride on quiet streets or roads so that you don't have to worry about traffic.
2. Get used to shifting gears smoothly. Shift only when the pedals are rotating with light pressure on them. As you shift upward and downward, do it one gear at a time and don't allow the chain to grind on the sprockets.
3. Ride without coasting. Coasting breaks your pace and eventually makes cycling a lot more difficult.
4. Learn to ride in a straight line without wobbling from side to side. This indicates a mastery of steering and an ability to apply even pressure to the pedals.

## DISTANCE

After about a week of fifteen- or twenty-minute rides, you are ready to work up your distance. This is the most crucial aspect in touring, for you must be able to pedal consistently over long stretches without becoming fatigued. Start with half-hour rides. Don't be afraid of taking one in the morning. You'll be amazed how much more efficiently and alertly you function at work or in the home if you have ridden before you begin your day. On the weekends try to work in longer rides or two half-hour rides a day. After a week of half-hour stints you will find that your seat is no longer sore, nor are your back and leg muscles getting as tired.

At this point you have made it through the first, and most important, barrier. Your body is now used to the new demands that you are placing on it, and you can start building greater time and distance goals. The initial one will probably be your first day-long trip. This, in fact, may or may not last a whole day, but if you feel like taking that long, do so. Set a reasonable goal, say 20 miles or so, and make a picnic of it. Stop and have lunch when you've gone a little over halfway, relax, then ride home. Whether you know it or not, you've completed your first tour. Some people never cycle farther than this when actually touring.

## MORE ADVANCED TECHNIQUES

While you are increasing your distances and presumably covering different terrains, you will have the chance to start practicing some cycling techniques that, once mastered, really make riding a lot easier. With some practice these techniques will become second nature to you, and you will be in the realm of "serious" cyclists, those who know their bicycle so thoroughly that riding well and easily is second nature to them.

1. *Ankling.* Ankling is a way of moving your feet and enlisting the aid of your ankle muscles while you pedal so that less overall leg energy is needed. If you ankle properly you will find that your cycling becomes about 25

percent easier. The ankling process starts when the pedal is just past the twelve o'clock or vertical position (see illustration). Your toe should be slightly above your heel. As the pedal starts downward you help it along by pushing with your toe. By the time the pedal is in the six o'clock position, your toe is lower than your heel. As the first foot has completed its downward journey the other one begins. When you are first learning to ankle, practice in a traffic-free area so you can concentrate on it and watch your feet move. At first you may find that one foot adapts more easily than the other, but with practice this will even out, and you will be pedaling with a consistent rhythm. Once you have mastered this technique you will find that it is much easier to climb hills that used to seen difficult because now your feet are helping push you up instead of being dead weight.

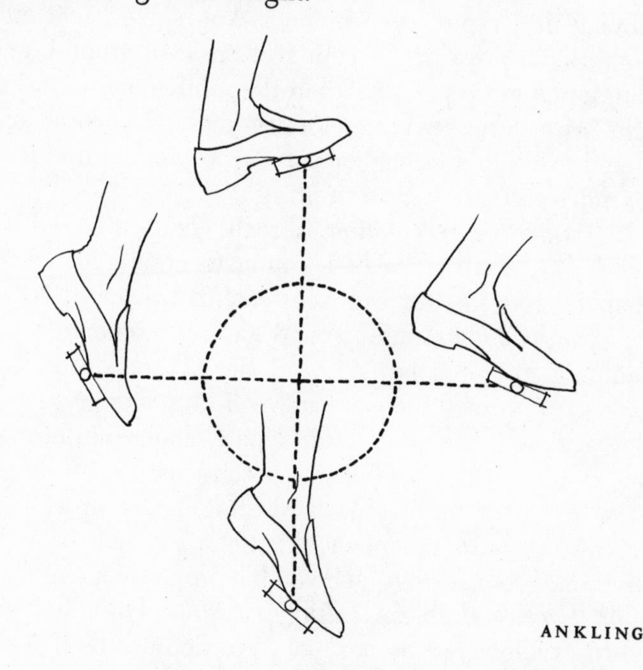

ANKLING

2. *Find your natural cadence.* Cadence is the number of revolutions your feet make in one minute of riding. Your riding efficiency will increase once you find the cadence that is natural for you and then learn to hold it all the time you are riding. This is why it is important to learn to ride without doing much coasting. A natural cadence allows you to expend energy at an even and economical rate which coasting disrupts. Scientific studies and the experience of cyclists have shown that bodies operate most efficiently when the cadence is between sixty and eighty-five revolutions per minute. Your cadence will depend on a number of different factors—age, temperament, size, and agility—and finding it will be a matter of trial and error. Once you have mastered shifting, start keeping track of your cadence. If it is too low (common among beginning cyclists), start riding in lower gears. Get used to your legs moving in a rapid, even manner. You should feel only a slight pedal pressure on your feet on level ground, and if you notice more pressure than this, shift down to a lower gear. After a few days of practice you will become accustomed to the higher cadence and you will be able to ride for miles with little or no strain.

3. *Proper gear selection* is really connected with cadence and is a matter of learning to anticipate when to change gears so your cadence remains constant. Shift before you lose your cadence and natural momentum when climbing hills. As you descend the other side and your cadence becomes too fast, move into a higher gear and slow it down. Learning to anticipate changes in terrain in this fashion will soon become second nature to you, and soon you will find yourself shifting gears upward and downward without much thought attached to it—the rhythm of your feet will tell you the proper moment.

4. *Practice different riding positions.* Different riding postures allow you to vary your position on the bicycle so

that the parts of your body that have been working can rest and the other parts take over. It is important to change regularly to prevent cramping in your hands, back, and neck muscles. Riding posture is determined by the position of your hands on the handlebars. There are a number of different positions, but learn to use at least these three.

5. *Learn to pace yourself.* Pacing is important because it is the factor that gets you accustomed to covering long distances. As you begin your 20- or 25-mile rides, try to cover at least half the distance before you take a break. If you must take a break before then, try to make it a short one, perhaps just stopping and straddling the bicycle. If you've ridden to the point where you have to flop panting on the grass, you've pushed yourself too hard. Cycle more slowly, use lower gears, or cycle less distance. But get used to sustained cycling. Perhaps one day you'll even cycle for 20 miles before stopping.

Two things that help pacing and keep your muscles in better trim are proper warming up and slowing down habits. When you start a long ride your heart and muscles need some time to build up to their maximum efficiency. Often the first mile or so of a ride is the very hardest. Begin slowly. Start your ride in a low gear and shift to higher gears only as you loosen up and riding becomes easier. Another habit that will help you maintain a constant pace is to taper off gradually after vigorous exertion. After climbing a hill or sprinting, don't stop immediately. Such sudden stops strain your heart because it is still pumping an extra amount of blood and you are no longer using it. Continue pedaling at a slower rate for a while. Sometimes this means pedaling down a hill and not coasting, or riding easily for a block or two if you have sprinted on the home stretch.

*Position 1.* Hands resting on the top of the bars midway between the stem and the curved part. This lowers your body sufficiently to reduce wind resistance and yet leaves you upright enough so there isn't too much pressure on your back and neck muscles. This is the most popular touring position.

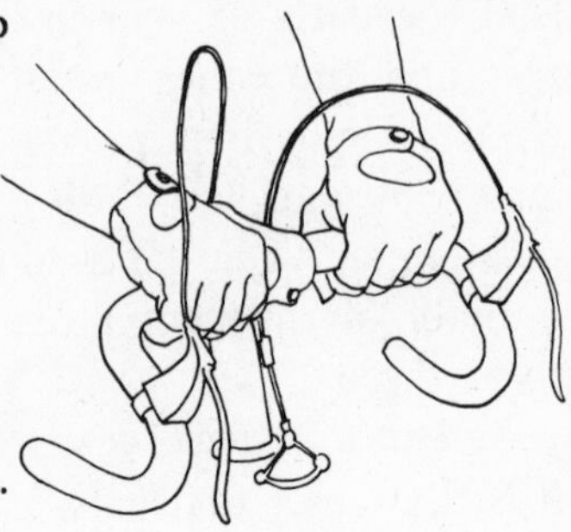

*Position 2.* Hands resting on top of the brake levers with thumb and forefinger extending on either side. This lowers the body, is a good trade-off from the first position, and provides a good position for riding downhill as your body weight is forward and you have free and ready access to the brake levers.

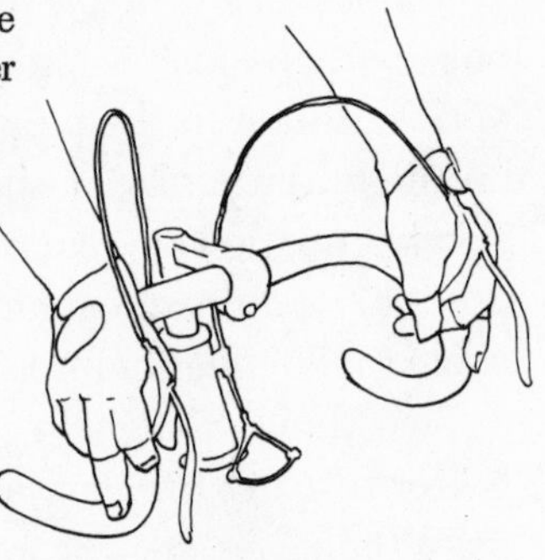

*Position 3.* Hands resting near the ends of the lower bars. Your body is in the lowest possible position. This is used when riding against the wind or for maximizing pulling efficiency for hill climbing. You will need to practice this position more because it puts an extra strain on your back and neck muscles. So practice a little on daily rides even if terrain or wind do not require it. It will come in handy someday.

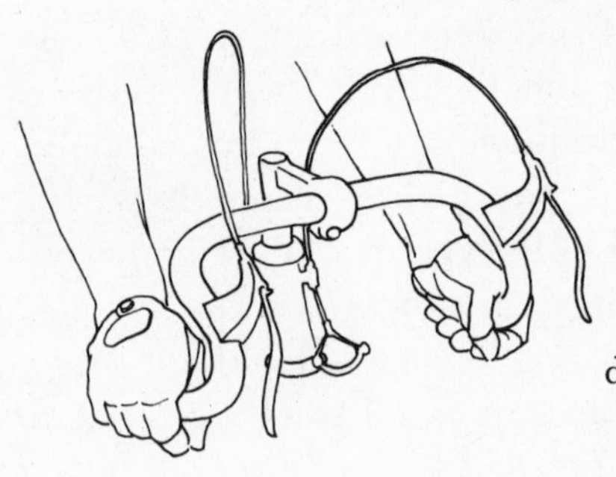

## CYCLING PSYCHOLOGY

By the time you are beginning to master these cycling techniques you should also begin to develop an attitude toward cycling that will help you along. Since your attitude toward riding is determined by the kind of experiences you have while doing it, try to make them positive ones. This is why it is important to ride at first where there is no traffic and never to push yourself to the point where you feel exhausted. It may help you to know that nearly everyone who bicycles was just about where you are now when they started, if not worse off.

The real key to developing self-confidence and good feelings about bicycling is just to do a lot of riding. The two aspects build on each other—the more riding you do the better you are able to ride, and the better you are able to ride the better you will feel about the whole idea. For instance, if you have never ridden up a steep hill it looks forbidding, but if you manage to climb it, the next one is easier, and the one after that will be easier still. The hills don't get smaller, you are just better equipped to handle them.

At first you may have to generate a little extra discipline to make yourself keep going. Part of this is accomplished by setting realistic goals for yourself. Obviously you will not be able to ride 10 miles the first time you get on a bicycle—at least not comfortably. You shouldn't even try. If you have had less than a month to train and condition yourself, you shouldn't set out to travel 40 miles the first day of your tour. Try always to set goals you have reason to believe are realistic for you, based on your past performance. Then begin stretching those goals in reasonable amounts. By this method you will nearly always guarantee yourself some successes, and these more than anything will give you that extra will power to push a little harder to get over that last hill in the evening or make the last mile into the village where you can rekindle yourself over a cup of coffee.

## CYCLING WITH OTHERS

Learning to ride with someone else can be one of the most satisfying, and at the same time trying, problems in either a training period or on an actual tour. Few people are so perfectly matched either in physical abilities or in traveling temperament that they will fit each other exactly or escape the need to make some adjustments. One person may have to reduce his or her expectations and the other increase his, one person travel a little more slowly than normal, the other ride a few more miles than usual. No one should ever push himself or others to the point of exhaustion. Exhausted people tend to be poor company.

There are some practical things you can do to facilitate this adjustment period. The stronger rider might take some of the weight or allow the slower person to set the pace. The most important consideration in making satisfactory adjustments is that they be done in the spirit of friendly cooperation. Talking about the different things you are all feeling about the trip will be the best way to ensure that the adjustments will be made. Communication is important in all relationships but especially when you are planning to spend part of the summer riding together day in and day out. With a little work on both sides your relationship will seek its own level and then you will be able to travel miles and miles together without effort or strain between you.

We have used these techniques when bicycling with

others who have different natural paces or inclinations from our own.

1. Work out an overall plan in advance and then try to stick to it. Agree, for instance, that for a certain number of days your trip will be slow-paced, with frequent stops to visit châteaux, museums, churches, and the like, and that a later portion will be geared more toward distance. This can give everyone's tastes some satisfaction.

2. If the group numbers four or more, split up and let the persons with more compatible paces ride together, with longer or shorter route alternatives. Always make sure each group knows where the others are going, and always establish a definite meeting place. We plan rendezvous points during the day at intervals of 10 or 15 miles. Our rule of thumb is that if we become unexpectedly separated, everyone is to retreat to the last place where we all were together and wait there.

3. Slower riders in particular need to guard against the feeling that there is something wrong with them. Certain aspects of our culture have emphasized speed over leisure, endurance over curiosity, record setting and professionalism over quiet and individual pleasure. There is some evidence that these predominating values actually account for a good bit of unhappiness in our society.

You should, however, make a distinction between exertion and pain. Within limits, there is nothing at all wrong with exerting yourself.

One thing we have found that helps slower riders build their confidence is to be the *first* ready in the morning. If you are straddling your bicycle, already packed, while everyone else is zipping panniers it can help your own and their perceptions of you. Even a cheery "I'll get a little head start. Meet you down at the end of the block" will do wonders for your morale.

4. If you are one of the faster riders, remember that someone going slowly often is exerting as much or more energy than you. Vigorous riders tend to forget the days when they have felt rotten, and when a fast pace or horrendous exertion would have ruined everything for them. Try to remember those days.

## FOR WOMEN

The body of a woman is especially suited to activities requiring consistent energy output over long periods of time. The extra layer of fat most women have just below the skin is converted to food energy once other supplies are exhausted. This gives them the ability to carry out prolonged physical activity with relatively less need for food intake to replenish lost supplies. The number of women who excel at endurance events such as marathon running or distance swimming attests to this natural advantage. Bicycle touring puts much the same kinds of demands upon the body.

*In training.* Training is a duel process of getting mind and body in shape. If you haven't done much physical activity lately you will find that you get to know yourself a lot better as your program progresses. Make your riding time pleasant and consistent, and set realistic goals for yourself. Evaluate yourself on a concrete basis, not according to abstract or arbitrary standards. How much farther did you go this time than last? How much stronger were you? How is your technique improving?

If you are training or riding with a man, avoid getting bound into comparisons of strength, especially at first. A man, even if he has sat doing nothing for five years, may be able to outride you at the beginning of training. Riding with other women from time to time or as a regular part of your training program will give you a better perspective on yourself.

As you get into shape you will reach your own level. You may find, as we have, that you are much less prone than some men to sugar loss and related heat exhaustion during hot weather. After exceptionally long rides, you may also find that you have more energy left at the end of the day. This has been our experience, and we have observed it with others also.

*On the road.* One of the earliest long-distance bicycle trips was taken by a woman from Ireland who went overland all the way to India. By herself. Bicycle touring offers women an excellent way to get off the beaten track. Europe is generally a safer place for women than is the U.S., but you should follow some basic guidelines and exercise some common sense.

First, know the basic mechanics of the bicycle—changing flat tires, broken brake cables, installing and adjusting derailleur cables, and tightening the nuts and bolts that work loose. This will keep you free of "helpful strangers."

Secondly, keep in mind the impressions clothing may make on certain societies that are more conservative than our own. Very skimpy halters or short shorts will attract attention, some of it unpleasant. Riding shorts and a cotton T-shirt or blouse will attract less.

Given all this, should a woman bicycle by herself in Europe? This is difficult to answer. In most countries, under most circumstances, the worst you are likely to encounter is verbal behavior and the inevitable, but often annoying, man who is overly helpful or obtrusive. Anyone on a bicycle must pass long periods when she is off on side roads with relatively few other people around. As such, a woman is vulnerable to harassment. There are certainly circumstances where such harassment can be physical, and possibly violent. A woman who takes off on her own should realize that.

A much better solution is for two or more women to travel together, which takes most risk out of the adventure and still leaves the pleasure.

In the event a woman is traveling by herself or with a small group of other women, she or they should stay in organized lodgings, be it hotel, hostel, or campground. If you are staying in hotels, you may want to check out the room and make certain you feel comfortable in it. One travel guide oriented toward young people estimates that women who are alone will spend up to 25 percent more than men for lodging, just because they have to be more choosy. Organized campgrounds or youth hostels provide obvious and very safe solutions.

## RIDING WITH WEIGHT

Learning to ride with additional weight on your bicycle should be a part of your training period. When you first add weight to your bicycle it will cause changes in balance and control that are important to get used to before you begin touring. Particularly when weight is added to the rear carrier, you will notice a tendency to wobble a bit. Pedaling also will seem more difficult at first, but once you learn to shift down earlier and ride in lower gears than normal, this too will disappear.

You also need to become accustomed to some new ways of handling the bicycle. When riding down hills you will need to start braking earlier, and you won't be able to bank as sharply on turns as you did before. Apply your brakes in soft, even spurts and avoid having to slam on your brakes, which will cause you to fishtail. When you start riding with weight you may find that your knees are sore. This is normal and just one of the indicators that your body is working harder. If it persists, cut down on your daily distance. Lowering or raising the seat may also help. If these fail, you may want to consider laying off for a few days and beginning again with less weight.

## THE SHAKEDOWN TRIP

If you can, fit in an overnight trip before you leave. This trip should be planned as nearly as possible to resemble the touring style you plan to follow in Europe. Try and cover approximately the same distance you anticipate covering on a daily basis, but leave yourself some leeway for unexpected events such as rearranging luggage or getting lost. Your saddlebags or panniers should be the same as or resemble the ones you anticipate using so you can make certain everything fits inside them. If you plan to ride with someone else in Europe, try to bring him or her along too. In other words, do everything you can to make it a realistic, pleasant experience. If you are going to tour lightweight-style make reservations in a nice motel and eat in a nice restaurant. If you are a camper tourist plan to stay in a good campground and cook one of your favorite meals for dinner.

SIX

# Days of a bicycle tourist

What you encounter in a typical bicycle tour will depend a great deal on what kind of touring style you adopt and where you happen to be. In this chapter we try to give you some idea of what things to expect.

To begin with, we take you through a portion of one of our own tours, as the two of us, our 2-year-old son Benjamin, and our 26-year-old nephew, Ken, worked our way south through France in mid-May, our destination the Basque city of San Sebastián on the Atlantic coast of Spain.

Later on we discuss some of the conditions we encountered as well as some others one is likely to encounter on a bicycle tour. These include ways to handle hills, weather, traffic hazards, and using the train to ship your bicycle from point to point.

## CALAIS TO SAN SEBASTIÁN

*Calais, May 9.* It was cold. We had pitched the tent in the lee of a hill to protect it from a constant wind off the sea. Ships and boats in the harbor nudged into the docks as if huddling from the gale coming in off the Channel. Until later in the morning, the four of us stayed in the tent studying maps, calculating a route south to Spain. We believed it would take us three weeks of riding to get there, given the fact that it was still early spring and we were bound to get rain.

*Calais, May 10.* Complications. After our last trip, we had left our bicycles in France. Friends shipped them north. One was really only a frame that had to be equipped. The dealer in town said he would do it, but it would take at least two days, probably more. In the afternoon we found out that he did not have a large freewheel that we needed. Calais is too flat. It took a morning's trip to Boulogne (a hillier region) to find a dealer that had one.

*Calais, May 11.* With the one functioning bicycle we took Benjamin for his first short ride in the trailer. The road along the Atlantic coast was dusted with sand blown in by the winds. Benjamin peered uncertainly over the side of the trailer, with constant admonitions from us to keep his hands off the wheels. The curious stopped in their tracks to watch us go by. The beach resorts had the deserted appearance of winter. The cafés were empty, the bright little changing rooms shuttered and boarded up.

*Calais, May 12.* Just at noon, with a whoop of exhilaration, we headed out of town, fully loaded with gear. Outfitting the bicycle cost about $200, but the $350 frame, given to us by a friend, made it worth it. We were officially on tour.

Clouds chewed at the low hills lying ahead of us, but we went on, hoping it wouldn't rain. It did. We rode through two light showers, with Benjamin unmindful, as he was facing rearwards and couldn't feel the drops. To keep him amused we tied toys on his trailer with strings, and filled a small plastic sack with peanut butter sandwiches, raisins, and other snacks so he could eat when bored. One or two of us rode behind him, chattering and pointing out the wonders of the green French countryside, all with a little edge of hysteria in our voices, as we pushed a little hard to make him think it grand. Fortunately he had more equilibrium than we and just began enjoying it on his own. He napped against a knapsack we had wedged in the corner of the seat. When he was awake, we stopped every forty-five minutes or so to let him run around and to give ourselves a chance to stretch and ease rear ends unused to saddles. Riding with weight seems to accentuate this problem. We made liberal use of the baby powder at night, and during one two-day stretch one of us even made use of a handy paper diaper applied to a particularly sensitive spot where bicycle meets body.

*May 13.* Just as we pulled into the campground at Hesdin, a rather charmless village set in rolling hills, it started to rain. We got the tent up quickly and ducked inside to cook. All the next day we were pinned down, but people invited us into their trailers for drinks in the afternoon, and the kids played with Benjamin during breaks in the showers. When we arrived at the camp we were ready to sit down and relax, and he was ready to explore. How do you set limits for a 2-year-old when every night is a different physical layout? We didn't, or couldn't, and usually herded him around or took him down to the play area most campgrounds have, amusing him there. The amazing thing is that he was no trouble at all during the day, chattering, taking naps in his trailer, playing with his toys. Only after we stopped did we have problems. We chased him with good humor for the most part, as he was turning into a superb traveler otherwise.

*May 14–15.* We were on the road again, under a high overcast but rainless sky, climbing rolling hills but trying to pick roads that stayed up high on the plateaus. At Amiens, a great cathedral town, we were preoccupied by a lack of cash, having foolishly forgotten to cash travelers checks, and to add to it, an extra day had been tacked onto the weekend by the Feast of the Ascension. All the banks were closed. Fortunately, Ken had some extra francs, and we ate omelets in the train station restaurant. This is not usually the best choice for a meal out, but after comparing menus (usually posted on the window or by the door of restaurants throughout Europe), we found that the station was the best and least expensive. Amiens, like a good many European cities, has a campground within its limits, so the train station and the cathedral were all within walking distance.

*May 16–18.* Three more riding days through northern France, a stretch made better by the fact that we were always on side roads, riding next to the famous hedgerows of Normandy. A druggist and his wife hailed us to a halt one afternoon and invited us back to town to chat with them. We offered instead to chat along the road, as we didn't want to lose time.

*May 19, Dreux.* Rain. It had started again just as we were finishing the previous day's ride, a fairly typical pattern. Then it kept us holed up the next day. We took periodic walks into town, saw the university, sat in cafés and watched an international assortment of students bustle by, bought some bicycle parts, and wrote letters.

*May 20.* Clear, and we were off again. At Chartres, Karen watched Benjamin while he was asleep in his trailer and the others toured the cathedral. A couple hesitantly approached the baby, left, then the woman came back again.

She was fascinated by the fact that we were touring on bicycles. Benjamin added his own element to our entourage.

"Where will you sleep tonight?" she asked.

"South of here," we replied. We dug out our map and indicated a general destination about 40 kilometers to the south of Chartres.

"Why, that's right near our country home. There's loads of room there tonight. You must join us!"

Danielle, the woman, and her husband Robin were Parisians who, like many French, have a second home.

Several hours later our hosts were waiting as we walked our bicycles over the rough gravel path leading to a 300-year-old farmhouse in the upper reaches of the Loire valley. It was set in a deep copse of trees, just then beginning to flesh out with the thick green they would bear later on in summer.

With some understanding of the desires of bicyclists, our hosts ushered us immediately inside to a modern bathroom, complete with a luxurious supply of hot water that we reveled in with total abandon. An hour later all of us were sitting before a fireplace in the heavily beamed living room. Robin grilled meat over the live coals, a good French country tradition. Later, we walked the alleys cut through the heavy forest, then talked long into the night, eyes fixed on the flames flickering up the ancient chimney.

"I grew up in England," Robin said, in something of a rusty English. "My grandfather was the French ambassador there. But at eighteen I ran away to sea. Of course my family thought I was mad. When I got out, I took up interior decorating." His eyes darted up as he spoke, away from a heavy damask material he was sewing into curtains for a U.N. employee stationed in Paris. He was short, as are many French men, and there was an impish quality in his face, a half smile, as if he was mischievously delighted with himself.

We turned in upstairs, the huge beams of the roof above our heads.

"The French today know nothing about architecture," Robin said. "Look at this." His hand swept around the ancient room. "Now *these* people knew how to build a house to live in!"

As we nestled down deep in our blankets late that night, we agreed—the person who built this lovely place knew something about living as did our hosts who now inhabited it.

*May 21–26.* We crossed the Loire the next morning, something of a geographical barrier between northern and central France. We idled through some of the châteaux country, showing Ken one of our favorites, Chenonceaux, which straddles the river Cher with delicate splendor. South of the Loire, we fell into very jumbled terrain, unlike the mildly rolling north. We had an infinite choice of back roads, and using our Michelin regional 1:200,000 maps, we actually were map-reading a little too well. We had picked such minor roads that, while absolutely deserted of car traffic (about a car an hour), they had been laid out by a Sherman-like engineer who believed that the best route was the shortest, no matter what the pitch of the hill. Over lunch in a park one afternoon, we scrutinized the map some more and found another route that, while less secluded, ran along a railroad track, then down one of the main tributaries of the Garonne river, our next major pathway. That afternoon we switched routes, and cycling was about a third less difficult the rest of the trip to the Garonne.

*May 27, Les Landes.* This is a vast, timbered region reclaimed from marshy soil by planting millions of pine trees, now forming steep, fragrant alleys over our heads. We asked some locals for a good place to camp, and after talking for a moment, they directed us to a stream off a quiet country lane where we set up on a sandy shore. We washed in the cold water and made boats for Benjamin to send down to the Atlantic as forewarnings that we were on our way.

Evening set in and we nestled inside the tent, Ken joining us to keep away from the mosquitoes. He was carrying only a rainfly and groundcloth, neither really rain- or bug-proof. He bunked with us when adversity struck.

"Pssst." The noise was just outside our tent.

"Pssst," it repeated. It was a human voice, just inches from our door. We glanced at one another, and Ken was somehow chosen to investigate. He zipped open the oval door of the tent and stuck his head out into the inky night.

"Sorry to disturb you," the voice said in French. We could see the silhouette of its owner, hunkering down a few feet from us.

"What do you want?" we asked.

"I just wanted to tell you," he whispered, "that some friends are coming down later. We're having a *fête*."

None of us had any idea what they might be celebrating.

"That's fine," we said. We were beginning to be relieved. We had never had trouble camping out in the woods, but there was always a feeling of uneasiness.

Our eyes grew accustomed to the darkness, and we made out a man in his late twenties, dark hair, wide face, broad mouth.

"We're having fireworks as part of the *fête*," he continued.

"Fireworks? Where?" Instantly visions of falling debris, smoldering with flames, filled our heads. It was all heading straight for the roof of our nylon tent. "Can't you have them somewhere else?"

"No. This is where the *fête* is," he whispered secretly. "We wanted to tell you. Someone noticed that you had a child. We wanted to tell you so he wouldn't be frightened."

The personage in question was sound asleep. But the whispering visitor had saved the best till last.

"The fireworks start at midnight," he said.

"Not before?" we howled.

"No, at midnight."

He vanished back into the darkness. Later we could hear footsteps passing some yards from us, and the tittering of unseen voices as the crowd increased.

We gripped the edges of our foam pads until an uneasy slumber overtook us.

Exactly at midnight, a shriek went up in the night, and the sky was illuminated with bright phosphorous oranges and whites. Benjamin instantly sat up in his improvised sleep sack, eyes wide open. He applauded with tiny baby hands. Then just as quickly he lay back down and was asleep. The fireworks continued.

After about fifteen minutes they stopped. We were all still intact. The celebrants carried on late into the night, but we listened only with a somnambulant attention, feeling that the worst had passed. The baby had no recollection of the pyrotechnics the next day.

*May 28.* We broke out of the fireworks campsite early, determined to get as far south as possible. We had no choice but to take a main road that day. On a Sunday, we knew, the route would be uncrowded until noon, then all hell would break loose as both French and German tourists beelined down it on the road to Spain. Europe was having one of its wettest Mays in history, and we weren't the only ones thinking of getting out of it.

We succeeded in getting most of the busy highway out of the way by the early afternoon, and pulled into another makeshift camp at 2 P.M. A sprinkle started during the night but was gone in the morning. We packed up the tent wet, a bad practice for nylon, but one we couldn't avoid if we wanted to be on the road much before 10 A.M.

*May* 29. We threaded our way through the endless forest, the sky gray with coastal fog. Roads were nearly deserted, and we could almost taste the flavor of Spain, barely two days' ride away. Then, just before noon, Ken looked down to see his right pedal drop off. He had misthreaded it after the flight to London, and it had taken it this long to work its way out and strip loose. It was a cotterless crank, completely ruined. The small shop in the village had no replacement, and a 40-kilometer hitchhiking trip to the nearest large town was necessary.

"We'll wait for you here," we said.

"No, go on," he countered. "We're almost to Spain. I don't want to hold you up."

"But how can you get the parts when you barely know how to say hello and good-bye in French?"

"I'll manage," he said grimly. But there was also a certain tone of anticipation in his voice.

He had been unhappy for much of the trip. While he was used to cycling, he had never cycle-toured before. An inquisitive and vigorous man, he yearned for some of the things he was not finding in the small villages and hamlets we were stopping in. And although we were more friends than relatives, and there was not much difference in our ages, still there was some nagging distance at being the neophyte with uncle and aunt. Not to mention his 2-year-old cousin.

"He needs an adventure," one of us said. "Maybe he'll meet some girls."

We were uncertain. We didn't like turning him loose with such little knowledge of the language, but finally decided we were being overprotective. He seemed eager to be on his own. We scribbled the name of the nearest town, Dax, on the back of a map, and watched him disconsolately as he trudged down the road. A farmer agreed to store his bicycle in a shed for him until he could return with the part and make repairs.

We headed off for Spain on our own, disappointed that things hadn't worked out better. We had made arrangements with him to meet again at the campground in San Sebastián.

That night the two of us and Benjamin camped in relative luxury in the historic French watering spot of Cap Breton. While the wine was good in Spain, we knew it was not nearly as good as the best the French could offer, and we celebrated what was to be our last night in France with a bottle of St. Emilion, a fragrant, earthy wine of Bordeaux, whose vineyards we had skirted on our way south.

*May 30.* The road into Spain was an enormous funnel into which thousands were pouring, and we were being drawn inexorably toward its spout. Finally we couldn't avoid it any longer; it offered the only means of reaching the frontier. We could have taken the train over the last 60 miles, but we were too stubborn, wanting to do it all on bicycles.

Even at that, we were unprepared for the ferocity of the traffic. Trucks, cars, and trailers screamed past us in a frantic rush to reach the border. After some 60 miles of awful traffic, our bodies gritty with dirt and diesel fumes, nerves stretched to the breaking point by the badly paved road that left no room to swerve away from potholes, we pulled to a stop on one of the gracious, shaded streets that stretch languidly through downtown San Sebastián. Our faces were drawn and our mouths were dry.

"Where's the campground?" we asked some people.

"Up there," a moustachioed policeman in white pith helmet said. His finger pointed to a mountaintop rising from the other side of the bay.

"He's got to be joking," one of us said.

He wasn't. We picked up the campground signs down the street. The symbol is an inverted "V" which is used universally throughout Europe. We followed them and they led us, faithful to the policeman's directions, straight up. The pitch was so steep we could barely keep the pedals moving. It seemed a harsh and capricious ending to an already grueling day.

The campground attendant greeted us warmly, but with a knowing smile. We wheeled our bicycles over the graveled road to a spot where we were surrounded by the shrill but comforting cries of English schoolchildren, off with their parents on an early holiday.

We flopped on the grass, watching high cumulus clouds drift in off the Atlantic, heading somewhere for the interior of Spain. We would too, in a few days. But for now, we remained perfectly motionless, letting Benjamin frolic with new friends, the first children he could understand in three weeks.

We had come some 725 miles in nineteen days, had two days of enforced idleness because of rain and repairs, had struggled with steep routes and fireworks in the night, experienced the generosity of strangers, and were now high and dry atop one of the loveliest cities in the world. We had made it! But there was a lingering sense of the bittersweet in our satisfaction. We knew our trip was over. Ken woke us up the next morning.

# TOURING TECHNIQUES

The conditions encountered on your own tour will certainly include some of the ones just described as well as others we didn't experience. Let's begin by talking about one we did encounter, and one you will encounter to some extent on most tours—hills.

## HILLS: THE UPS AND DOWNS

If you haven't bicycled much, or if you haven't carried weight on a bicycle, the thought—or fear—of pedaling up hills may preoccupy you. The simple fact is that it takes energy to go up a hill. And while you can condition yourself, have your bicycle geared properly, and pace yourself, you cannot change geography. There are hills in the world, and on all but the shortest or most unusual tours you will encounter some of them.

But hills do not have to mean physical agony, either. You can avoid the number and steepness of hills that you do climb by careful route-finding. You can pedal more easily over the ones you do meet if you use a combination of good riding techniques. Finally, you can bicycle primarily in flat country or take trains across difficult sections of your route.

*Route-finding.* You often can reduce the number and steepness of the hills you do climb by some careful map-reading prior to the day's ride. Begin by turning your attention to the most obvious notations about terrain. If your map is color-coded, areas with higher elevations are easy to distinguish. If the elevation changes abruptly, you obviously will be climbing. On the other hand, high elevations in and of themselves do not mean hills. There are relatively long stretches in the high Alps, for instance, that, while not perfectly level, are quite easy cycling. Of course it is the getting there that is difficult, but this can often be done on a train. High plateaus are another example of elevated areas where the cycling is not necessarily rugged. The important thing in your route-finding is often not so much avoiding hills as avoiding going back down *after* you have climbed. Look for roads that maintain a basic elevation rather than rising and falling out of river valleys or across stream beds.

Some maps, such as the Michelin 1:200,000 series, indicate the steepness of grades by the use of small arrows etched across the road. These indicate pitches of certain grades, one arrow for a grade of 5–9 percent, two arrows for grades of 9–13 percent, and three for grades of more than 13 percent. One arrow means a difficult but not impossible pitch for the average cyclist, two indicate a real workout, and three are for people who are in top physical condition. You should be careful, however, not to overestimate a route's difficulty by counting the arrows you'll have to go over. On some roads, an arrow means a steep but short pitch. The appearance of a good many of them, or clusters of them, means stiff bicycling country.

In addition to noting these factors of elevation changes, you should always be on the lookout for things on a map that denote the easiest pathway through hilly terrain. Streams and rivers are the first things to look for. River beds in particular mean gentle or moderate climbing in almost all instances. Following a smaller stream upward usually means that the route will be moderate cycling for a while, then get hard as you go up over the crest of a ridge. How hard it gets usually depends on the nature of the terrain and the skill of the road engineers. Often it is a matter of how much money was spent on grading the road. Canals are the second kind of waterway to look for on your map. Not all European countries have them, but France and Holland have many, and they denote excellent pathways for the cyclist. Finally, look for roads that parallel railroad tracks. Railroad grades are usually minimal, and roads that follow them take advantage of most of the same geographical characteristics of an area.

Finally, let us make another recommendation. This is a personal preference, and may not be the same for everyone: We prefer far and away to take one long hill over a series of short ones. On a long hill you can get into a pace, keep it, and not really worry about whether the top is just around the next bend. You know it will be a long haul and you just accept it. Worse for us are short hills where you climb and fall, climb and fall, all day long. Finally we begin resenting the fact that just as we crest one hill we see another looming on the horizon. The ride down doesn't seem to take any of the sting out of it.

Naturally there are some regions where all the hills will be of this short, steep variety. In this case there is nothing you can do. But in terms of longer-range route-finding, you often have several choices of terrain, where crossing a major mountain pass may in fact be easier psychologically and perhaps physically than crossing lower terrain cross-hatched by streams and valleys.

*Hill-climbing techniques.* Finally, you come to the hills themselves. As with much else on the tour, a great deal of how easily you climb them depends on how you approach them mentally. Part of this mental perspective is really visual. We are inclined to judge a hill to be steeper than it really is because we pay the most attention to it either as it first comes into view from the top of another hill or from its bottom as we are about to start up. In addition to being psychologically bad moments, both vantage points give you an erroneous perspective on the hill. The only place for a truly accurate view of the pitch of a hill is from its middle, where you have a view of it both up and down. Wait until you get there before worrying about how hard it is to climb. (By then you can also take some comfort in the fact that you are halfway up it already.) Secondly, when you are on the hill, don't rush it. Remember you are on vacation. Look down and watch your feet revolve. If you are traveling with someone, and he or she is nearby, discuss things.

Once you have adjusted your attitudes toward hill-climbing, you can begin to work on some cycling techniques that will make hills physically easier on you:

1. *Keep ankling* (see Chapter 5). If you are still unused to ankling, hills are a good place to practice, since your speed is slower and you can think about it more.
2. *Select a gear that allows you to maintain your normal cadence*, or as close to it as possible.
3. On small, short hills where you rise and fall rapidly, it is difficult to keep an even cadence. You can help do so if you *keep your rear sprocket constant and simply shift to your small front sprocket as you lose momentum, then back to your large front sprocket as your speed increases on the downgrade.* If you shift quickly enough you should have very little strain using this method.
4. *Alternate standing and sitting.* Standing up and pedaling relieves the strain on legs and knees. Keep your weight forward and your arms flexed. When your pedal is just past the "up" position, throw your weight on that foot

and allow gravity to pull the pedal down. Reverse the process for the other foot.

5. *If the road is quiet you can weave from side to side.* This cuts the angle of the grade for you and, once you develop a rhythm, gives you a pleasant swinging sensation.

6. *After a long climb, avoid the temptation to stop suddenly at the crest or just coast down the other side.* Coasting cools your muscles, which have been working hard and rhythmically to get you up. A sudden stop also is harder on your heart and circulatory system. Instead, stay in your lower gear and, if it is safe to do so, take a turn around the crest of the hill. Then, within the limits of safety, keep the pedals moving as you go down. As speed increases, ease your brakes on and off and keep a tight hold on the handlebars. Anticipate curves, remembering that the extra weight you may be carrying as baggage will lessen the effectiveness of your brakes, and rear panniers particularly will not permit you to bank as far as you normally would. Remember, too, that the wind whistling past your ears is likely to obliterate the sounds of cars overtaking you from the rear. Don't let the exhilaration of the descent cause you to forget and drift out in the middle of the road (this happens with most cyclists unless they consciously correct the tendency). Not only can you not hear cars from the rear, you will be uncomfortably close to cars coming up the hill, and they, too, are inclined to slide over a bit in your direction, particularly on curves.

7. As you lose momentum going up the next hill, *drop down a gear or so at a time* so that your cadence stays about the same. Whatever you do, don't wait until you've almost stopped before shifting from your highest to your lowest gear. By then you will have lost all momentum, and shifting will be nearly impossible.

8. *Avoiding hills entirely.* You can avoid very hilly country by traveling only in areas or countries that are flat. Many regions of England, most of Holland, the plains of Spain, and the many broad river valleys of France and Germany offer largely level cycling. The best way of connecting the easy areas is to cover the rugged stretches on the train.

Railroads are the best-developed form of transportation in most European countries. And Europeans use railways all the time to carry bicycles. Many trains have cars with special racks in them. Large train stations even have special carts used only for transporting bicycles from the check-in point to the designated baggage car. While there is no guarantee against damage when shipping your bicycle on the railway, our experience has been that they are well treated. If you have a frame you are particularly anxious about, tape newspapers on your main tubes and stays to give added protection from scratches.

Regulations and costs vary. In England, you load the bicycle into the baggage car yourself and it is carried for free (assuming you have a ticket). In Germany and Holland, you also load the bicycle yourself, but a small fee is charged. In France, Italy, and Spain your bicycle is checked as on-board luggage and is handled by station personnel. You pay a modest fee for this in France and Italy, but in Spain it is carried free of charge. Because of this wide variety in procedures, how much it will cost you will depend on where you are and how far you are going. But in most cases you can expect to pay from $1.50 to $4 to have your bicycle carried on the train with you while traveling within one country.

To put your bicycle on a train, buy your ticket first and then inquire about specific procedures. Sometimes you will have to purchase a separate ticket for your bicycle, sometimes you simply wheel it through the gate with you and put it in the luggage car. If the bicycle is being handled by railway personnel, allow at least forty-five minutes to an hour before train time to get everything done. If you are loading the bicycle yourself, it is helpful to have a length of nylon cord or a stretch cord for securing the bicycle to the wall of the baggage car. Attach a sturdy tag with your name and home address and, if possible, a reliable European address. Some identification on handlebar pack and panniers is helpful too; a piece of surgical tape with name and address on it secured to the inside somewhere will do.

In most cases, your bicycle will travel on the same train with you. If you are traveling on an express train and getting off at a small station, the bicycle often will follow on the next local train. This may mean a wait of some hours or even overnight. At certain times of the year, particularly in Holland, you may experience even longer delays. Inquire first. If necessary, ship your bicycle on ahead of you a day or so before you leave.

Should you be traveling to a large city and want to spend some time sightseeing, you can leave your bicycle in the station's luggage room. There is usually a twenty-four-hour grace period after its arrival until you begin paying storage fees on it.

## WEATHER: THROUGH RAIN, WIND, HEAT AND COLD

No matter how carefully you have planned your trip, you will not be able to forecast exactly what your weather is going to be like from day to day. You will eliminate or minimize many unfavorable aspects of weather by having the right clothing and equipment along and adjusting some of your riding habits to account for the weather.

*Rain.* Rain tends to be the weather factor most people

worry about when considering bicycle touring. In truth it seldom is a consistent problem. Few summer rains last all day, and if necessary you can use a "ride and hide" method about 90 percent of the time and still get in a reasonable day's ride. Even the onset of rain tends to work in your favor, as many—but not all, of course—summer rains begin in the afternoon. This gives you some chance to get your riding out of the way before it starts.

Should you wish to avoid the likelihood of rain entirely, you can cycle in southern Europe where summers, although not absolutely rainless, are essentially so.

But most bicycle tourists will sooner or later be caught on the road as it starts raining. What to do? First of all, get to shelter before it starts to soak things through. Anything you can stand under and stay dry will do. We carry two or three plastic garbage bags slit open and use these to cover panniers and handlebar packs if the bicycles must remain out in the weather. We strap the plastic down with stretch cords to keep it from blowing in the inevitable wind.

We normally keep riding in a drizzle or a light rain. We wear nylon shell windbreakers that, while not waterproof, keep enough of it off. If it's also cold, we add a wool sweater underneath. Our eyes usually are the first to tell us that it's raining too hard and we should stop. We start blinking excessively. When this happens, we head for shelter. We never seem to be able to keep track of weather forecasts, so we normally just try to guess how serious a rain is going to be from the looks of the sky. If it looks absolutely hopeless, we head for the nearest town. We either dry out in a café, find a hotel, or camp for the night. If you are camping, incidentally, it is much better to wait for a lull in the rain before putting up your tent. Nothing is worse than putting one up in a howling rainstorm. Everything, including your panniers and sleeping bags, seems to get wet.

If you do ride during a rainstorm, ease your brakes on periodically to keep your rims dry, and be very cautious when crossing railroad tracks or even painted lines on streets. Railroad tracks particularly become very slick and, unless crossed exactly at right angles, can cause a spill.

The usual pattern with rain is that it will force you into shelter for a while, then break enough for you to ride some more. Although it is annoying to have to keep stopping for rain, this method of moving during the breaks will usually allow you to get to some permanent haven relatively dry, leaving you, at the worst, with an extended ride the next day to make up distance. If necessary, make up the distance by train.

There are many people who ride in ponchos or rain capes, although we have found that condensation builds up on the inside and you end up getting wet anyway. Newer, waterproof yet breathable materials such as Gore Tex are much better, keeping you dry without excessive condensation unless you are cycling moderately hard for long distances. If possible, try out a rain cape before you leave and form your own impressions.

*Wind.* While most people worry about rain, we have found that wind is a more serious physical and psychological weather problem. Without presenting you with any visible challenge it can tire you out. Worst of all, it seems to frustrate most people psychologically because it causes them to work hard in covering terrain that normally requires much less effort. You can't understand at first why you aren't doing better. Here are some suggestions to cut down problems caused by wind.

First, try to get as early a start in the morning as possible. Most heavy winds rise sometime after noon. If you have most of your ride out of the way by then it will go much easier for you. Secondly, when riding in the wind it is important to readjust your daily goals. You won't be going as fast as usual, nor perhaps as far. To counteract both fatigue and frustration, take breaks more often, and if at all possible take them out of the wind, preferably inside a café or some enclosed place. Finally, keep as low a profile as possible, riding with your hands on the lower or dropped part of your handlebars and your head well down.

There is one positive note to the whole matter of wind, however, and that is when you get a direct tailwind pushing you down the highway. These are magic moments. You reach speeds much above what you normally can do, and best of all, the speed of the bicycle often matches exactly that of the wind. You ride in a world of nearly perfect stillness, with only the sound of your tires singing up to you from the road.

*Sun and heat.* These seem to be easier for most people to handle psychologically, but they can take a heavier toll on you physically than any other weather factor. Riding in heat is deceptive. The cooling factor of the wind passing over you can disguise how hot you are really becoming, including making you unaware of a state where you actually stop perspiring. Moreover, the regulatory mechanism within your body causes thirst to lag behind real need for water. What this means is that you won't *feel* thirsty until your body has lost important quantities of fluids. Severe water loss can reduce muscle strength, lower plasma and blood volumes, reduce cardiac function, lower oxygen consumption, deplete liver glycogen, and increase the losses of electrolytes from the body. In extreme cases, it can damage the ability of your brain to regulate the body's responses to heat.

What most cyclists will feel, however, is weakness, nausea, and severe headaches. If this happens, stop immediately, douse yourself with water, get in the shade, and sip small quantities of fluid. Stay in the shade until you feel better. When the day has cooled off, cycle to the nearest convenient place and stop for the night.

Most cyclists will not get in this kind of a strait. And no one should, if reasonable care is taken when riding in the heat.

First, and most obviously, take care to drink frequently. A small amount of glucose in the water on exceptionally hot days will help offset sugar loss in the blood. We normally mix some powdered drink mix in our water bottles after lunch break for drinking during the afternoon heat. This gives the water a refreshing taste and gives you a little lift at the same time. Try to anticipate when your bottle is getting low, and fill it before it runs out. We fill ours in gas stations, from fountains, from people's homes, or from cafés if we can't find anything else.

We have never had problems with water in Europe, nor did our 2-year-old, and we draw from any source where local people are taking water. If in doubt, or if you are susceptible to stomach disorders, you can buy bottled water, available all over Europe.

In terms of hot-weather clothing, it is helpful to wear cotton rather than synthetic fabrics, and most people benefit from wearing a hat, although one of us who is prone to headaches significantly reduced them by wearing not a hat but a bandana soaked with water on extremely hot days. A scarf tied around your neck and soaked with water, particularly if allowed to lie on the nape of your neck, is also helpful.

Finally, you can do most about the heat by not riding in it. In hot-weather climates get on the road as early as possible. During a blistering tour of Sardinia one August we geared ourselves to wake up just before sunrise, had quick breakfasts, and were on the road just as it was getting light. We stopped every day before 2 P.M., and if that wasn't possible, we sat out the worst part of the day, between 2 and 5 P.M., sightseeing, resting in the shade, or swimming in the sea. We continued on after five. If you are very sensitive to heat, treat it the same way you would rain. When it becomes too oppressive, just don't ride in it.

*Cold weather* is not much of a problem when cycling, since you normally generate enough body heat to keep yourself warm. Wear at least two layers of clothing. They should be loose-fitting and allow your body to breathe—for example, a wool sweater over your usual riding outfit. If you feel cool at all in your torso area add a third layer in the form of a windbreaker. As you warm up, start removing extra layers. Legs can be left uncovered unless it is really cold, but cover them if you stop for a long rest.

The more crucial factor about riding in the cold is what you do once you have stopped. You must avoid cooling off too fast and getting chilled, especially in the torso area. If you are stopping for a five-minute rest, keep upright, lean against a tree, or pace around a little so your muscles don't cool off. For longer rests try to stop in a warm café where you can have something warm to eat or drink. Drink alcohol only if you are through riding for the day. Drinking and riding can leave you colder than you were before. If you are stopping for the day, change all your damp clothing immediately, including socks and underwear; otherwise you may never get warm.

## ROAD SAFETY

With any sort of reasonable care, a bicycling holiday should not be marred by accidents. Sticking to small roads with little traffic eliminates the major hazard. You decrease your chances of having an accident even further by practicing good safety habits. While most of these are common sense, they should be reviewed from time to time anyway. Here are a few that helped us out.

*Riding in the country.* Unless the road is exceptionally quiet, ride single file. In any case, always ride with the flow of traffic, and ride well over to the side of the road and watch for farm equipment and cars entering from the small side roads. Loose gravel is also a problem. Watch for it on turns and on the shoulder of the road. If you do find yourself in deep gravel, try to stop without slamming on your brakes. Since bicyclists usually ride near the edge of the road, one particular hazard is dropping off the pavement onto the shoulder. If the shoulder is more than an inch lower than the road level, don't try to steer back on. Stop first and lift your wheels onto the pavement. Our one accident in touring came as a result of not doing this and ended up with four stitches and a night in a French hospital. You must also be careful about drifting too far toward the center of the road, particularly if you are riding side by side and talking. Just as a normal precaution, keep periodic checks on the road both ahead and behind. A final general rule is that if for any reason you are knocked off balance—running into your partner or getting a flat tire—don't slam on the brakes. Try to right yourself first.

*Riding in the city.* When riding in the city loosen your toe clips and be extra cautious regarding traffic. There are two particular hazards for cyclists. The first is when riding past parked cars. Keep enough clearance from them so that if someone in one decides to open his door on your side you won't slam into it. The other hazard is at intersections. When crossing them be on the lookout for cars making right-hand turns. Often they will not look before turning and turn into you.

If the city is very large, a quarter of a million or more, it is often best to avoid it entirely; if you want to sightsee, check your bicycle at a suburban train station and go in via rail. Industrial cities are particularly hectic, as truck traffic is heavy and road surfaces are often deformed, particularly near the edge of the pavement.

Unless we have some reason for going there, we usually just plan our route around a large town of any size. This sometimes means extra miles (although not necessarily), but much more tranquil riding.

Should you have to ride through, certain times are better than others. The optimal period in much of Europe is from noon until two in the afternoon, when most Europeans take their main meal. Particularly in southern Europe, city streets are often deserted. Sunday mornings are also good times for traversing large cities. Next in line is the morning, either well before the daily rush or just after it.

In some instances, in very large cities such as Paris or London, we have ridden just before dawn.

*Dogs.* This is the most refreshing note we can add to this list of safety hazards. The waters of civilization have flowed long enough in Europe so that people keep their dogs fenced or tied. It is very unlikely that some beast will chase you, yapping at your feet and foaming at the mouth.

If it does happen, try to ignore him. He will usually tire faster than you. If you have a good downhill run you can try to outdistance him. There are aerosol dog repellents, but these are bulky to carry and never seem to be around when you need them. Kicking at dogs tends to throw your balance off and could cause you to tip. If things get really serious, your best bet is to dismount and look for help. If none is available try throwing rocks. Don't run—he is faster than you.

## CAMPING OUT

We discussed organized campgrounds in Chapter 2. But often the question is asked, How safe is it to camp out in Europe? Frankly, the question is not so much one of safety as of being annoyed or chased off.

To begin with, outside of Scandinavia and some of the mountainous regions of Europe, there are no vast expanses of wilderness or untracked terrain. Most of the land you see belongs to someone. If you pull off the road and go into the woods and camp, you are doing so on someone else's land. It is possible that they will ask you to move if they discover you, although in most instances the presence of your bicycles and a harmless (or helpless) appearance will persuade them to allow you to stay. Make it clear you're not setting up camp for the summer, but only for one night.

There are some countries where it is forbidden to camp outside organized campgrounds. This rule is usually loosely enforced; Yugoslavia is the one place we know of where authorities are more strict. You are inviting trouble, however, if you camp in a public park, or along beach areas where there are organized campgrounds available.

Given these factors, the best course is just to ask a farmer if you can camp on his land. We've met with success every time we've asked. Sometimes it is the start of a unique person-to-person experience.

But often you will see what seems to be a perfect area and there's no one around to ask. Should you camp there anyway?

This is what we do: We wait until there are no cars on the road, then wheel our bicycles into a lane or through the woods. We don't camp within sight or sound of the road. If we are exceptionally uneasy, we even wait until dusk to put up the tent, fixing dinner, relaxing, or reading with only partially discharged bicycles. In case someone complains we have little to do before moving on.

When camping like this—and we have done it often in areas such as the interior of Spain, Italy, and Greece where campgrounds are rare—we always carry a collapsible container that holds a gallon and a half of water. We need this to cook with, wash dishes in, and, if there is no other source of water, to wash ourselves with. This requires exceptional conservation, and it is a skill we have enjoyed mastering. Incidentally, we have found that a portable plastic douche bag makes an excellent in-the-woods shower. It takes about a quart of water for an adequate cleansing.

Furthermore, we never, never build a campfire. In addition to being discourteous, it attracts attention and can be dangerous. We cook with a butane stove, discussed in our equipment section in Chapter 8.

These makeshift camps have been one of the delights of our camping experiences in Europe. We are completely out of sight, we do not harm things, and, to date, we have never been asked to leave or been annoyed, other than the fireworks display discussed earlier in this chapter. And that, frankly, is the sort of experience we are always hoping for anyway.

SEVEN

# Buying and equipping a touring bicycle

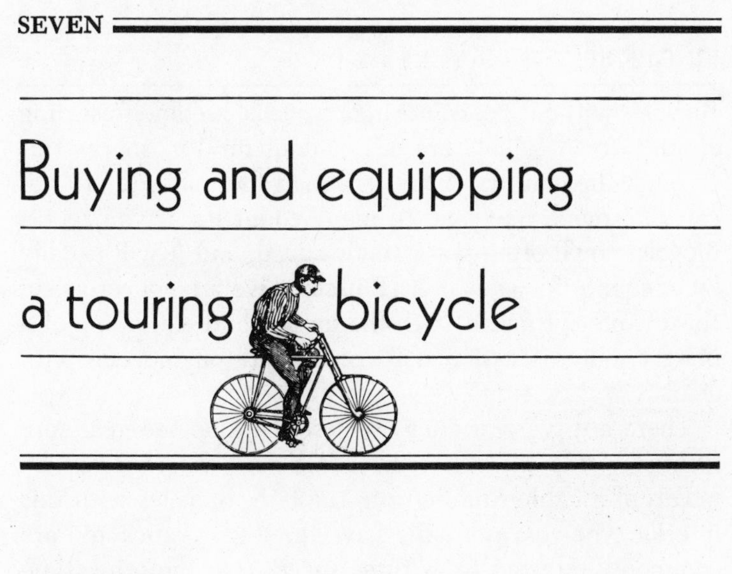

## GEARING

The most important thing about a touring bicycle is its gearing, including the number of gears on your bike and the range they cover. Every other consideration is secondary. Gearing is the ratio of pedal turns to turns of the rear wheel, and it determines how hard you will have to push in order to keep your bike going; whether or not you will be able to climb certain hills or will have to get off and push the bicycle up; how much weight you can carry comfortably; whether you can get into a natural riding cadence and keep to it; whether or not you can even cycle in certain terrain. Gearing also determines how fast you can go; whether you can keep up with a group if you have a strong tailwind and the riding is easy; whether you are obliged to coast down a long grade rather than pedal and build your momentum before starting up the next.

## SINGLE-SPEED BICYCLES

Bicycles without gears, or single-speeds, are fine for riding around town. They are also adequate for short trips through the country if the terrain is flat and you are not carrying much baggage. In many countries, if you rent a bicycle, you'll often get a single-speed, and it will usually be adequate for your uses. But since we are concerned in this chapter primarily with the buying and equipping of a bicycle, our discussion will concentrate on bicycles with gears.

There are two varieties of these. On one the gears are located inside the rear wheel hub and are changed by means of a cable running into the hub. Bicycles with this interior type gear normally have three-gear ratios and are commonly referred to as three-speeds. On the other type of bicycle the gears are changed by engaging the chain on different front and rear sprocket combinations. The chain is changed from one sprocket to another by means of a derailleur, and bicycles with this kind of gearing are commonly called derailleur types.

## THREE-SPEED BICYCLES FOR TOURING

In addition to their gearing, three-speed bicycles have other features that make them easier to pedal than the balloon-tire bicycle you probably rode as a kid. Their frames are lighter, and their tires are thinner, causing less road friction. You can tour on a three-speed bicycle, and many Europeans do, but our experiences with them have been mixed. With light loads and in level, windless country they are fine. In a headwind or in hilly country pedaling is difficult or even impossible. The three-gear ratios do not give you adequate options for any significant variations in terrain, particularly when the bicycle is loaded. The lawnmower-type handlebars on most three-speed bicycles put you automatically in an upright position. This causes excessive wind resistance and makes it physically harder to pedal. The seats on three-speeds often have springs, which at first appears more humane than the hard and unsprung seat of a lightweight derailleur bicycle, but the sprung seat also makes pedaling more difficult by reducing leverage. Taking all these factors into consideration, we would not recommend three-speeds for general European touring. In no case would we recommend them if you are carrying a full complement of camping and cooking equipment, no matter where you are touring. This just makes bicycling more difficult than it has to be. A better all-round choice for touring is a derailleur bicycle.

## DERAILLEUR BICYCLES

Derailleur bicycles have more gear combinations than three-speeds. Some of them come with five gears, most of them come with ten, and if you want to go all out you can even have one with eighteen gears! Other aspects of construction in derailleur bicycles also make them better touring choices. Some are obvious things such as lighter frames, thin, hard tires, firm seats for easier pedaling, and dropped ("racing-type") handlebars for a more efficient riding posture. Other invisible differences—such as stronger pedal assemblies or more finely machined interior components—make cycling more trouble-free.

If you already own one of these bicycles you are aware of their qualities and advantages. In fact, if your bicycle is a good one, and you are used to it, you most likely will decide to take it with you. If you are new to bicycling and will be buying one for your tour, you should know something about what goes into a good derailleur bicycle.

*Gearing and cadence.* The main purpose and advantage of having five or more gears is to allow you to pedal with about the same amount of effort and at the same cadence (revolutions of the pedals per minute) over varying terrains. Studies show that if we expend our energy at a more or less even pace it lasts longer. Another way of looking at it is that you will feel less tired covering the same distance if you do it with an even amount of energy than if you do it with heavy spurts followed by periods of coasting. You can try out this theory by running up a very long flight of stairs, stopping midway and resting briefly, then running again to the top. After you've recovered, do it again, this time climbing them at a steady and moderate pace. You'll feel better doing it the second way.

The most important factor in a touring bicycle is that it have a wide enough range of gear ratios so that it will allow you to maintain this even and economical kind of pace for sustained periods of time over different kinds of terrain. With this in mind let's look at what you can expect from five-, ten-, and fifteen-speed bicycles.

*Five-speed gearing.* A five-speed bicycle has five sprockets fixed to the rear wheel and a single sprocket attached to the pedal assembly. The five gears give you a minimal range that allows you to climb moderate hills when loaded, and your top or highest gear is high enough to give you good speed on level ground. If you are not climbing steep grades or carrying much weight this will be sufficient. The limitations of a five-speed are at the top and bottom ends of the gear span. Low gear is not really low enough to allow easy hill climbing, and the highest gear is too low to allow you to maintain a fast pace going down slight inclines or steeper hills. The lack of a good low gear is the more serious limitation in that it makes hill climbing difficult. But not having a good high-speed gear is also a limitation. If you are covering any distance at all in a day it is not a good idea to puff up one hill and then coast down the other side without pedaling. Coasting breaks your pace and causes your leg muscles to cool off too quickly, especially after they have worked hard pulling you up a hill. One additional feature that detracts from some five-speeds is that their frames are rather heavy and they are generally equipped with lower-quality derailleurs and brakes.

*Ten-speed gearing.* Ten-speed bicycles have seven sprockets, two attached to the pedal axle and five attached to the rear wheel. You change gears by working one of two levers fastened to the frame or handlebars of the bicycle, usually on the tube that runs downward toward the rider from the handlebars to the pedal casing. These levers control two derailleurs, one for the two front sprockets, the other for the five rear sprockets. The derailleur is like a hand that allows the chain to slide through its fingers while it lifts the chain from one sprocket and engages it on another, thus changing the gear ratio. With proper sprocket sizes on both front and back, you can climb 90 percent of the hills in Europe, including the mountain passes if you don't mind a little physical workout.

Since the seven sprockets on a ten-speed give you an extremely wide choice of gear ratios, you should know something about the specific sprocket sizes that are best for touring. The general rule is that you need a wide range of sizes in both front and rear sprocket sets. Your small front sprocket should have thirty-two or thirty-six teeth, with forty as the uppermost limit. Beyond forty your bicycle is not geared low enough to allow easy hill climbing. The large front sprocket should have between forty-six and fifty-two teeth. The small front sprocket is used for hills and for riding into headwinds, the large one for level terrain, going down hills, or riding with a tail-wind. We prefer a small front sprocket with thirty-six teeth and a large front sprocket with fifty teeth. If you are new to touring you should have a thirty-two/forty-eight combination. If you are in excellent condition, or touring with light loads (five or seven pounds maximum), you might use a small front sprocket of forty or even forty-two, and a large front sprocket of fifty-two.

Of the five sprockets attached to the rear wheel the most crucial one for touring is the largest one, since this, in combination with your small front sprocket, gives you your lowest gear. The largest sprocket, which is closest to the rear wheel, should have at least twenty-six teeth. If you are not used to touring twenty-eight teeth or thirty would be better. The others should be scaled downward to a small rear sprocket of about fourteen teeth, with the remaining three sprockets spaced between the two. Your dealer can best decide these sizes since an endless set of variations is possible and the size of your wheels also makes a difference. But you should make clear to him that you will be using the bicycle for touring and that you want your lowest gear to be at least a "thirty-three" (a figure calculated on the basis of sprocket sizes and wheel diameter).

With the exception of climbing steep grades, where you obviously must labor more, touring on a properly geared ten-speed means that you feel about the same physical strain all the time. Once accustomed to this you are free to enjoy the scenery.

*Twelve- and fifteen-speed gearing.* Twelve-speed gearing is achieved by having six plates or sprockets on the rear wheel and two sprockets on the crank. Fifteen-speed gearing is reached with five sprockets on the rear and three on the front. In most cases, the use of twelve or fifteen speeds does not increase the total gear range of a bicycle. The additional gears give you closer gear ratios in the spread between the highest and lowest gears.

There are some bicycle tourists who are in exceptionally good condition or who are traveling very light (or both) for whom closer gear ratios will be beneficial. Cadences can be kept more constant, pacing will be easier. But unless such a gear combination actually increases the overall range of your gears, the extra ones represent primarily a convenience, not a necessity.

## OTHER ELEMENTS IN CONSTRUCTION AND PARTS

### FRAME CONSTRUCTION

There are small but measurable differences between a bicycle frame created for touring and one designed for faster paces or for racing. These have to do with the weight of the frame, the stiffness of it, and the rake of the front forks.

The most common ground for judging the desirability of a frame is its weight. Weight varies with the kind of tubes used in construction and the metal used to make the tubes. The stiffness of the frame relates to the length of those tubes and how they are joined together. The rake of the frame refers to the angle at which the front wheel forks slant. The more the slant (deviation from vertical) the softer the ride, and the less responsiveness.

If you shop very long for a bicycle, you undoubtedly will hear a great deal about frame construction and about the alloy compounds used to create the frame tubing. Our feeling is that for the average bicycle tourist these considerations are of secondary, not primary, importance.

To begin with, most of the refinements in frame construction are spurred on by a concern to build the fastest, most responsive bicycle possible for racing or high-speed roadwork. Neither of these qualities is excessively important to the tourist.

Secondly, the weight advantages and the responsiveness gained via frame construction—always at considerable expense to the buyer—are obviated by the weight most tourists add to the bicycle in the form of carriers, packs, and equipment.

Of course it will make a difference to you if you are hauling 21 pounds of bicycle up a mountain as opposed to hauling 28 pounds of bicycle. But you can do more, and at less expense, to reduce weight by reducing what you carry on the bicycle. Deciding to leave a 900-page paperback behind at a youth hostel, wearing jeans made of synthetics rather than heavy cotton denim, opting for a smaller and lighter tent will all produce effective results. The cost of shaving that much weight off a bicycle frame will be very steep.

In addition, the weight of a bicycle frame is essentially static. A more important area in which to work for weight reduction is on anything that moves. A wheel rim, for instance, has its own inherent weight, and requires additional energy (from you) to keep it spinning. The same is true of tires, tubes, sprockets, and pedals. Even the weight of your riding shoes is a factor; it takes far more energy to move them around all day than it would if you carried them in your pack as static weight. Over the course of a day, as these things are lifted or made to revolve thousands and thousands of times, the energy required to do so multiplies accordingly. Because of this, if we have a given number of dollars to spend on a touring bicycle and must make a choice between an alloy frame and moving alloy components, we will spend it on the latter.

*Tandem frames.* You may, if you wish to tour with a friend or spouse, buy a tandem bicycle. If you do, we would strongly suggest that you borrow or rent one before you make your purchase and get some long rides in to see if you really enjoy this kind of togetherness. If you do, then go ahead and buy your bicycle built for two. Look for the same qualities you would in any good ten-speed. The main disadvantage with tandems is that you will have a luggage capacity only a little greater than with one single-seat bicycle.

## TIRES

Bicycles can be outfitted with two kinds of tires. The first is a standard tube-type tire, with which most of us are familiar. In bicycling terminology these are called clincher tires. The other kind of tire has a tube completely encased within it. These were developed specifically for racing and are called tubulars or, more commonly, sew-ups, due to the fact that the tire is actually sewn around the tube. Sew-ups are extremely light and can be inflated to high pressures. This gives a fast, responsive ride. Their disadvantages are that they puncture easily and require considerable skill and time to repair. Our one experience with them on tour was a three-week nightmare of a flat a day, with half an hour or more spent each evening trying to repair them. Some people tour on them. We recommend clinchers, however. In addition to being easier to repair, recent technological advances in rim and tire construction have made clinchers nearly as light as some sew-ups. They will inflate to 90 or even 110 pounds of pressure, are less costly, and, should one be ruined, can easily be replaced. This brings us to a final important point about tires as they relate to touring abroad.

Most bicycles sold in the United States and Great Britain use a standard 27-inch-diameter tire. In continental Europe, the standard tire is 28 inches (700 centimeters) diameter. This divergence often makes 27-inch tires difficult to find outside of Great Britain. If your bicycle is equipped with 27-inch wheels, make certain the tires are new or in excellent condition before you go on tour. It is not that common to ruin a tire, but it does happen, and getting a 27-inch replacement in much of Europe can mean a delay of some days unless you happen to break down in or near a large city.

While most tourists do not carry an extra tire, we always carry an extra tube (the 27-inch tube fits both 27- and 28-inch rims) simply to avoid having to patch a tube should we get a flat on the road, or when we are traveling in places (Yugoslavia and Greece, for example) where bicycle shops are rare except in large cities.

## HANDLEBARS

Almost all ten-speed bicycles sold in this country and in Europe are equipped with what are called "dropped" handlebars. They curve downward like ram horns. Novices, or people getting back on bicycles after years of absence, invariably find them uncomfortable. Some people find they feel too insecure to use them. Nonetheless, we strongly recommend that you get used to them. Their advantages are important. First, they put your body in the best possible position to deliver maximum power to your pedals. They allow you to use your arms when cycling, which is important in that it disperses energy expenditure over a larger portion of your body. In addition, the old "upright" handlebars place all your weight on your seat, which will fatigue you in other ways. Finally, dropped handlebars allow you to adapt to varying conditions, such as wind or very steep hills. In wind particularly you will find them crucial in reducing resistance as you bend low over the bars.

However, if you just can't ride with them, then go to the other kind. Your pace will be a little slower, and you won't do as well in the wind, but on level stretches or at a slower pace they are quite sufficient. One advantage to them is that they reduce the pressure on arms, shoulders, and neck caused by dropped handlebars. You can also look around more easily with upright handlebars. Of course you pay for these advantages by some loss in cycling efficiency.

*Padded handlebars.* Soft foam-rubber sleeves can be mounted on dropped handlebars to cushion the rider's hands, arms, and shoulders from road shock. Over an extended touring day this padding will alleviate fatigue and numbness in these areas and make riding much more comfortable. We recommend it highly to anyone inclined to these problems. You can produce the same effect by cutting short pieces of foam and wrapping them around the handlebars, then taping it all down in the usual way with regular handlebar tape.

## SADDLES

More than any other aspect of touring bicycles, the seats strike the uninitiated as well-designed instruments of torture. In fact, until you are used to them, they are. They are narrow, hard, have no springs, and are made of unpliable leather or plastic. Their saving grace is that they are more efficient than seats constructed in other ways. They are hard and unsprung because one needs a firm base to push from when pedaling. When cycling, the body functions as a lever. The arms exert an opposite force as they push down. The middle point, or apex, in this lever is your rear end. A saddle that has springs or too much give to it reduces the efficiency of the lever action much the same as a teeter-totter loses efficiency if the board keeps sliding on the middle bar. The seat is narrow because if it were wider the inside of your thighs would be chafed after riding some distance, particularly if you were grasping the low part of your handlebars.

When you first ride on a new saddle, your body will have to develop some toughness to a new demand upon it. After a hundred miles or so the saddle begins to get broken in, much the same as a new boot is broken in after walking in it for a time.

Saddles developed specifically for touring reduce these discomforts to a great extent. They are wider in the rear than the traditional racing saddle, and most have a thin layer of foam padding on them. There are also especially contoured touring saddles for women riders. All padded saddles require less breaking in, and reduce to a great extent the week of soreness you get if you haven't been riding much before you start on tour. We've had particularly good experiences with Avocet touring saddles.

## DERAILLEURS

There are a number of good derailleurs for touring bicycles, some fabricated in Europe, some in Japan. We have toured using a variety of European brands, but prefer the Japanese Sun Tour by far. They are better equipped to handle the great divergencies in sprocket sizes necessary to the touring bicycle.

Until recently, however, it was difficult to find replacement parts for Japanese derailleurs (and other Japanese components as well) in Europe. This has changed considerably in the last five years, and most shops that stock a wide variety of bicycle parts will have Japanese parts as well.

## BRAKES

Brakes are important on a touring bicycle, since you often have additional weight that makes stopping even more difficult. Therefore, equip your bicycle with the best brakes you can afford.

Brakes may either be side pull or center pull. A side-pull brake, if it is well constructed, is superior. The Japanese Dia-Compe and the Italian Campagnollo are examples. Cheap or poorly made side-pull brakes are not very efficient. Among the variety of good center-pull brakes on the market, we have had good success with Mafac. Weinmann is another excellent brand. Keeping the brake shoes adjusted so they pull into the rims evenly, drying the brakes frequently in wet weather, and keeping the rims free of oil are as important as the quality of the brake, and are routine maintenance and riding procedures that should be attended to when touring.

## FENDERS

If you are riding in absolutely arid climates you won't need fenders. For most of Europe, however, they will make your bicycle more versatile. Even if you don't ride in the rain, you frequently ride after a rain with puddles on the road. Fenders give you and those following you some protection. Riders following you closely will be particularly appreciative of your fenders when in dairy cattle country, where herds often cross the road or walk on it. Avoiding the residue of their passing is a difficult, and at times impossible, cycling feat.

## OTHER ACCESSORIES

*Lights.* Most bicycle lights, either generator powered or battery operated, do a better job at making you visible than they do at making the road visible. We choose not to ride at night. We do, however, carry a square bicycle light with a small handle on it which we use primarily as a flashlight but in emergencies tie to our rear carriers, covering the light with a red handkerchief. All European countries require that you have both front and rear lights for night riding. If you are contemplating much night riding, then a generator-operated front and rear light is best, despite the drag it puts on your tire.

*Toe clips.* Toe clips are metal and leather attachments for your pedals. They hold your feet in place and make riding easier and safer. Using them guarantees that you always have your foot correctly centered on the pedal (ball of the foot directly over the pedal axle). You don't have to employ any muscle power to keep them there. The clips also help you ankle automatically, a technique discussed in Chapter 5. Ankling greatly increases your cycling efficiency.

While toe clips look ominous and require some getting used to, their advantages are so great that we recommend that every tourist equip his or her bicycle with them.

*Tire pumps.* Your bicycle will probably come fitted with a tire pump. You need one to keep your tires firm from day to day and for repairs. Make certain yours fits your particular tube stems, as there are two types used, the English and American Schraeder and the continental Presta. Most tubes sold on the Continent will have the latter kind of valve. Some better-quality tire pumps come with Presta adapters.

*Kickstands.* Kickstands will do an adequate job of holding up a bicycle, but many people don't want to be bothered with the extra weight. We are of the latter category, but our bicycles bear the scars of many proppings and leanings against trees, posts, and buildings. You might want to try out your present kickstand to see if it will effectively support your bicycle while fully packed with gear.

*Locks.* If you have a good lightweight lock, take it with you. Generally speaking, you will not find the same quality in lock design in Europe that you will find at home. This is because theft is not as significant a problem in Europe as it is here.

Still, bicycles are stolen there, and you don't want to be the victim of such a theft. Depending upon the country and the individual circumstances, we follow these procedures: In large towns, we never leave our bicycles unattended (even if locked). We check them in the train station. In villages or middle-sized towns, if we want to have a look around, or we know we are going to be away from the bicycles for periods of a half hour or so, we lock them, take our passports, money, and other portable items such as sunglasses, but leave the bicycles packed. For short stops to shop in stores, we usually just lean them against something. We have never had any problems with this system, but you must use your judgment and act accordingly. In campgrounds, we lock our bicycles to a tree or fence, or if that isn't possible, we lock one bicycle to another if we are away for very long, or if the campground has a lot of in-and-out traffic. In a few situations in large city campgrounds we have actually put our bicycles inside the tent if we were going to be out for the evening. Hostels normally have places where bicycles can be put. Lock them there. In hotels, ask if there is a hotel garage you may use, and put your bicycle in there and lock it. Some people touring on very expensive equipment will insist on taking the bicycle into the room with them. This may raise a few eyebrows, but your bicycle will be safe.

Generally speaking, you don't have to exercise the paranoia about theft that one must exercise in some parts of the United States. Particularly in small towns and villages, it is most unlikely that your bicycle will be stolen or things taken from it. On the other hand, there is a decided lack of romanticism about locking things in Europe. We were given prudent, and typical, advice from an old man in a French campground on one of our first tours: "*Tout dedans, tout fermé.*" Everything inside, everything closed up!

*Water bottles.* This is one of the most crucial items on any touring bicycle. Bottles are made of either aluminum or plastic and fit snugly into wire holders attached to the frame. Since keeping an adequate water balance is essential in hot weather or when you are working hard, the clip-on bottle is a very good investment. You can drink while riding, and even when stopped you are not forced to root around in your pack to find a water bottle or canteen. You can also squirt water on yourself while riding, which is refreshing on hot days.

If you don't carry a regular bicycle water bottle, a simple one-quart polyethylene bottle carried in your front pack will do. The two-quart metal canteens sold in many sporting goods stores are fine for a Sahara expedition but unnecessary as long as you stop and replenish your supply whenever it gets low.

*Bicycle trailers.* There are a number of companies within the United States and in Europe that manufacture trailers for bicycles. Only one is adequate for the bicycle tourist, and that is manufactured in Massachusetts by the Cannondale Corporation (see Appendix 8). It comes in two models, one for carrying gear, the other for carrying a child. Costs range from $120 to $165. It is doubtful whether most tourists would have need for a trailer just for carrying gear if normal loads are anticipated. These can be handled by panniers, rear racks, and handlebar packs. But if one person is carrying gear for two or more, the trailer is a most efficient way of doing it, and we have known people who have toured this way.

Carrying a child is quite another matter. The Cannondale "Bugger," as the trailer is named, will carry one or two children 5 years of age or under, plus gear. As far as we know, this is the only safe and humane way of doing so on long trips. A seat belt holds the child or children in, and there is room underneath the seat and at the bottom of the trailer for storing other gear. We carried about 70 pounds on the trailer, including Benjamin, on our most recent trip.

In addition to being much safer for carrying children than the traditional child's seat mounted on the rear carrier of a bicycle, the trailer allows the child to move around a bit, gives him or her an unobstructed view, allows for napping, and encourages playing simple word games and talking. It is exceptionally stable and will protect the child in case of a fall (one experience—absolutely no damage done). It is also easier for motorists to see and does not upset the equilibrium of the bicyclist as does a child seat on a rear carrier. We mounted a bicycle flag to the trailer in such a way that it jutted upward and outward toward passing traffic. We also put Day-Glow tape on the rear. We never rode at night.

Whoever is pulling the trailer will notice additional drag, caused by the extra weight and the friction of two additional wheels passing over the pavement. On level ground, with a moderate load, this usually required using one gear lower than normal. On steep grades or in the mountains, the difference was considerable, and took some getting used to. Some cycling in the Pyrenees and the Alps was very difficult. If much mountain work is contemplated with loads of this kind, a 30-inch gear or lower should be used.

We have commented elsewhere (Chapter 4) on the pleasure we found in traveling with our son. In almost all cases, he was willing to make whatever adaptations were necessary. An unobstructed view of the countryside, the opportunity for games, the adventure of a new place each night, all kept Benjamin pretty occupied. The few modifications in our own routine that we had to make—some care in shopping for special foods (peanut butter!), using sterilized rather than fresh milk (he had some reaction to the latter), a willingness to entertain him when we were tired at the end of the day—were small prices to pay for the joy we found in being on a great adventure together. We would recommend it to anyone.

*Tool kit.* Unless you are skilled at doing your own repairs, have any important work done in a bicycle shop. They are plentiful throughout Europe. For tightening an occasional nut or replacing a broken cable, you need to carry only a few things. Your bicycle may come with a set of combination wrenches. If not, get one that has a variety of nut sizes on it. In addition, carry these tools and spare parts:

*Tools*

1 4-inch crescent wrench
1 pair small pliers
1 freewheel remover. You probably won't be using this yourself but one is needed to replace broken spokes on the freewheel side (sprocket side) of the rear wheel. Any bicycle dealer can replace spokes, but many in Europe do not have a freewheel remover.
1 spoke wrench (optional)
1 tire patch kit
1 set tire irons (some of the combination wrenches can be used as tire irons)

*Spare Parts*

2 extra brake cables
1 long derailleur cable (will fit either front or rear)
4 extra spokes
2 extra brake shoes
1 extra tube

## WHERE TO BUY YOUR BICYCLE

There are a number of advantages to buying your bicycle here and taking it with you to Europe.

*Buying the bicycle here* insures that you can get exactly what you want and have a good chance to try it out to see if there is anything wrong with it. You will have time to break in the saddle, make proper adjustments for saddle and handlebar height, ascertain if the gearing you have selected is low enough, and get the feel of riding it before you add weight and start touring. You also will know exactly how much you must pay, or have paid, and will be in for no surprises that will dent your touring budget.

*Buying your bicycle in Europe.* The cost advantages that used to exist for bicycles purchased in Europe have shrunk greatly over the years. Wages in the Common Market countries have gone up considerably. In addition, all Common Market countries add a luxury tax to bicycles. As a foreigner taking the bicycle out of the country, you can avoid this tax, but most dealers are small and are unfamiliar with the forms they must fill out. Our suggestion is that if you wish to take advantage of this tax rebate, do so in London where language problems are nonexistent and where some dealers, especially larger ones, are familiar with the procedures. Kensington Bicycle Company is one such firm (see Appendix 6 under *London*). The Scandinavian Tourist Bureau (see Appendix 4) also has advice for purchasing Crescent bicycles in Sweden on a no-tax basis.

With careful shopping, you can still save some money if you buy your bicycle in Europe. Generalizations are difficult, but this will normally run in the area of 10 percent. If you decide to buy abroad, we recommend the following:

1. Allow yourself enough time to shop. Even if you find what you want in the first shop you enter, you should compare prices elsewhere just as a matter of principle.

2. Plan to buy your bicycle in a country where you have at least a good working knowledge of the language. This prevents misunderstandings about price, equipment, and delivery dates.

3. Buy your bicycle in one of the major cities of a well-known bicycle racing country (France, England, Belgium, Italy, Holland, and Spain), where you will find numerous shops selling ten-speed equipment. While it is

available in other countries, choice is limited. Even in the supposedly great bicycling countries such as Denmark, most bicycle shops cater to the wobbler set—those who toddle back and forth to the market on heavy black machines.

4. Take your broken-in saddle with you! (Make certain the dealer discounts the cost of the saddle already on the bicycle.)

5. Have the dealer write down the cost of the bicycle along with the equipment you want on it. Get a final price on paper before you agree to buy. This is sound advice no matter where you buy, but particularly so in a country where your knowledge of the language may be imperfect.

6. Remember that most European bicycle shops are small and selection will be limited. This may mean going to several shops to find what you want, or waiting a day or two for parts to be interchanged to give you the combination of gearing, frame size, and accessories that you want.

## TAKING YOUR BICYCLE ON THE PLANE

If you are taking your bicycle to Europe with you or bringing back one you bought there, you can take it on the plane with you as part of your luggage allocation. There is no charge for this.

Airline regulations vary as to what you must do in order to get your bicycle on for free. All major carriers will permit you to count it as one of the two items you may check in as on-board luggage. The difference comes in terms of whether you must put it in a carton or not.

Officially, most U.S. airlines require that you put the bicycle in a carton. Technically, the dimensions of the carton's width, length, and height should be 62 inches or under *when added together*. In practice, we have never seen this rule enforced, and most bicycles cannot be made to fit in a carton of this size anyway.

In addition to your cartoned bicycle, you are allowed one other item of checked luggage, whose added dimensions should not exceed 42 inches. We have never seen or heard of this rule being enforced either.

Practically, all you need to do is show up with your bicycle in a carton and have one additional piece of luggage. Get the bicycle carton from a local dealer. Take your panniers or handlebar packs with you as carry-on luggage (they should fit under your seat or in the overhead compartment on wide-bodied aircraft).

To get a bicycle in most bicycle cartons, you must turn the handlebars sideways, take off the pedals, remove the wheels and tape or secure them to the bicycle frame. Take care to pad anything that will rub, and add extra padding or wooden blocks to axles and other protrusions from the bicycle. Remember when taking off the pedals that the left-hand pedal has a reverse thread.

Putting a bicycle in a carton is, frankly, a bother. First of all the carton doesn't really protect the bicycle in a crunch. The only damage we've ever had done to bicycles was when they were in cartons (bent quick-release skewer, bent chainring on the crank). Moreover, unless you have someone with whom you can leave a carton, you have to spend some time just before coming back looking for a replacement.

Some transcontinental airlines will permit you to take the bicycle along without putting it in a carton. Others that require a carton may in practice ignore the rule, or enforce it here but not for the return trip. Check to make certain.

In either case, the airline usually wants you to break the bicycle down by turning the handlebars sideways and removing pedals and wheels as described above. Some want you to pad protruding parts such as axles.

If the airline insists that you put your bicycle in a carton, try suggesting that they permit you to wrap it in heavy-gauge plastic. With fiberglass strapping tape, this makes a good package and will give your bicycle better protection than a carton. It also is easier to store for reuse on the flight back.

If they will not accept this, then our advice is to go along with them. In addition to satisfying requirements and avoiding explanations at the check-in counter, you can use the carton for packing other unwieldy items such as tents or sleeping bags that may be difficult to fit into your other piece of allotted luggage. These other items will also give your bicycle some protection. But do check with your airline—particularly if it's a charter flight—for confirmation on all regulations.

EIGHT

# Your wardrobe, packs, roof, and bed

Some experienced tourists will go to any length to cut an ounce or two off their total weight—sawing toothbrushes in half, carrying tooth powder instead of toothpaste (lighter and lasts longer), using nylon rather than cotton underwear, carrying a comb instead of a brush. Your touring bicycle has enough carrying capacity that you don't need to turn equipment selection into a fetish, but you are not going on an African safari either. You need to exercise some common sense. In this chapter we give you some idea of the things you'll need to take along.

Avoid starting out with much more than is recommended. If you find later on that you need something else it is usually easier to buy it than it is to carry something uphill and down that you never use. Purchase the things you know you need to take touring with you. You will use them for a shakedown tour anyway and you may not be able to find what you want in Europe. American synthetic clothing is usually better than you'll find abroad. The same is generally true of camping equipment. Good panniers and saddlebags are difficult to find in most European countries. If your bicycle shop or your outdoor equipment shop doesn't carry the items you want, you can order them from one of the mail-order supply houses listed in Appendix 8. They will send you a catalog to help you choose things.

## YOUR CLOTHING

You will need two outfits—one to ride in and something to change into after you stop. If you select your clothing carefully there will be some items that will double—for example, a warm wool riding sweater that can also be worn with slacks or dress in the evening.

What qualities should you look for in selecting clothing for touring? First of all it must be light and should fold or roll into as small an area as possible. A good example of this is a nylon shell windbreaker with a roll-up collar hood. It weighs only a few ounces and when folded can almost be kept in your pocket. Yet when worn with a sweater it keeps you warm, whether you are riding or strolling around in the evening. It also does an adequate job of shedding rain.

You should also look for clothing that is easy to wash and that dries quickly. Synthetics are natural for this, particularly in items such as a short sleeve "dressy" shirt for men or a jersey dress for women. Unless the air is very humid, both will dry overnight.

Another quality you need in clothing, particularly that worn next to your skin, is that it breathe. Here you must make some deviation from synthetics because nothing parallels natural materials. Cotton is the best thing to wear in warm or hot weather. It allows air to circulate through the material and over your body to keep you cool. Wool is the best fabric for times when it is cool or damp. It will insulate even when wet.

Finally, you need outfits that you can live with from

day to day. You can add a splash of color or change of mood by adding an extra head scarf or a tie to your luggage, but put aside any worry about being seen in the same thing each day. If you are traveling with others they are in the same boat, and the people you see en route change from minute to minute. To them you are always wearing something new.

*Riding clothes.* Selecting riding clothes is in some ways the simplest of all—there just isn't that much to wear. Both men and women will most likely ride in shorts and cotton tops. When it is cool you add sweater and windbreaker and, if your legs are cool, your slacks. You will also need something to cover your head on warm days and to keep your hair from blowing. We also recommend riding gloves, which have leather palms, half fingers, and cotton tops. They give you a firm grip on the handlebars and absorb a good bit of the riding shock. You can get ones with padded palms that do an even better job of this. The gloves also protect your hands in case you should fall. The half fingers allow you to manipulate shifting levers and brakes easily.

*Footwear.* While riding you may use either a regular cycling shoe or some lightweight alternative, such as a running shoe with a flat sole. The advantages of a bicycling shoe are its light weight and narrow profile, both of which make pedaling easier, and a thin steel plate between the outer and inner sole which will keep the pedals from cutting into your feet. Its disadvantage is that it was not designed for walking, and a bicycle tourist does quite a bit of that while on the road—going into small stores for snacks, looking around a wayside church, or just strolling around a park after midday lunch. Bicycling shoes with cleats on them are even worse.

A reasonable compromise is a regular bicycle touring shoe, which keeps some of the construction qualities of a racing shoe but has a flexible sole for walking. A number of companies make them.

Our own favorite is a lightweight running shoe with a flat, relatively stiff sole. Don't buy the kind with square nubs on the soles if you mount toe clips on your pedals, however. Your feet can get jammed and won't pull out.

The advantage of running shoes is that they are lightweight and, if well built, will resist the tendency of the pedal edges to cut into them. They are quite acceptable all over Europe as casual shoes, too. Their primary disadvantage is their width, which gives us a feeling of always hanging out too far over the pedals, particularly once used to narrow-profile cycling shoes.

*Shorts.* Most cyclists prefer shorts to long pants or slacks, as they give more freedom to the leg. We ride in regular cycling shorts with a chamois crotch for increased grip on the saddle and less chafing. Some manufacturers are now making these shorts in colors other than the traditional dreary black. Some are also making them with a terry-cloth crotch for greater moisture absorption.

*Other riding clothing.* Beyond your shorts, gloves, and footwear, ride in whatever feels most comfortable. Hats keep the sun off and prevent your hair from drying out. Be certain to get one that will stay on in a 30-mile-per-hour wind, as that is what you'll reach going down hills. On exceptionally hot days we also wear bandanas soaked in water around our foreheads or necks. Sunglasses will reduce glare and keep bugs out of your eyes. They should fit snugly enough not to keep sliding down on your nose, particularly if your bicycle has dropped handlebars. We wear a breathable nylon shell windbreaker on cool days or for drizzle. Ones with roll-up hoods are exceptionally convenient, keeping you warm when cold, shedding rain, and keeping mosquitoes off your neck.

*Casual clothes.* For evening wear, a pair of slacks is

practical for both men and women. Lightweight cotton or polyester fabrics are good. Denims are heavy and not too versatile. Women can add an uncrushable lightweight dress. Men can carry a wash-and-wear short-sleeve dress shirt or sport shirt. Sandals are a good choice for after-riding footwear for both sexes. They are light to carry, compact, and, like running shoes mentioned above, are perfectly acceptable informal wear all over Europe. If you want to swim, carry a quick-drying suit. The bottoms will double as riding shorts if you wish.

Make all your clothing selections on the basis that you will not find laundromats at most of your stopping points. Except in large cities, they are rare throughout Europe. You will be doing most of your laundry by hand. Therefore quick-drying and/or drip-dry fabrics are best.

*Women's clothes.* Your riding shorts can be of any soft, flexible fabric that is relatively free of seams and allows unrestricted leg movements. Cotton knit shorts, culottes, or anything that is comfortable and easy to care for will do. Whatever you choose to ride in be sure to try it out ahead of time, as there are many sports clothes on the market that are better kept for poolside cocktail parties. Your slacks can be of lightweight cotton or polyester. Anything that is light and doesn't wrinkle easily is appropriate. Your dress should be of lightweight material that can be folded into a bundle and come out looking like something you would want to be seen in. The list of materials is endless—the only real criterion being that you like it, since it is the only one you'll have along. The wind and sun can be very hard on your hair so ease their impact by wearing a scarf or hat most of the time. Hand and face cream will help men and women's skin after a long day in the wind and sun. You can ride either with socks, light wool peds, or golf socks. Your legs will tan, so you will not have to wear hose unless you feel more comfortable in them. One pair of panty hose will do. You can find replacements anywhere in Europe.

## CLOTHING CHECKLIST

*For both men and women*

1 pair of riding shorts
2 pairs of riding socks
1 nylon windbreaker with roll-up hood
1 wool sweater
2 cotton T-shirts
1 pair of riding shoes
1 pair of riding gloves
1 hat or scarf
3 changes of cotton or cotton/polyester-blend underwear
1 pair of sandals or casual shoes
1 pair of cotton or polyester slacks
1 bathing suit
1 pair of sunglasses
*1 rain cape

*For men only*

1 pair of dress socks
*1 wash-and-wear short-sleeve dress or sport shirt
*1 tie

*For women only*

*1 wash-and-wear light dress
*1 pair of panty hose

* optional item

## TOILET AND FIRST-AID ITEMS

You need to exercise the same care in selecting other items of personal luggage as you do with clothing. Keep things as light and compact as possible. Many small loose items can be packed in nylon ditty bags. These can be stuffed into nooks and corners more easily than rigid containers. All liquids should be carried in containers that won't leak. It will also help to pack them so they ride in an upright position. If you can manage it, buy these items in square-shaped containers or buy square containers for them. These pack more compactly than round ones. Pliable plastic containers are less likely to spring leaks. Carrying anything in a glass container nearly guarantees that you'll have it all over everything sooner or later. Whenever possible substitute things in tubes for those in containers. They carry better, and the tubes can be rolled as the item is used, reducing carrying space. Here is a checklist of toiletries:

Waterproof toiletries bag
Hand soap in leakproof container
Toothbrush and paste in fold-up container
Deodorant
Metal mirror
Towel (small size, absorbent, quick drying)
Face cloth
Nylon cord or travel clothesline
Toilet paper
Safety pins (double as clothespins)
Suntan lotion
Sewing kit
Tweezers
Small scissors
Tube of good hand/face cream

*First aid.* You need to carry a minimal first-aid kit. If you don't want to bother making up your own, many companies have ones made up in compact containers. If you are traveling with a group, only one person need carry a kit. All kits should include these items:

Band-Aids
Gauze
Adhesive tape
Liquid antiseptic
Aspirin
*Vitamin C
*Elastic bandage (good for sore knees)

* optional item

## PANNIERS, SADDLEBAGS, AND HANDLEBAR PACKS

All of your clothing and personal effects will be carried somewhere on the bicycle. Some people tour wearing knapsacks, but doing so causes unneeded agony. The straps cut into your shoulders and reduce or entirely cut off blood circulation. The weight of the pack adds additional strain to your arms and back. It can also be dangerous. Since you ride with your back at an angle, when you turn around to check for traffic you are usually staring right into the top of your knapsack. For these reasons your bicycle should be equipped with luggage packs.

These fit on four different places. Packs that fit on either side of your front or back wheels are called panniers; packs that fit immediately below your bicycle seat are called saddlebags; and packs that fit on your handlebars are called, for want of a better term, handlebar or front packs.

*Panniers.* For most cyclists, panniers are the primary means of carrying gear, and their choice is important. You must first of all estimate how much clothing and equipment you will be carrying in them, as they come in a variety of sizes, ranging from ones that will carry little more than a thousand cubic inches to some that will carry well over twice that amount. Panniers normally fasten over the rear wheel, but smaller sets are made for the front wheel. These allow better distribution of weight if you're carrying a lot of equipment. Prices range from $25 or $30 to well over $100.

In general, resist running out and buying the largest set you can find. You will be amazed at how easily you fill them up with things you may not need. Our nephew arrived in England for a tour with the largest, most expensive panniers then on the market. He was carrying, in addition to all the things any cyclist might think of, a wool peaked hat, three pairs of shoes, and, hoping to appear as English as possible, a herringbone tweed sports jacket. Fortunately, he was able to ship most of this back home before he set out touring.

You might lay out the things you expect to be carrying in your panniers, put it all into a paper bag, and take it down to the bicycle store when you do your shopping. In addition to this general advice, keep these things in mind when shopping, and try to compare at least two brands before buying (a list of mail-order businesses selling panniers is given in Appendix 8):

1. The panniers should be made of sturdy waterproof nylon pack cloth. We recommend a cloth of at least six ounces, and eight-ounce cloth is better. The panniers should be double-stitched at all stress points, and zippers should fully open when the pannier is on the bicycle so you can take things from it.

2. The panniers should have a reasonable number of

auxiliary pockets in addition to the main compartment. One such additional pocket is minimal, two are better.

3. Panniers should detach easily from the carrier. This will allow you to remove them if you are staying in a hotel or hostel or shipping your bicycle on the train; as well, it will permit you to put them inside your tent if you're going to be away from camp for a good while.

4. The pannier should be designed so that it allows your foot to swing upward on the backstroke without your heel touching it.

A number of companies sell kits for sewing your own panniers. Many of these are quite good, but are difficult to sew unless you are adept at it. Frostline kits are one brand available in most cities.

*Saddlebags* attach beneath the bicycle saddle and usually have about a quarter or a third the carrying capacity of a set of panniers. Sizes range from ones in which you can carry only a transistor radio to others large enough for the needs of a lightweight tourist. If the saddle bag is well anchored and supported it rests in an ideal place for carrying weight and gives better balance than a set of panniers. Look for the same qualities in saddlebags as you would in panniers: outside pockets for additional storage, durable, waterproof nylon fabric, and strongly reinforced fasteners.

*Handlebar packs.* These are so useful that we regard them as necessary for the cycle tourist. Almost all of them are made so that the flap opens away from the rider, allowing him or her to reach in for an occasional snack or to get out a pair of sunglasses or lip balm. Most also have a map pocket on top, absolutely crucial for navigating on back roads. In addition, they are so convenient for carrying windbreakers, cameras, passports, and money that we couldn't imagine touring without them.

Most handlebar packs are made of waterproof nylon pack cloth, although a very good French one is still made of heavy canvas. We have used one of the latter for seven touring summers and it may still have one more trip left in it.

In shopping for a handlebar pack, make certain it has these features:

1. The flap should open away from you.
2. The bag should fasten to your handlebars or come with a rack so that the top part of your handlebars is accessible for resting your hands on. This is the most common riding position, and if you are denied it, you will quickly notice the difference. Some packs fasten just close enough to the handlebars that they leave them free, but also allow you to jam your fingers into the pack on cold days. This makes a big difference.
3. The bag should have a map pocket. Don't buy one without it. The pocket should have a plastic or acetate covering that is flexible and yet sturdy, since you will be taking the map out frequently to turn it or to study it more closely at a crossroads or after a day's ride. The map pocket should be at least 5½ inches wide by 11 inches long. When we first started touring, the road networks were so confusing that in addition to the map, we inserted a small piece of paper in the map pocket with the roads and turns we were to take that day written out. We've become skillful enough since to abandon the practice, but it's a good one for novices on back roads. This is impossible without a decent map pocket.
4. If your bicycle frame is short, make certain that the pack doesn't rub on your front wheel or cause your fender to rub on the front wheel. Most of the handlebar packs that come with support racks will lift the pack high

enough to avoid this problem. If not, you can buy a small rack to support the bottom of the pack.

5. It's useful to have at least one extra pocket on the rider's side of the front pack for carrying small items such as chap stick, a pocket knife for lunches, silverware, a length of nylon cord, etc.

*Rear carrying racks.* Most bicycle shops both here and in Europe carry an assortment of rear carrying racks. As they support a good bit of weight and are subject to considerable strain, the better constructed they are the better off you'll be. Persons with either large or small bicycle frames should make certain that the rack will actually fit their bicycle. If not, the rack may tilt either backward or forward and throw the panniers off balance. Some judicious bending of the stays that attach the carrier to the tubes below your seat is sometimes necessary.

## CAMPING EQUIPMENT

If you are going to be camping you will need something to sleep in (sleeping bag), on (foam pad or Ensolite), and under (tent or tarp). Everything should be as light and compact as possible. This will not be difficult if you shop wisely.

*Sleeping bags.* The most important thing about a sleeping bag is the material it is filled with. When you go to buy a bag you'll probably find them filled with either an artificial fiber or with natural goose or duck down. The filling forms hundreds of thousands of tiny air pockets which retard the loss of your body heat, thus keeping you warm. Pound for pound, down is the most efficient at doing this. It also packs tighter and in general will have a longer life than a bag with artificial fill. Its disadvantages are its cost and its limitations when wet; some artificial fibers do a better job of insulating under those circumstances. Down is also more difficult to wash.

How much of either filling—down or artificial fibers—you need to keep you warm in Europe during the summer, late spring, or early fall depends upon a number of other factors: how the shell of the sleeping bag is made, its shape, and its size. But assuming that the coldest night you will face will be about 40° Fahrenheit, a well-constructed down bag with 1¼ pounds of down filling will do the job well. Its total weight will be only a little above 2½ pounds. An equivalent fiber-filled bag, equally well constructed, will weigh from 3 to 5 pounds and will occupy proportionally more space when packed. While a down bag costs at least twice as much as the other kind, many people feel it is worth the investment because of the great weight and space savings.

Whichever kind you choose, keep these things in mind:

1. Nylon shells are lighter and easier to turn in.
2. Side zippers at least 70 inches long allow you to ventilate the bag easily. Double zippers are particularly useful.
3. The outer and inner shell of the bag should not be stitched together quilt-fashion. This constricts the loft or thickness of the bag to zero at these seams, and leaks cold air.
4. The bag should be tapered toward the feet. This saves on weight and is more efficient since your feet are your body's poorest heat-producers.
5. If you are traveling with someone, you can get bags that zip together. Some of these zip along the side zippers, others unzip completely before being joined. We now carry only one bag on most of our tours; we unzip it

completely and cover ourselves with it, sleeping on nylon-covered foam pads. The covers are easy to remove and can be washed. We have used this combination in the high Alps, the Pyrenees, and for camping in England into late October. We have been cold on only a few occasions, at which times we added extra clothing. This recommendation may not be for everyone, and our advice is to try it before you start. Its primary advantage is the weight and bulk you eliminate by carrying only one bag.

6. Make certain your stuff sack is waterproof. Seal the seams. If you leave the bag on your bicycle during a rain, cover the stuff sack with a piece of waterproof plastic.

The best bags, either of artificial fill or of down, are usually found at shops specializing in mountain sports. Costs will vary widely, but a rough guide is that artificial fill will cost from $40 to $85, down fill from $110 to $200.

*Sleeping pads and air mattresses.* Some people sleep right on the ground, but this is rather Spartan and in cold weather makes it difficult to keep warm. You have a choice of three beds, all of which are comfortable to sleep on once you are used to them.

1. Air mattress. If you use an air mattress, buy a hip-to-shoulder-length one of coated nylon. All others are too heavy. There are some disadvantages to an air mattress, however. Most obviously, they can go flat. But in addition, in cold weather they conduct heat away from the body—you can actually feel the cold creeping in from underneath. There have been some recent innovations in inflatable beds, one a combination air mattress that has closed-cell foam built into it. Not only does it not go flat, it is a good insulator. Their cost is rather high, however, running between $25 and $30.

2. Foam pads. These are a better choice of bed than an air mattress. They are light, less expensive, and roll up for easy carrying. They insulate better and don't go flat. We find them more comfortable. Most mountain shops sell foam pads with a nylon covering. The best ones have a waterproof bottom and a breathable nylon/cotton top. They roll up to about 6 inches diameter and have ties for keeping them rolled. Our present set has lasted us six years. We simply change foam every season.

3. Ensolite pads. Ensolite is a closed-cell material that will not absorb water. It is a superb insulator, rolls up into a small space, and is light. It takes most people some time to get used to them, as they are ⅝-inch or ½-inch thick, and just take the edge off the ground. They are extremely versatile and can be thrown down on the ground for noon-time lunches or put on a boat bench to make sitting easier.

*Tarps and tents.* If you are traveling in rainless country and are camping out only occasionally, you may want to sleep under the stars. Most people want some kind of covering, if only to keep the dew off and some of the bugs away. Remember to keep your nose tucked in, as mosquitoes are an international insect. How much of a covering is right for you depends on where you are touring and what kind of night comfort you demand. A tarp is light in weight and will keep light rain off you; most of them are not good for downpours; none is good for keeping out bugs. If you choose to carry only a tarp, get one with grommets for easy tying. Carry a length of nylon cord to string between two trees and use as a ridgepole. You will increase your tarp's versatility as a shelter if you carry collapsible aluminum poles, since trees don't always grow where you need them.

A better choice than a tarp might be a single-shell

nylon tent. These have their limitations, since they sweat on the inside where your breath and body heat condense. Unless they are well ventilated with mosquito netting, they normally will leave you or your bag moist wherever you happen to touch. Their great advantage when compared to a tarp is that they do not weigh much more, can be set up anywhere, give excellent protection from rain, wind, and bugs, and give some measure of privacy. Most European campgrounds are open areas, and your nearest neighbor is sometimes only a few feet away.

A recent innovation is something called a sleep sack or bivouac bag. This is a waterproof yet breathable sack that you slip your bag into. A fiberglass wand and a window of mosquito netting give you some space around your head. The sack weighs about 2 pounds, and rolls up to about 3 inches in diameter. Cost is rather high, usually over $80.

A better choice than all these for extensive camping is a nylon tent with a separate waterproof rainfly. These tents breathe and yet are watertight. Tent making is a more advanced science in the United States than anywhere else in the world, and top manufacturers have been able to build spacious two-person tents that weigh only 5 or 6 pounds. Some have interior stays of fiberglass or aluminum that allow the tent to be pitched anywhere without either ropes or stakes. Good ones will keep you dry in just about anything short of a flood.

You can buy a simple single-shell nylon tent for as little as $40. A good two-person tent with an extra rainfly will run anywhere from $150 to $225. For our last trip with our son, since we knew we would be on the road about six months, we opted for a high-quality six-person tent that weighed about 13½ pounds. It cost well above $300. There were a few times when the weight seemed excessive, but the extra comfort it provided over that long stretch of time, including space for a 2-year-old to romp, was worth every penny and every ounce.

When buying a tent, look for these things:

1. It should be all nylon.
2. If it is made of waterproof nylon and has no rainfly it should have net-covered openings that allow it to breathe.
3. The flooring should be made of completely waterproof material. If this reaches partially up the tent walls it makes for an even drier tent.
4. The end flaps should zip completely shut. Better-quality tents have zippered mosquito netting immediately inside the outer flap.
5. The tent should be wide enough to accommodate you and your sleeping bag and long enough to give extra room for gear. Although the tent may taper in height toward the rear, the front should be roomy enough to sit, eat, and cook in during rainy weather.
6. Poles and stakes should be made of aluminum, and the poles should collapse for easy carrying.

NINE

# Eating and touring

## WHERE TO EAT

Where you will be eating depends on your touring style and your finances. For anyone eating in European restaurants, troubles will be few. Most of them avoid the mass-produced atmosphere and taste in food that is so common with American restaurants. You will find a wide variety of prices, but food is generally cheaper than at home. Most restaurants place a menu on an outside wall or window that lists prices. This saves you from being surprised when the bill comes.

But almost all cycle tourists will find themselves spending some time shopping for their own food. Some will do it out of economy, but even lightweight tourists may prefer to buy their own food for breakfast and lunch. European breakfasts are often skimpy—coffee and bread in most countries—and most people find that eating a heavy restaurant meal at midday makes cycling more difficult in the afternoon. Whatever the case, you will often find yourself shopping for your own groceries and in need of some special guidance if you haven't done it before when abroad. Be ready for a fascinating experience.

Supermarkets aren't rare in Europe, but shopping may involve going from one small specialty shop to another. Each country has its own customs, style, and techniques, so don't take your old shopping habits into the store with you. Italian and French storekeepers are there to wait on you, and if you start rooting through the fruit display you may receive disapproving looks or be told quite directly to leave things alone. In Scandinavian and German stores you could stand for hours before someone would run around and fetch all your items. If you aren't sure about what to do when you go in, just stop for a minute to watch the regulars and then follow suit.

When you arrive in the country find out the general trend of store hours. These differ from country to country and within countries. Many stores in southern Europe are closed from noon until two o'clock. Some are even closed from noon until three or four, then reopen until eight or nine at night. Usually, the farther south you go, the longer the afternoon closing time and the later the stores are open in the evening. There are also weekdays in some countries or sections of countries when stores are closed all afternoon and in some cases closed all day. A good guide or phrase book will give you the specific details about the countries you are visiting. You'll usually need the phrase book anyway for the names of different foods.

It is much easier to stop and buy food close to the time you plan to eat so you don't have the weight and bother of carrying it around with you. This means that you will shop for lunch before noon, and shop after you have arrived at your destination in the evening, or just before you get there. Many small stores do not package your groceries. You can save yourself the trouble of carrying loose items by investing in a shopping bag. Plastic, string, or anything that is light, strong, and easily packed when not in use will do.

Once you have an idea about the style you can start remembering what you are shopping for. If you don't know the language try at least to know the numbers so you can ask for pieces, slices, and weights. Throughout Europe the measurement system is the same—grams and kilos (see conversion chart in Appendix 10). If you don't know the number system take a pencil and paper with you and write the numbers for the clerk. This way you can almost be assured of getting what you want. Knowing the numbers will also make keeping track of your money easier. Unless you are going to be in a country only a day or so, it is more convenient to figure up in the local currency how much you are budgeted for each day or each meal, and keep track of your spending this way. Trying to convert everything into dollars and then back again can leave you hopelessly confused.

You may feel somewhat insecure at first about making financial transactions if you aren't fluent in the language; or perhaps you have heard rumors about Europeans charging higher prices and not giving correct change if they know you are a tourist. This is very rarely so with the small shopkeepers you will deal with on a daily basis when touring. Nearly all of them are humane, honest, friendly, and considerate, particularly when treated that way in return.

O.K. You're in the store, money ready, but what to buy? It all looks so good. We found that the answer to this question was one of our most important considerations. Cycle touring places a lot of energy demands on your body, and therefore food—the right kind in the proper amounts—is strategic. If you are eating properly you will have a consistent, reliable supply of energy available to you, and this makes cycling easier and more enjoyable than if you have to haul around a tired, sluggish body. There are no set food formulae available that take into consideration all the radical fluctuations that exist between individuals. You have to develop your own formula by paying close attention to how you function and then manipulating the essential food groups to suit your needs. In our case one of us had to double his food intake, while the other's diet remained pretty much the same. This is usually a process of trial and error.

When cycling at a moderate rate over relatively even terrain your body is burning approximately 5 calories a minute or 300 calories an hour. Energetic cycling, high cadence, going against the wind or uphill can double these figures. This means that a large pear (100 calories) is good for twenty minutes of moderate riding and only ten minutes of energetic cycling. So you can see how many calories it is going to take to keep you going mile after mile. But counting calories is not, in and of itself, the answer. They have to be the right kind of calories—thus the need for a balanced diet.

A balanced diet is one that supplies your body with all the vitamins and minerals, proteins, carbohydrates, and fats it needs to supply you with energy and to rebuild itself. You don't have to pack health books and diet scales to insure eating a balanced diet. Most of us eat well-balanced meals at home and will continue that tendency on the road. There may be some problem with cyclists on a limited budget skimping on items such as cheese, meats, or fruits, as these are relatively more expensive than pastas and breads. But even here nutritionists are revising their thinking about how much of these high-cost protein foods are really necessary. Our advice is to use common sense, pay some attention to getting fresh fruits and vegetables, and avoid a tendency to stave off hunger *only* with sweets or high-carbohydrate foods such as cookies or breads. If in any doubt, keep some vitamin pills in your panniers and take them during your trip.

Your eating schedule will affect how well you cycle during the day. Your two most crucial times for eating well are at breakfast and dinner. Breakfast gets you going, and dinnertime allows your body to relax and rebuild. During the day you should try to avoid eating large meals. If you are so hungry that one medium-size midday meal won't satisfy you, then eat two medium-size meals, one in the morning and the other in the early afternoon. It is helpful for everyone to have snacks along to eat during the break time—peanuts, dried or fresh fruits, or candy. There is absolutely no food value in coffee, but it sometimes helps to give you a lift if you find yourself getting too cold or tired during the day.

To help you eat well and inexpensively we have provided you with some basic meal plans and recipes. These vary in the amount of equipment needed and time required, but you may find them helpful when you want a break from hostel or restaurant food.

## BREAKFAST

The first meal of the day is going to be a major determining factor in how your riding will go. A lopsided breakfast —all protein or all carbohydrates—will present you with problems. The first won't get you going, and the latter won't keep you going for long. You can choose a balanced meal that includes cheese, cottage cheese, or yogurt; fresh fruit; local pastry; tea, coffee, or juice. Using these groups as a basic pattern you can have a different breakfast every morning by varying the individual choices of fruit and pastry. Shop, eat, and then rest awhile to give the food a chance to start digesting. Study your maps and plot your course for the day, wander around and watch the town wake up.

Anyone who has a small cook kit, access to a stove, and some time in the morning can prepare any of the old cooked breakfast standbys: eggs, French toast, cooked cereal, and the like.

## LUNCH

The fellowship of cycle tourists is split on the subject of midday meals. One group emphatically refuses to eat anything but light snacking food between breakfast and dinner, and the other group eats lunch. Your view on the subject will be formed by your dietary needs, disposition, and style of touring. If long distances and constant riding are the most important considerations you will probably opt not to eat very much while riding, since you must give yourself time to eat and to digest the food. If, on the other hand, you are touring without strict daily deadlines you may want to take the time to enjoy a light lunch. If you are in this latter group, as we are, here are some suggestions for lunchtime.

There are two basic guidelines—eating a balanced lunch that (1) doesn't require a lot of preparation or cleanup and (2) doesn't leave you feeling heavy at the end of the meal. The first guideline cuts out cooking food for lunch. If you want something warm, such as soup, it is much easier to buy it than it is to cook and clean up. But this lack of hot food for lunch doesn't mean meager eating —the list of possibilities is endless. Good country bread is a start, and you will find a wide variety of it in Europe. But in addition each country abounds with delicatessen specialties: cooked meats, cold sausages, and an endless variety of cheeses, pickles, and spreads. Your real problem will be what to try next. Whatever you decide, try to include something salty, especially if it is warm, as it will help maintain salt/water balance.

The second guideline means that you don't overdo it. The more you eat the longer you have to sit and wait before you can start to move again. Try to eat before you feel any deep hunger pangs and then stop short of leaving yourself with a stuffed feeling.

In addition to these guidelines, here are some specific suggestions that should be of some use to you when shopping and planning your meal.

1. Keep your utensils (knives, forks, spoons) handy so you don't waste time looking for them.

2. Bread is usually sold in kilo measures. Half a kilo is the size of a normal U.S. loaf. If you buy fresh bread you will probably have to slice it yourself. A good sharp knife such as the Swiss Army "Spartan" knife suggested below under Cooking Equipment will help you with this chore.

3. Mustard, mayonnaise, and other spreads are frequently sold in tubes. They are easy to carry and will last for several days if kept out of direct sunlight.

4. Juice is recommended over alcohol because it doesn't make you sleepy and over soft drinks because it supplies natural sugar and vitamins.

5. Butter can be bought in small quantities in many countries. If you don't see a small package ask the clerk and he may cut you a piece.

6. Ready-made puddings, custards, and yogurt are found all over Europe and are usually made with fresh and

genuine ingredients. All these items give additional protein and are usually not expensive.

7. When you stop for lunch buy your snacking food for the afternoon so you won't have to stop again until the evening.

## DINNER

Your evening meal should be a leisurely affair. Eat a satisfying dinner with emphasis on the high-protein foods so your body will have material to rebuild itself while you rest. If your intake of protein hasn't been very high during the day, now is the time to make up for it.

The following meal plans are divided according to how much preparation they require. The first ones require no cooking and a minimal amount of equipment. They can be used by everyone. Next are the recipes that require a minimal amount of cooking and can be used by those who have access to a stove and a small mess kit. Finally, there is a discussion of the more elaborate meals the camper tourist can prepare on a one-burner stove. At the end of the chapter is a list of the equipment you will need for each kind of eating.

You can add considerable zest to all your food if you carry just a few extra items such as bouillon cubes, packaged sauce and soup mixes, small containers with garlic powder, seasoned salt, and so on. Once they are out of their original containers and into plastic bottles or sturdy plastic bags, they weigh very little and require almost no space.

### NO-COOKING DINNERS

These can be eaten cold and take advantage of the many excellent prepared foods you find in specialty stores found throughout most of Europe. Here are two of our own favorites.

*Chicken Dinner*

Roasted chicken (sold all over Europe, usually naturally fed chickens, and good even when cold)
Yogurt and cucumber salad
Bread and butter
Milk or local wine (Even if you never drink wine at home you might give it a try in Europe. It is usually excellent and inexpensive.)
Prepared custard pudding

*Ham Dinner*

Ham slices
Potato, beet, bean, or macaroni salad (You will find a great variety of these from country to country, and they often are the most distinctive national dishes.)
Lettuce salad
Milk or local wine
Fresh fruit yogurt

Salads are refreshing supplements to any dinner, and most take little preparation and few ingredients. If you want to turn one into a whole meal, add meat, cheese, and hard-boiled eggs.

### MINIMAL-COOKING DINNERS

These can be handled by anyone having access to a stove and a simple cookset. Here are two suggestions. You can improvise many others on your own.

*Soup and Omelet*

Packaged soup mix (These are usually excellent. Maggi and Knorr are found throughout Europe and are the best.)
Omelet
Bread
Coffee or tea
Wine or milk
Prepared pudding or yogurt

*Green Beans and Sausage in One Dish*

Green beans and sausage (Fresh beans are available throughout most of the summer. Sausages are almost always distinctive of the region they're purchased in.) For link sausage, poke it with a fork and parboil it before adding to cooked beans.
Dark bread
Tomato salad
Milk, wine, or beer
Custard

## CAMP-COOKED MEALS

You can munch beef jerky or eat a can of stew at the end of the day if you wish, but with only a little more effort you can cook creative meals that will let you explore the world of local foods and will leave you truly satisfied. All you need is an adequate cookset, a simple one-burner stove (wood fires are universally prohibited), a little imagination, and some time. The key to successful cooking on a one-burner stove is planning.

Don't set out to cook more than two courses. If you are going to have meat and a cooked vegetable eliminate potatoes and get your starch in the form of bread. If you want potatoes or rice with your meat then eat your vegetables raw in the form of salad or supplement your meal with a side dish from the delicatessen. Before you start cooking think about the order in which things should be cooked. Start with the item that will require the longest time. Potatoes, rice, carrots, etc. will stay warm and will continue to cook if you remove them from the heat a few minutes before they are finished. Keep them in a container with a tight-fitting lid and wrap them in a towel to retain the heat. Then set about cooking the meat. If you cut meat into smaller pieces it will require less cooking time. For more tender meat cut it against the grain or marinate it in a little wine while you wait for the potatoes to cook. The marinade can then be used in a sauce. If you are cooking chops, meatballs, or other items that won't all cook at the same time you can keep the cooked ones warm by placing them on top of the ones being cooked. With a little practice and forethought you can turn out delicious meals that are all warm and ready at the same time. If you are traveling with someone else, share the cooking tasks, and if you share a bottle of wine it won't seem like a chore at all.

## COOKING EQUIPMENT: WHO NEEDS WHAT?

### EVERYONE

1 set of interlocking stainless-steel silverware. Get one that comes in a vinyl case. 3 oz. About $1.50.

1 sharp pocket knife. The Swiss Army "Spartan" is the one we like best. It is small yet provides all the equipment you need: can opener, two knives, bottle opener, and corkscrew. 2 oz. About $13.

1 combination salt and pepper shaker with lids. 1 oz. About $1.25.

FOR NO-COOK OR QUICK-COOK MEALS

1 Boy Scout–type mess kit. This has a small skillet, a small pan with lid, cup, and plate. 1 lb. About $3.
1 sierra cup. This is a stainless-steel cup that is unmatched for drinking hot liquids. It can double as a small pan to heat coffee water or make bouillon soup. 3 oz. About $2.50.

FOR THE CAMPER TOURIST

1 one-burner stove. Bleuet is the best for Europe. 1½ lbs. About $16.
1 two-person nestling cookset (see below). About 1½ lbs.
1 Teflon frypan with folding handle. About $7.
1 collapsible water container. We use a flat polyethylene bag with removable spout at the bottom. Two-gallon capacity, rolls up into a scroll about 12 in. by 1 in. 8 oz. About $4.
1 ½-pint oil container. A small plastic whisky flask works well. It has a double lid that prevents leaking. 4 oz. About $2.50.
1 waterproof nylon food bag. The 14 in. by 18 in. size is good. 1 oz. About $2.

FOR DIRTY DISHES

1 Scotch Brite pad or other scouring pad.
1 dish towel. Buy one of quick-drying, absorbent material, such as thin cotton.
1 small plastic or nylon bag with powdered soap. A kind that dissolves in cold water is good. It will also double as laundry soap.
1 small nylon ditty bag to keep everything together.

## SPECIAL NOTE ON COOKSETS AND STOVES FOR THE CAMPER TOURIST

*Stoves.* To cook in European campgrounds you will need to carry a small one-burner stove. There are two general types suitable for the cyclist—those using some form of liquid fuel, usually white gas or kerosene, and those using a propane gas cartridge. Liquid fuel stoves are more compact, but white gas is not available in most of Europe and kerosene seems nearly as hard to find. You have to carry extra fuel in a metal container, and this has a tendency to leak. For these reasons a butane stove is a better choice. The one sold throughout Europe is the French-made Bleuet. This uses a "Camping Gaz" cartridge that is available everywhere. Cartridges there cost from 70¢ to $1.50 and last about 3½ hours, which for most people means two or three days. Buy a spare before the one in the stove runs out. Cartridge stoves weigh about 1½ pounds complete and fold into an area 3½ by 8½ inches. The optional heat reflector is worth the few extra cents and few ounces in weight.

*Cooksets.* We do all our cooking on a two-person cookset and carry extra plates and cups if traveling with one or two others. For a larger party you need a larger-capacity cookset. After experimenting with a number of kinds, we made up our own. If you do not now own one, you might try something in the nature of what we use. It is a heavy-gauge aluminum "Rover" set (available from Recreational Equipment, Inc.; see Appendix 8 for address), to which we added one extra plate and two sierra cups. It nestles to a 3¾ by 8½ inch size, weighs about 1¼ pounds, and contains these items:

1 1½-quart pot with tight-fitting lid
1 1-quart saucepan, 8 in. by 3 in. deep
1 ½-quart saucepan/plate combination, 7¾ in. by 1½ in. deep
1 8-in. aluminum plate
2 sierra cups
1 pot lifter (indispensable)
1 Teflon frypan with folding handle

TEN

# Fourteen European tours

By now you are prepared as well as can be for a bicycling tour in Europe; all that's left is to go. As a final sendoff to you, we have developed fourteen tours that cover some of the best cycling country Europe has to offer. They vary in distance, terrain, and climatic region. Some are best for high-season touring; some are better left until after the other tourists have gone home or taken before the hottest part of summer arrives.

You can also put these tours together in your own combination, or do our own "Grand Tour," combining a number of those offered prior to it—with some connecting stretches outlined—which will take you all the way from London to Athens. It is a tour for the cyclist who has several months to while away; to whom the thought of a continent sprawling before him or her is a challenge; or perhaps who, like ourselves, is lured by the promise of a different horizon each day, new people and new experiences around the next bend.

Whichever of the tours you may decide upon, long or short, easy or hard, or whether you choose to create one of your own, we hope that your riding days will reward you as richly and deeply as our own have rewarded us.

*Bon voyage.*

## HOW TO USE THE TOUR INFORMATION

We have not planned the tours to cover any certain distance per day. Only you can determine how far you want to go each day. Moreover, there is some advantage in leaving a little flexibility in your schedule. But to help you plan your daily itinerary we have indicated this information for each tour:

1. An estimate of the tour's difficulty. Here we have employed three terms: *easy cycling*, *moderate cycling*, and *hard cycling*. Easy cycling means mostly level or slightly rolling country. Moderate cycling means rolling country, where you may expect to climb and descend hills, but over well-graded roads that allow you to negotiate the hill while still seated on the bicycle and over terrain that should not leave anyone in average bicycling condition excessively tired. Hard cycling means either steeply pitched hills or mountainous areas. If you are not in good condition for cycling, you may do some walking over these stretches.

2. The mileage (and kilometers for the Continent) between major points along the tour. In most instances this is calculated on the basis of the most direct route between points. It will vary (usually it will be longer) if you choose the quieter side roads.

3. Total mileage for the entire tour and an estimate of how many days this will take you. Remember these figures are just guidelines.

4. The locations of principal campgrounds and youth

hostels found en route. These are given in the order you will find them if you follow the tour sequence. Hotels are so numerous throughout the tour regions that we have made no effort to catalog them. Almost all towns en route will have at least one, and most will have several, varying in type of accommodation and price.

Youth hostel users are urged to make advance reservations, in large city hostels, as they tend to be crowded in summer. A form is provided in the *Youth Hostel Handbook*, which you receive when you join the Youth Hostel Association. If you are camping, no reservations are necessary anywhere. Hotel reservations are advisable for the cities of Amsterdam for the Dutch tour, London for the English tour, Copenhagen for the Danish tour, and Athens for the Greek tour.

Your ride will be made more enjoyable if you use the detailed maps we have suggested for each tour. These show the network of tiny country roads that almost never appear on standard road maps and consequently never see much automobile traffic. If you make your way via these you will find your own Europe—the Europe of quiet places still largely unknown to the outside world.

## TOUR #1: A TASTE OF TWO WINES—THE BURGUNDY AND ALSACE REGIONS OF FRANCE

Distance: 250–265 miles
Time: 5–7 riding days
Degree of Difficulty: The entire section from Mâcon to Cernay is easy riding. From Cernay to Strasbourg the route is easy to moderate.
Maps: Michelin maps nos. 66, 70, and 87 (1:200,000)

Wine sets the mood for this tour, and in the space of a few hundred miles you pass through two of the most famous wine regions in the entire world, Burgundy and Alsace. Begin your tour at Mâcon, located on the winding and incredibly green Saône river. Follow the gentle river valley upstream, and you will begin passing through towns whose names recall the wine list of an elegant restaurant—Beaune, Gevrey-Chambertin, Meursault, Pommard, Morey-Saint-Denis, and Nuits-Saint-Georges. These wine towns are located amidst the rolling foothills on the western side of the Saône valley, and the valley itself is dotted with picturesque towns and gently rolling wheat and hop fields. As you leave Dijon, the countryside begins a gradual transformation, and by the time you reach Cernay and Colmar, you find yourself in one of France's most unusual regions—Alsace—where German is spoken as often as French and where the light Alsatian wines are cultivated. Stands along the roadside offer free samples, as do the wine cellars found in even the smallest villages. (Take care: young wines in the heat of the day can play havoc with your cycling.) Half-timbered houses, ancient belfries, archways, cobbled streets, flowers sprouting from the window boxes of every house, and an occasional stork's nest atop a chimney are all common sights. You end your tour at Strasbourg, a town where the influences of France and Germany are pleasantly mixed.

From here you may head back to Paris by either cycle or train, or turn eastward and connect with the tour of the Black Forest in Germany at Baden-Baden. If you do the tour in the reverse direction and end at Mâcon, you may head northwestward from there to intersect the Châteaux of the Loire tour at Cosne.

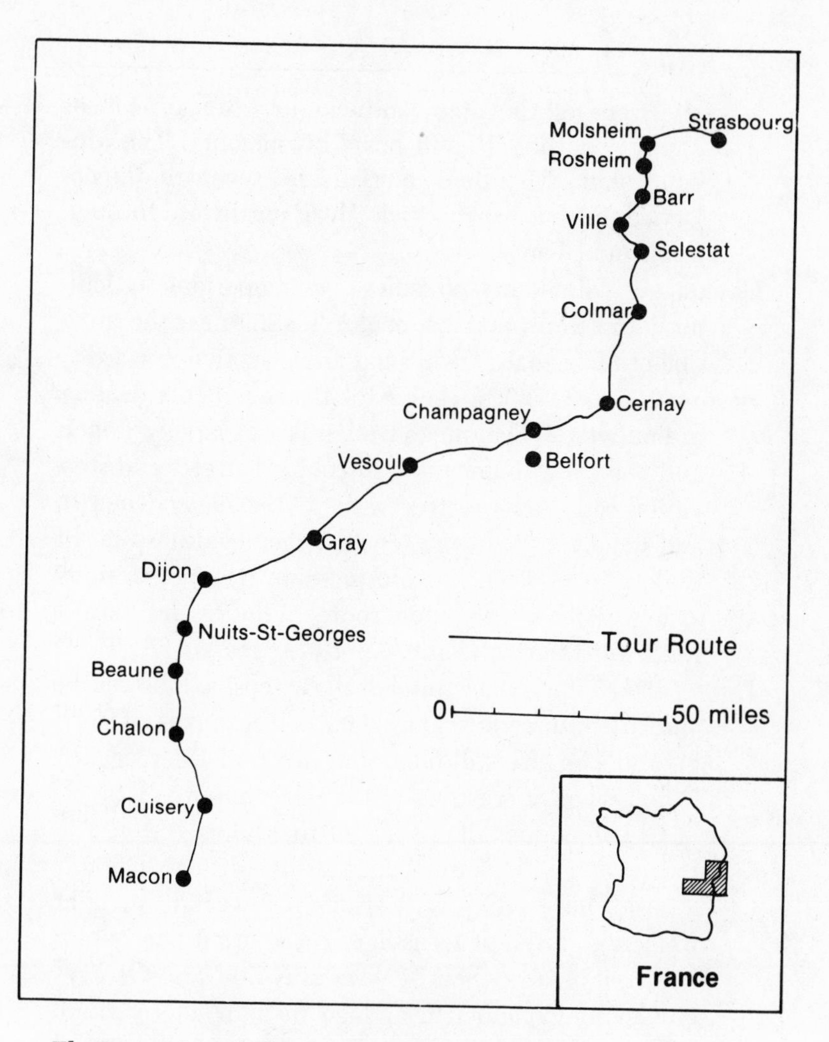


*The Burgundy and Alsace Regions of France*

ITINERARY

Mâcon. Home of the nineteenth-century Romantic poet Lamartine, the city still bears his memory. The Museum of the Ursulines, housed in a seventeenth-century convent, is worth a visit. Head northward through Lugny and Tournus to

Chalon (57 kilometers/35 miles), an important agricultural and transportation center, resting near the junction of two canals. Head away from the river toward

Beaune (33 k/21 m), a center for the merchants dealing in fine wines. The ancient town is still largely intact, and you can wander through cobbled streets and stop periodically to taste free wine at the many wineries and wine cellars in the town. A medieval hospital in the center of town, the Hospices de Beaune, is interesting. Follow the wine route ("*Route des vins*") northward through Nuits-Saint-Georges to

Dijon (38 k/23 m), the capital of the extensive fourteenth- and fifteenth-century kingdom of the dukes of Burgundy. The city still maintains much of the elegance it had when it was one of the most important towns in Christendom. The palace of the dukes, restored in the seventeenth century, may still be visited. Dijon is a large, busy city, and persons not wishing to fight traffic and attempt to navigate in and out may either bypass it or store their bicycles at Nuits-Saint-Georges or Gevrey-Chambertin and go in and out by train. Whichever the case, after Dijon turn northeastward and head toward

Gray (48 k/30 m). The old part of the town is perched on a hill overlooking the Saône River. From Gray you continue along the Saône, then dip slightly southward to Vesoul (65 k/40 m), then continue northeastward toward

Cernay (50 k/30 m). This is the starting point for the wine tour through Alsace. Leave Cernay north to

Colmar (50 k/30 m), the first major town in the Alsace region and a miniature of all there is to the Alsatian character—a unique mixture of German and French influences. Old homes with elaborate façades face each other across narrow streets. From Colmar, the best route to follow is the marked wine route (*"Route des vins"*) through the picturesque town of

Kaysersberg (10 k/6 m), birthplace of Albert Schweitzer. Continue north through Riquewihr, Sélestat, and the small wine towns of Rosheim and Molsheim, both lovely examples of flower-laden Alsatian towns. From Molsheim turn eastward and go to

Strasbourg (54 k/33 m). The end of the tour. If you arrive on Saturday, leave your bicycle in the railway station and walk through the center of the old town. The entire area is closed off and becomes one huge outdoor market. You can walk literally for miles through stalls selling everything from flowers to monkeys. The soaring rose-colored cathedral with its striking portals and clock, which puts on a show at noon each day, is a major attraction of this pleasant city.

## ACCOMMODATIONS

*Locations of Youth Hostels*

Chalon
Dijon
Vésoul
Belfort
Colmar
Sélestat
Strasbourg

*Locations of Principal Campgrounds*

| | |
|---|---|
| Mâcon | Champagney |
| Chalon | Cernay |
| Beaune | Colmar |
| Dijon | Sélestat |
| Gray | Molsheim |
| Port-Sur-Saône | Strasbourg |

## TOUR #2: SOUTHERN ENGLAND—A QUIET VISIT TO BRITAIN'S PAST

Distance: 503 miles
Time: 10–17 riding days
Degree of Difficulty: Easy to moderate
Maps: Bartholomew National Map Series (listed in order of use): 10, 6, 5, 8, 7, 14, 19, 20, 15 (1:100,000) or Bartholomew GT Map Series 5, 2, 4 (1:253:440)

This tour of England stretches out in a wide arc from London and takes you through the most concentrated historical area of England. It puts you in direct contact with some of the most famous castles, cathedrals, cultural centers, and colleges in the Western world. Because you are touring on your own you have the opportunity to visit these sites leisurely, unruffled by the pace of those who march in and out in throngs from their tour buses. You also have the added advantage of getting to experience the small villages and the people of the present.

The tour starts from London and heads southeast to Canterbury. As the roads in this area tend to be heavily traveled by Continent-bound traffic you may opt to take the short train ride to Canterbury. From here we head south through Battle, the site of the Battle of Hastings in 1066, and move slowly down the coast to Arundel. Next on the agenda are Winchester, with its impressive cathedral, Stonehenge, and Salisbury. From Salisbury you continue northwest to Bath and then head due northeast for Oxford, famous for its centuries-old university. Out of Oxford you move into "Shakespeare country" and visit Stratford-on-Avon. The tour then heads east to Cambridge,

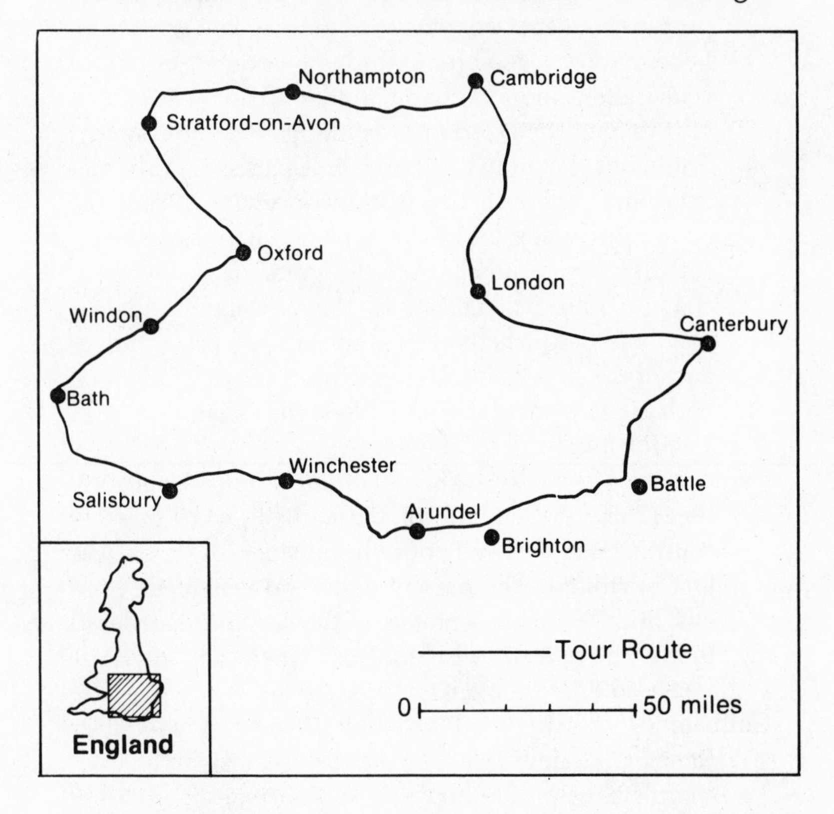


*Southern England*

England's other famous university town, and from there returns to London.

ITINERARY

London. Start of tour. There are so many sites and points of interest in London that we aren't even going to attempt to single out the most important. We will, however, offer some suggestions for things that are fun and can be had for free. If you like markets and want to experience the Cockneys and other market people there are two very good markets to visit. Portobello market is good for Saturday mornings, and Petticoat Lane is most lively on Sunday. Also on Sunday a visit to Speaker's Corner in Hyde Park is entertaining. The main downtown squares and parks are different from any others in the world, especially during the noon hour when all the clerks and shoppers congregate for picnic lunches on the grass. If you want a change from typical English food, wander into the Soho district, where restaurants of all price ranges and of all nationalities crowd next to each other on both sides of the street. Follow the Thames out of London and head southeast to

Canterbury (52 miles). This city dates from prehistoric times. The present site of the cathedral has been in constant use as a religious shrine since the area was first inhabited. The present cathedral was made famous in 1170 when Thomas à Becket was murdered there. You can still visit the spot where he was slain. Leave southwest and pass through

Chilham (4 m). Reputed to be the "prettiest village in Kent," Chilham has been restored recently and comes complete with a hilltop castle. Continue south from Chilham to the moated castle at Bodiam, built in 1386, and then on to

Battle (40 m), the site of the Battle of Hastings in 1066. From here continue along down the coast through Lewes, an ancient hilltop town with an imposing castle, then west along the coast to

Arundel (45 m), the site of the great castle of the dukes of York. From here start a slight climb northward and proceed to

Winchester (50 m), the ancient capital of Alfred the Great and the site of a beautiful cathedral, whose structure dates from 1079 and contains the great mortuary chest of the Saxon kings. The evening Sound and Light show held during the summer is well worth attending. Also of interest in Winchester are the oldest public school in England, dating from 1382, and The Great Hall, which purportedly has the remains of King Arthur's round table. Leave Winchester and head due west onto the Salisbury plain to

Stonehenge (30 m). This perplexing stone circle is reputed to have been built by Bronze Age sun worshipers. It is an astronomically perfect structure. Leave for the town of

Salisbury (10 m). This is a geometrically planned city that grew as the residents from Old Sarum moved away from the military fort. Today it has a beautiful cathedral that dates from 1220. You can visit the remains of the old town. Leave for

Bath (39 m). Bath is famous for its spa. The first community was established there in 863 B.C., and in A.D. 54 the Romans developed an extensive town there. You can still visit the Roman spa. Another point of interest is the abbey, which was built in 1499. Leaving Bath you have the alternative of going on into Wales (see the following World of Wales tour) or of continuing with the English tour via the river Avon out of Bath through the woods to

Oxford (60 m). Oxford is an industrial city but is also the location of a world-famous university, which is in fact a collection of thirteen separate colleges. These colleges are gathered together behind medieval walls, and there are many written and guided tours of them available. From Oxford head northwest through Tudor villages of the Shakespearean countryside into

Stratford-on-Avon (40 m), the literary shrine of the Western world. Shakespeare died here in 1616, and anything and everything having to do with his life and times has been preserved. Throughout the summer his plays are performed daily Monday through Saturday at the Memorial Theatre. The price of admission is not high, but you should try to secure reservations in advance. Leaving Stratford you ride to Cambridge, the gateway to East Anglia, which in the ninth century was a Saxon kingdom and for you is a gateway to

Cambridge (80 m), a very pleasant town that is famous for its university. The colleges seemed to grow with the town instead of being confined by it, and the total effect is more pleasing than Oxford. Proceed south to

London (53 m). The end of the tour.

## ACCOMMODATIONS

*Locations of Youth Hostels*

Canterbury
Hastings
Black Boys
Alfriston
Brighton
Arundel
Winchester
Salisbury
Bath
Inglesham
Oxford
Charlbury
Stratford-on-Avon
Greens Norton

Cambridge
Saffron Walden
Harlow
Epping Forest
London

*Locations of Principal Campgrounds*

London
Herne Bay (Kent County)
West Hythe (Kent County)
Hastings (Sussex County)
Brighton (Sussex County)
Bath (Somerset County)
Stratford-on-Avon (Warwick County)
Pavenham (Bedford County)

## TOUR #3: THE WORLD OF WALES

Distance: 300–320 miles
Time: 6–10 riding days
Degree of Difficulty: Moderate to hard
Maps: Bartholomew National Map Series (listed in order of use): 7, 13, 17, 22, 23, 18, 19 (1:100,000) or Bartholomew GT Map Series 4, 3 (1:253,440)

The countryside of Wales is full of prehistoric sites, Roman remains, castles looming from hilltops, and churches neatly tucked away in small wooded valleys. The cycle tourist is offered an endless stream of scenery that is a blend of lonesome gray hills and gentle valleys and woods. Legally a part of England, there is still something quietly different about Wales. Cross over the well-established point of demarcation—the Black Mountains—and see for yourself.

The tour begins in England at Bath. Go there directly by train from London or reach it by following the appropriate section of the English tour just described. You then make your way across central Wales to the coast, then turn eastward and follow the moors and the valley of the Dee to Froncysylltau, then southward back into England to the tour's end at Stratford-on-Avon. You may make connections here with the tour of England if you wish.

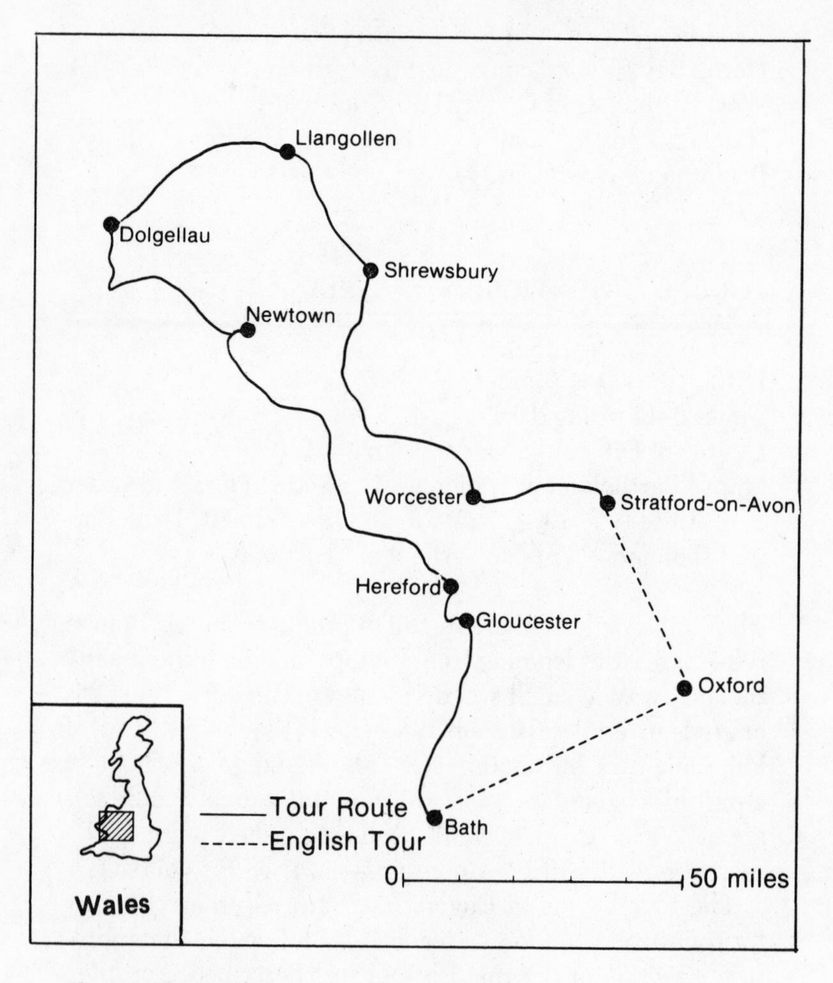


*The World of Wales*

ITINERARY

Bath. Beginning of the tour. (See description in previous tour.) Leave northward through the national waterfowl trust area and pass through Slimbridge to

Gloucester (45 miles). Founded by the Romans in A.D. 96, Gloucester is a town of narrow streets and timbered houses. Its cathedral dates from the eleventh century. Leave westward to

Hereford (35 m), on the Wye river. The Wye valley is full of beautiful old timbered houses and Tudor buildings. The city of Hereford has an excellent old market and a cathedral in a variety of architectural styles. Continue northwestward through the craggy moors to

Newtown (55 m), a town with a rich history of Welsh political struggles. The town is set in a commanding position between England and Wales and once had a large fortress. Now it is a market town. There is a good museum in the town center. Continue westward to

Machynlleth (30 m). The history of this town is continuous from the times of the Iron Age. Its military position is strategic, as it guards one of the main corridors into the Midland country of England. Now it is an agricultural and livestock center. The main street in town is Maen Gwyn. It takes its name from a stone signpost that dates from pre-Roman times. The street itself is a display case of seventeenth-, eighteenth-, and nineteenth-century houses. Leave via Dyfi, a picturesque town of old houses, and continue to

Dolgellau (15 m), a small town of narrow winding streets

and old rock buildings that take on the character of the surrounding countryside. The main bridge in town dates from the seventeenth century. The town was one of the last holdouts in free Wales. Continue north up the Vale of Bala and into the softer countryside of the Dee to

Llangollen (39 m), another town that dates from the Roman period. The wooded countryside surrounding it has many beautiful remains of half-timbered houses. The bridge over the river Dee is quite old and very well known. Two miles outside the city is the Valle Crucis Abbey, which was founded in 1189 and has been the scene of continual turmoil and destruction since it was first built. It is now in ruins but is still very awesome in feeling. Guarding the city is the Castell Dinas Bran, which still stands on its original Celtic foundations. We now head eastward and back into England. Follow the river Dee to Froncysylltau and then leave the river and head south to

Shrewsbury (31 m), a town noted for its multitude of half-timbered houses and well-cared-for streets. Its famous castle is now the location of the municipal offices. Surrounding the castle are a number of buildings dating from the time of Henry VI. Continue south along the river Severn through numerous English parklands to

Worcester (50 m). This is supposed to have been the favorite city of King Arthur. The cathedral dates from 1190, and some of the early Norman work can still be seen. The tour concludes in

Stratford-on-Avon (20 m). (See English tour for description.) Make your way back to London by following the English tour itinerary, or go directly by train.

## ACCOMMODATIONS

*Locations of Youth Hostels*

| | |
|---|---|
| Slimbridge | Llangollen |
| Staunton-on-Wye | Shrewsbury |
| Newtown | Malvern Wells |
| Dolgellau | Stratford-on-Avon |

*Locations of Principal Campgrounds*

| | |
|---|---|
| Howel (Radnor County) | Bala (Radnor County) |
| Towyn (Merioneth County) | Rhyl (Flint County) |

## TOUR #4: THE SONG AND ART OF ITALY'S NORTH

Distance: 680 kilometers/408 miles
Time: 9–12 riding days
Degree of Difficulty: After crossing the Appenines in the first 16 kilometers of the tour, almost all the rest is easy riding. There are a few hills on the Adriatic coast of moderate difficulty.
Maps: Kümmerly+Frey *Northern Italy* (1:500,000) is generally available in book or map stores in this country, and is adequate. The Touring Club Italiano has a series of 1:200,000 maps, available in bookstores within Italy or at the border crossing outside Menton.

The tourist who ventures into Italy's north is in for a number of pleasant surprises, beginning with the verdant countryside. The Lombardy plains that angle southwest between the Appenines and the Alps possess some of the richest soil in the world. The beautiful farms and pasture-lands that result make a pleasant backdrop to the journey.

The tour route also takes you through a series of cities that, while less visited than the more noted art centers of Florence and Rome, are nonetheless worthy of exploration in their own right.

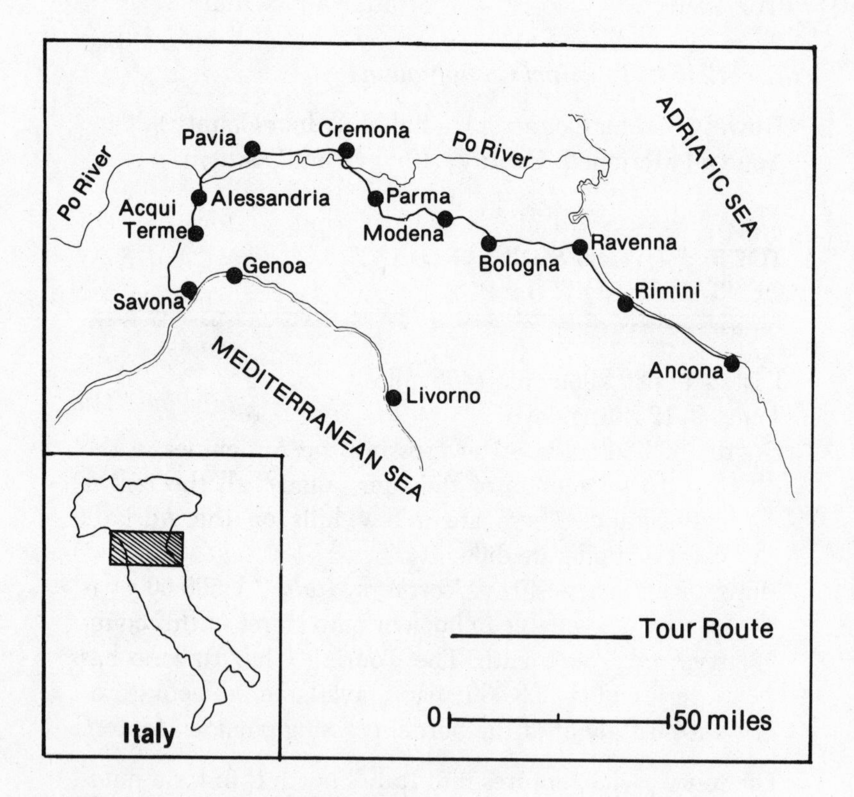


*The Song and Art of Italy's North*

Finally, the tour of Italy's north provides a pleasant passageway for cyclists on their way to Yugoslavia or Greece, or for those interested in further exploration of either Florence or Venice, both of which lie only a day or so's ride from the tour route.

The best times to bicycle are either in late spring or in the fall, when the weather is cooler and there are fewer tourists than during the summer months. If traveling during the high tourist season, be certain to obtain the recommended maps and travel on the smaller roads, as the main routes all bear considerable traffic during these periods.

You begin in the Italian Riviera town of Savona, some 45 kilometers northwest of Genoa and about 120 kilometers from the French/Italian frontier. Unless you are traveling in the off-season, Savona is best reached by train, as the coastal road is very crowded in July and August.

Within some 10 miles of leaving Savona, you cross the highest part of the tour, a rather low pass over the Appenines. From here on, with the exception of a few hills along the Adriatic coast, the ride is level and easy. The tour route roughly parallels one of Rome's most famous roads, the Via Emilia, and brings you into contact with a number of interesting towns, such as Cremona, the home of the famous Stradivarius violin; Bologna, a city rich in art and cuisine; and Ravenna, a charming poet's city that provided a final sanctuary for Dante and was the home for some time of the English poet Byron. From Ravenna you head south along the Adriatic coast, with some pleasant seaside resorts en route, and ample opportunities for dips in the cobalt blue waters of the Adriatic. The tour ends in Ancona, where ferry connections are available for Greece or Yugoslavia and rail connections to other parts of Italy and Europe.

ITINERARY

Savona. Beginning of the tour. A busy town on the Ligurian Riviera that has little attraction for the tourist but is the place from which the easiest crossing into the Po valley can be made. Take the road toward

Cacare (20 kilometers/12 miles), by which time you will already have crossed the high point of the tour. From Cacare you begin a long, winding descent into the plains of Lombardy, with the first major stop at

Acqui Terme (54 k/32 m), a noted spa and center for some of northern Italy's best wines. The cathedral here dates from 1067. Leave to the north for

Alessandria (34 k/20 m), a busy industrial city that may best be navigated between 1 and 3 P.M. Leave to the north via the road to Valenza, just outside of which you will cross the Po for the first time. From Alessandria on you never really leave the Po basin, with its vast expanses of cultivated fields and pasturelands. Proceed along the Po via any number of small roads to

Pavia (70 k/42 m), a typical Lombardian city of brick buildings. Its university dates from the fourteenth century. Leave eastward via Codogno to

Cremona (75 k/45 m), a city of music. The famous violin-making families the Stradivari, Guarneri, and Amati all produced their wonderful instruments here. The Stradivarian Museum has an excellent collection of instruments as well as displays relating to the work of Monteverdi. The Piazza del Comune is one of Italy's most impressive town squares, with a pretty twelfth-century Duomo. Leave Cremona via side roads to Casalmaggiore, where you cross the Po once again, then south to Colorno, where you have a choice of two quiet roads to

Parma (60 k/36 m), the birthplace of Arturo Toscanini. Its university dates from the eleventh century, and the present buildings there were constructed in the sixteenth century. It is at Parma that you intersect the Via Emilia, begun in 187 B.C. by the consul M. Emilius Lepidus. This road runs all the way to the Adriatic Sea. It is not the best choice for bicyclists, as it supports a considerable degree of traffic, although there are wide moped and bicycle lanes along much of it. There are a variety of alternative side roads along either side of the route. Leave Parma southeast via the towns of Monticelli Terme and Montecchio to

Reggio nell' Emilia (45 k/27 m), which has a nice thirteenth-century cathedral. Leave southeast to

Modena (26 k/16 m), a city of wide, arcaded streets and large squares. Its cathedral was begun in 1099 but only completed in the thirteenth century. The campanile is 285 feet high, one of the tallest bell towers in Italy and the most distinctive feature of the town. Leave northeast via the road to Nonántola and S. Giovanni to

Bologna (45 k/27 m). This is something of a midway point in the tour and deserves a stop for the day, if for no other reason than to enjoy a meal out in this center of northern Italian cuisine. Cyclists wishing to avoid the bustle of the town center may do so by taking one of the ring roads that circle to the north. For those in search of an engrossing experience, go to the city center where you can pass through the Piazza Maggiore and perhaps visit the famous university, founded in the fifth century, making it the world's oldest. It was here that anatomy was first taught, in violation of the church's orders. Bologna is a town of porticoed streets and elegant private palaces, the latter found primarily on the Via Zamboni. Its two leaning towers, one of which is 350 feet high and 11 feet off center at the top, can be climbed for an eagle's eye view of the city.

A long and rather hard day's ride south will take you to Florence, should you wish to make such a side trip. Otherwise, leave Bologna northeast via the towns of Medicina and Lugo to

Ravenna (80 k/48 m), a final resting place for Dante and home for a while of Lord Byron. Dante's tomb adjoins the Franciscan Church of San Francesco. Dante died here in 1321.

Ravenna was conquered by Byzantine emperors in the sixth century, and it still retains numerous examples of Byzantine art, some dating from the sixth century. The Oratory of St. Andrew in the Episcopal chapel has some of the best mosaics from that period. Leave south via the road to Borghetto, then take any of a number of side roads to

Rimini (64 k/38 m). On your way here, perhaps without noticing it, as it is almost dried up in summer, lies one of the most historical of all rivers, the Rubicon. (The Via Emilia crosses it near the town of Savignano.) Rimini itself is a pretty seaside town, with elegant resorts stretching to the south of it. There are remains of a large Roman amphitheater, which supposedly seated some 12,000 people. From Rimini, make your way along the sea via the towns of Bellaria, Riccione, and Cattolica to

Pesaro (48 k/29 m), a pleasant seaside town. From Pesaro, it is possible to weave a course south on small mountain roads, but an easier and more direct (although more heavily traveled) route is the coastal road paralleling the sea. You will find frequent places to go in and take a dip in the cool, clear Adriatic before arriving at the tour's end in

Ancona (60 k/36 m), an interesting town rising on hills above the harbor where ships leave regularly for Yugoslavia and Greece. You may make connections here to Patras, where the tour of the Corinthian and Saronic gulfs begins, or to a number of towns on the Dalmatian coast of Yugoslavia, should you wish to tour there.

## ACCOMMODATIONS

### *Locations of Youth Hostels*

Finale-Marina (toward France from Savona)
Genoa (45 kilometers from Savona)
Parma
Bologna
Ravenna
Rimini-Miramare
Pesaro

### *Locations of Principal Campgrounds*

Savona
Castel Boglione
Alessandria
Cremona
Parma
Modena
Bologna
Ravenna
Cervia
Cesenatico
Gatteo a Mare
Bellaria
Rimini
Riccione
Pesaro
Fano Marotta
Senigallia
Ancona

## TOUR #5: FIELDS AND FORTRESSES OF DENMARK

Distance: 335–350 miles/534–560 kilometers
Time: 9–11 riding days
Degree of Difficulty: Easy
Maps: Geodastick Institut Maps of Denmark. Available in bookstores throughout Denmark. Kümmerly+Frey *Denmark* (1:300,000) is available in this country.

Denmark is primarily an agricultural country and is liberally endowed with quaint half-timbered houses, Viking fortresses, castles, and beautiful waterways. It appears at first to be like an enlarged fairyland. In this tour we route you through some of Denmark's more scenic and historic areas. You cover some of the distance over easy terrain by cycle, some of it via the efficient Danish ferries that crisscross the country's many waterways.

The tour begins in Copenhagen. However, if you are arriving by ferry from Germany and do not wish to cycle or take the train all the way to Copenhagen, you may make your way by cycle via Langeland and Svendborg to Odense and intersect the tour there.

You begin the tour by moving south from Copenhagen through a picturesque area full of the old-style half-timbered houses, then move westward for a look at Odense, the birthplace of Hans Christian Andersen, and then proceed through one of Denmark's most beautiful spots—the lakes around Silkeborg—then return to Copenhagen via lovely fishing villages, stopping en route to visit Hamlet's castle at Helsingör (Elsinore).

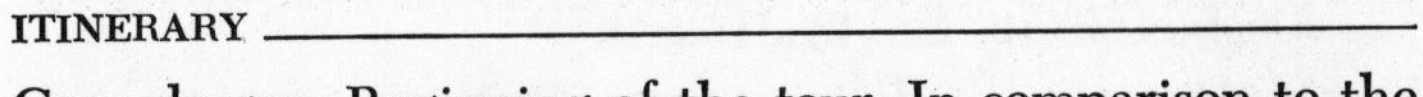

ITINERARY

Copenhagen. Beginning of the tour. In comparison to the history that surrounds it, the city is in many ways new.

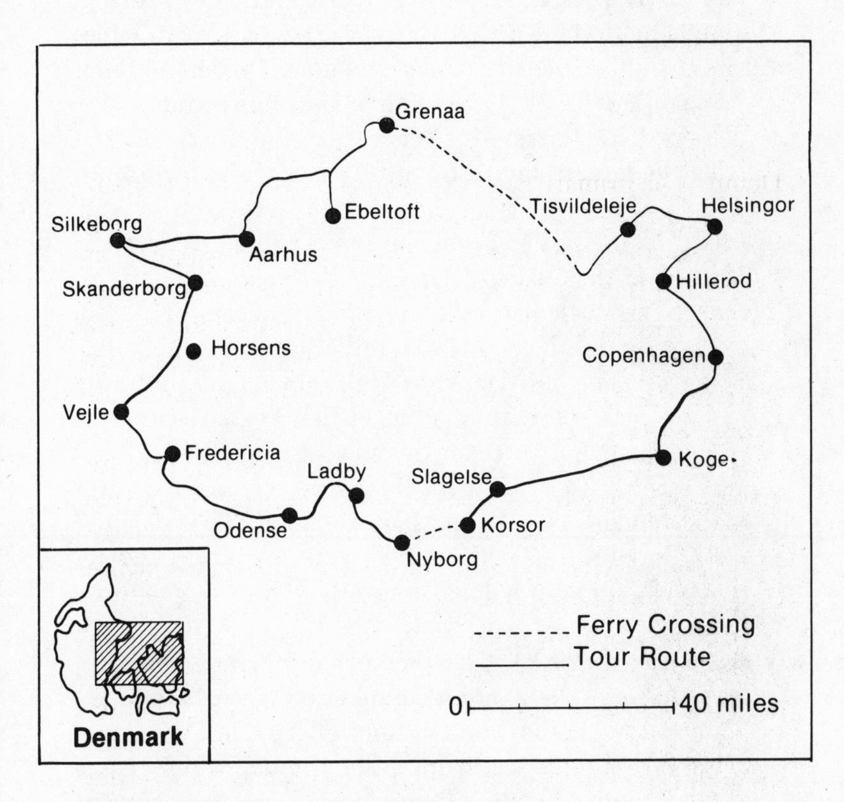


*Fields and Fortresses of Denmark*

Due to a continual series of wars, it has been destroyed and rebuilt a number of times. Special places to see are the town hall, the Tivoli gardens, and the Carlsberg brewery (with sampling part of every tour). Leave the city and head south for

Köge (24 miles/38 kilometers). This is an old market town that has many fine examples of old timbered houses. The town hall, dating from the sixteenth century, is pretty. Leave westward through Rinstead, passing through areas rich in pastoral scenery to

Slagelse (35 m/56 k). A slight detour to the north of Slagelse will let you see the Viking fortress at Trelleborg. This fortress is over a thousand years old and has been partially restored. From Slagelse turn south to

Korsör (17 m/27 k). From here you catch the ferry to Funene, the Garden Island. Land at

Nyborg. The castle here is intact and dates from 1170. The area around the city is also full of castles and country houses. The best known is Holckenhavn, dating from 1580 and set within a beautiful 30-acre park. On leaving Nyborg turn north and visit

Ladby (15 m/25 k). The local museum of Ladby houses the remains of a Viking burial mound. The remains? A 72-foot ship! The Viking king buried inside it along with his treasures lived a thousand years ago. From Ladby go to

Odense (12 m/20 k). The birthplace of Hans Christian Andersen. There are a number of town sites connected with the famous storyteller. There is also a famous Gothic cathedral, St. Knuds, which dates from the thirteenth century. Leave for the mainland of Denmark, known as Jutland, and for the town of

Fredericia (35 k/56 m). It is situated on a peninsula and is surrounded by good, sandy beaches. The town offers a blend of old and new Denmark. Continue north up the coast to

Vejle (12 m/19 k), an ancient town beautifully situated on the coast. Ride via Horsens to

Skanderborg (30 m/48 k). This is the gateway to Denmark's beautiful lake district. Ride through Emborg (and see the remains of the twelfth-century monastery) to

Silkeborg (20 m/32 k), on what is Denmark's largest river, the Gudenaa. The surrounding woods and lakes offer some breathtaking scenery. The city museum contains the remains of the 2,000-year-old Tollund Man and some excellent paintings. Go east to

Aarhus (26 m/42 k). Aarhus is located on a beautiful bay and is surrounded by woodlands. The old town is a collection of houses from all over Denmark that are decorated in the style of various periods. The town hall and university are two good examples of modern Scandinavian architecture. Move north and onto a tiny peninsula where you will find

Ebeltoft (40 m/64 k), a town of winding cobbled streets lined with old houses and shops. Walking there is really a stroll into the sixteenth century. Continue north to

Grenaa (30 m/48 k). Catch the ferry here back to Zealand and the town of Hundested. Move north to

Tisvildeleje (5 m/8 k). The first in a series of fishing villages and resort towns. Pass through Hornbaek to

Helsingör (33 m/53 k). This is one of the oldest cities in Denmark and the site of Kronborg Castle, better known as Elsinore, Hamlet's castle, even though it was built in the sixteenth century, 600 years after the prince's death. Leave Helsingör south via Hilleröd, the location of Frederiksborg Castle, and on to

Copenhagen. The end of the tour.

ACCOMMODATIONS

*Locations of Youth Hostels*

Köge
Ringsted
Slagelse
Korsör
Kerteminde
Odense
Fredericia
Vejle
Horsens
Skanderborg
Silkeborg
Aarhus
Rönde
Ebeltoft
Tisvildeleje
Helsingör
Fredensborg
Copenhagen

*Locations of Principal Campgrounds*

Köge
Slagelse
Körsor
Nyborg
Kerteminde
Odense
Fredericia
Vejle
Skanderborg
Silkeborg
Aarhus
Ebeltoft
Grenaa
Gilleleje
Helsingör
Hilleröd
Copenhagen

## TOUR #6: LOCHS AND MOORS OF THE SCOTTISH HIGHLANDS

Distance: 375–400 miles
Time: 8–12 riding days
Degree of Difficulty: Moderate to hard
Maps: Bartholomew National Map Series (in order of use)

nos. 45, 49, 52, 56, 55, 51, 48 (1:100,000) or Bartholomew GT Map Series nos. 8, 10, and 7 (1:253,440)

Touring in Scotland is an up-front experience. The Scots are friendly but they do not make great efforts to attract the outsider. And so if you find yourself there it is because you want to be there and are willing to accept the rugged honesty of the people and the countryside.

The following tour begins in Edinburgh, the capital of Scotland, and ends in Glasgow. You leave along the southern shore of the Firth of Forth, then wind northward through the heathered moors to Inverness. From here you turn southward, enjoying a long and relatively easy run along the shore of the fabled Loch Ness and Loch Linnhe to Glencoe, where you turn eastward and head toward the end of the tour at Glasgow.

Along the way you will see terrain that is wild, rugged, romantic, and beautiful. The Highlands are full of historic castles, and the towns along the lochs teem with mysterious tales and fables. The lowlands around the cities of Glasgow and Edinburgh are softer in their feel and perhaps more outgoing in their approach to the world.

## ITINERARY

Edinburgh. Beginning of the tour. Located on the Firth of Forth, Edinburgh has had a long history—reflected in its tourist sites. The castle that overlooks the city is a museum of Scottish history and affords a magnificent view of the city and the Firth. The old town can be seen from the castle. This is the section of Edinburgh that used to constitute the entire city and has a good representation of the architecture of the past woven into its narrow streets. The gardens in the town center are well kept and lovely. Just outside the town cen-

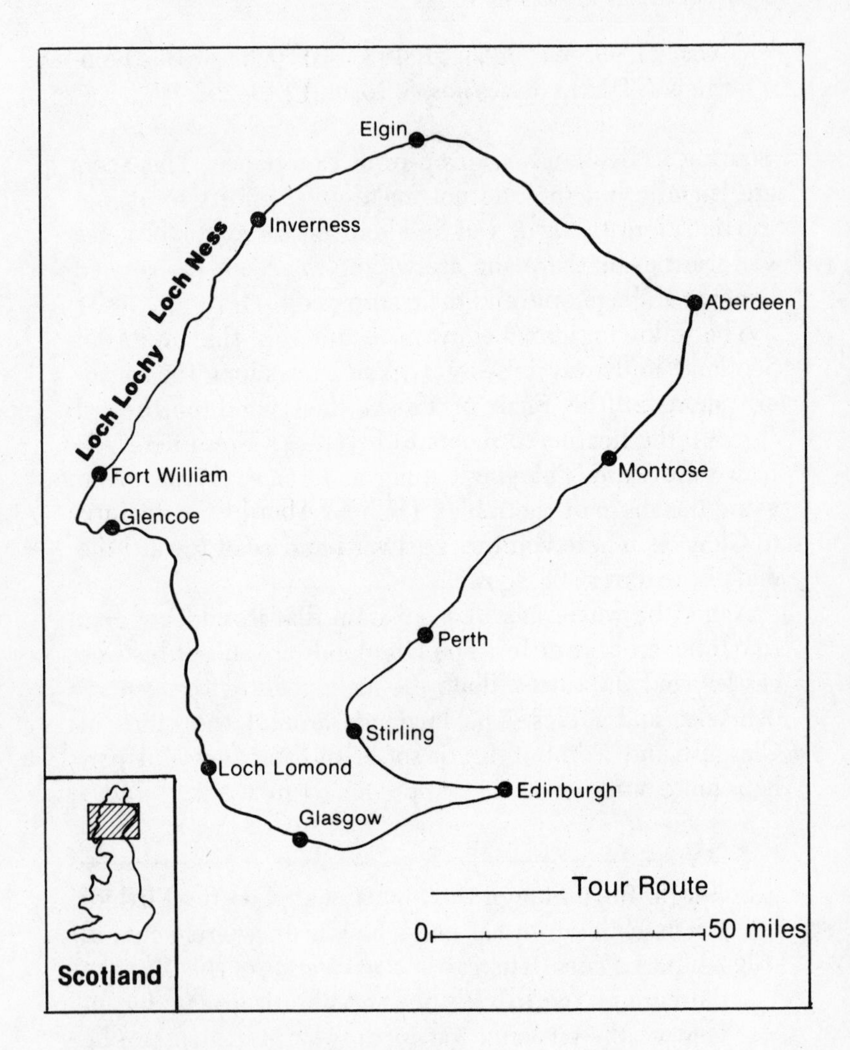


*Lochs and Moors of the Scottish Highlands*

ter is Holyrood Palace, the official home of the Royal Family when visiting Scotland. Leave the city and head west toward

Stirling (36 m), a very old, historic city with a sixteenth-century castle. Continue north to

Perth (34 m), a beautiful castled country town that was immortalized by Sir Walter Scott. Continuing north from Perth, you cross the imaginary line that separates the Lowlands from the Highlands. Our tour takes you northward along the coast to Aberdeen. If you want a more vigorous exposure to the Highlands, go to Aberdeen via Braemar, the site of the annual Highland Games every September, and then on toward Balmoral Castle and easterly to Aberdeen. This area is one of the wildest yet most tranquil in all of Scotland. Riding tends to be rugged. This side trip will add approximately 35 miles to the tour. The main tour continues up the narrow valley from Perth through Montrose and into

Aberdeen (87 m). Aberdeen is supposedly the most Scottish city in the country. It is the third largest in Scotland, has an active port and a university, and is surrounded by many popular resort areas. From Aberdeen continue northwest through the wooded hill country that is famous for its Scotch whisky and on to

Elgin (66 m), an ancient town with a famous castle that is now in ruins. It has the reputation for having the warmest, sunniest climate anywhere in the British Isles. Continue west through Nairn, the site of Cawdor Castle—it comes complete with drawbridge. Out of Nairn turn south toward

Inverness (38 m), a resort town that was once the site of Macbeth's castle. Presently it serves as the gateway to the Northern Highlands and the loch country. We continue south along Loch Ness—an area world-renowned for its scenery and wild tales of monsters, mythical and real. Continue south to

Loch Lochy (45 m). And on to Fort William, a resort town at the base of Britain's highest mountain, Ben Nevis. Continue east to

Glencoe (30 m), a lonely glen that is full of ghosts and tales of the ghastly murder of the Clan MacDonald in 1692. This area has inspired many artists with its vast panoramas of gaunt hills, soft clouds, and winding waterways. From Glencoe we proceed south to

Loch Lomond (57 m). Once again we are in the Lowlands, where the moors seem softer and greener and the people perhaps a bit less austere. The tour ends in

Glasgow (20 m), which was once one of the loveliest areas in Scotland. Now it is a sprawling industrial city that is best given only a brief glance. Worth a visit are its fine Gothic cathedral and art museum that houses some Rembrandt, Rubens, and Whistler paintings. There is an excellent rail service from Glasgow back to Edinburgh and to all parts of England.

## ACCOMMODATIONS

*Locations of Youth Hostels*

Edinburgh
Stirling
Glendevon
Perth
Glendoll
Glendsla
Aberdeen
Tonimtool
Elgin
Inverness
Loch Lochy
Glen Nevis
Glencoe
Loch Lomond
Glasgow

*Locations of Principal Campgrounds*

Edinburgh (Midlothian County)
Montrose (Angus County)
Peterhead (Aberdeenshire County)
Fraserburgh (Aberdeenshire County)
Lossiemouth (Morayshire)
Findhorn (Morayshire)
Inverness (Inverness County)
Spean Bridge (Inverness County)

## TOUR #7: CHÂTEAUX OF THE LOIRE

Distance: 235–250 miles / 376–400 kilometers
Time: 5–7 riding days
Degree of Difficulty: Easy
Maps: Michelin 1:200,000 series, nos. 64 and 65

More than anything else the valley of the Loire in France means castles (or *châteaux*, as they are called in French). On this tour of the Loire you can enjoy them to any degree you wish. There are so many châteaux from so many different periods that you can quickly become an expert on the entire subject if you apply yourself. On the other hand, you may just ride quietly past most of them and appreciate them for what they were intended to be: magnificent residences reflecting the opulence of a former age. Whichever way you decide to tour the Loire, you will most likely be convinced that few places offer so many attractions to the cyclist. In addition to the châteaux, there are thousands of miles of tiny roads interlacing the area. If you use any imagination at all in moving from place to place, much of your ride will resemble having your own personal bicycle path—except that this one will go on and on for hundreds of miles. The well-known châteaux such as Chenonceaux and Chambord are of course major attractions. But you will also be delighted at how often you round a turn in a small road and find, set off in the woods, an elegant mansion, an unheralded monument in its own right but probably unknown except to those in the immediate area and of course the family that lives there.

Between major sites you pass through dense woods, largely given over to hunting during the season. Occasionally you will see a field where asparagus is grown, and near Tours you pass through vineyards and by wine cellars cut into the banks formed by the river.

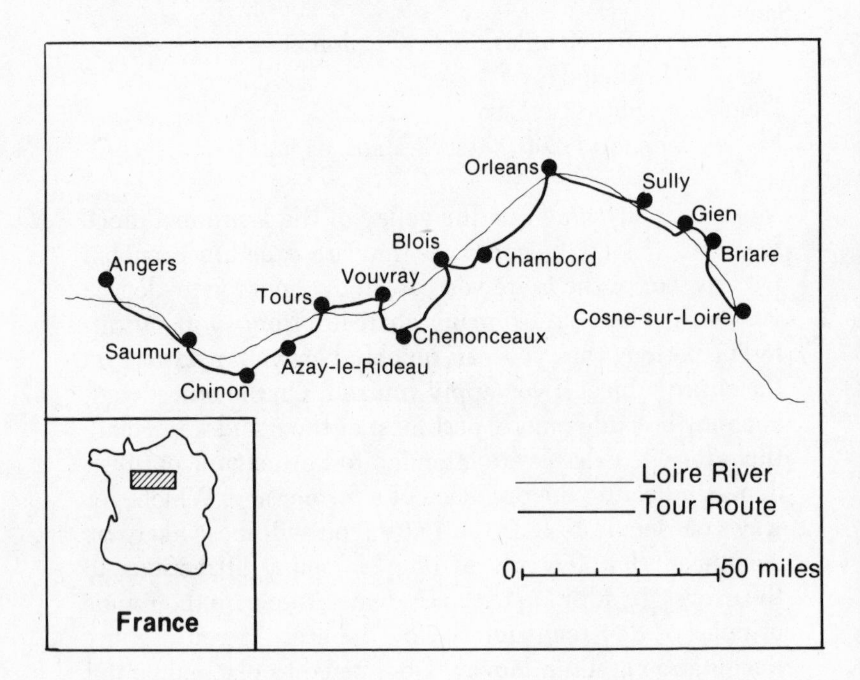


*Châteaux of the Loire*

The tour begins in Angers, not far from the Atlantic coast, and works upstream to Cosne. The fall of the Loire is so gradual that you are never aware that you are gaining elevation. By moving from west to east you also take advantage of the prevailing westerly winds that move up the valley.

## ITINERARY

Angers. Once an important Roman town with baths, circus, and amphitheater, it is now known for its cathedral and as a center for the mining of slate. Leave southward across the Loire through Ponts-de-Cé, where you pass numerous fifteenth- and sixteenth-century houses, and head up the Loire for

Saumur (30 miles/49 kilometers). Ravaged by invaders from the time of the Norsemen to that of World War II, the town still maintains an excellent château as well as numerous fifteenth- and sixteenth-century structures, including the elegant town hall and a military riding school. Continue on the same side of the river to

Fontevrault-l'Abbaye (10 m/49 k), site of one of the richest and most important abbeys to have existed in France, and one where both monks and nuns lived and worked under the same abbess. The abbey chapel is well preserved. Leave the river heading northeast for

Chinon (12 m/19 k), a lively tourist center with a campground giving memorable views of the château and the quays of the town. We found the best French pastry in the world at Chinon. You might try your luck. Head back toward the Loire, passing the château along the way, to

Azay-le-Rideau (13 m/21 k), which gives the feeling of an old Renaissance town, dominated by its château, with numerous winding side streets and interesting shops. Head north toward the river and then follow it via Villandry and Joue to

Tours (17 m/27 k). Badly damaged during the last war, Tours still has an interesting old quarter and university that give it a settled flavor contrasting sharply with the modern buildings and industrial areas surrounding it. Stay on the north side of the river, passing through Vouvray, a famous wine-growing region, then cross back to the south side of the Loire at

Amboise (15 m/24 k), dominated by its château built on a chalky escarpment above the river. At the foot of the château is the small manor where Leonardo da Vinci lived while working under the patronage of François I. The house contains a small collection of models of machines invented by Leonardo. Head southward through deep forests to

Chenonceaux (7 m/11 k), the jewel of all French châteaux. Even if you miss all the others, stop and see this one. It is built on a series of arched piers across the Cher river. Catherine de Médicis once owned it and gave lavish entertainments there. Once you see it you'll see why. Cycle via Montrichard to

Chaumont (22 m/35 k), not only an elegant castle, but one of the few on the Loire specifically built to withstand trouble by invaders. You still must cross an authentic drawbridge to reach the inner courtyard. From Chaumont ride the short distance to

Blois (13 m/20 k), built on the north bank of the Loire. A well-preserved château stands on the highest hill. Nearby are excellent views of the river. Leave southward, crossing the river, then turn upriver again to

Chambord (10 m/15 k). If Chenonceaux is the jewel, Chambord is the most impressive of the Loire châteaux. François I chose this isolated spot to build a structure that the Holy Roman Emperor Charles V termed "the epitome of the achievements of human endeavours." The roads leading to it from all sides make excellent cycling, passing through dense green woods. Leave toward Orléans, but keep away from the busy roads paralleling the banks of the river.

Orléans (26 m/45 k). A city filled with the history of Joan of Arc and how she liberated the town from the English in 1429. The Cathedral of the Sacred Cross (Sainte-Croix) is one of the best known in Europe. Cross to the south side of the river again, then continue eastward through Sully, then across the river once more to

Briare (46 m/74 k). Near here you can see one of the more interesting water projects in Europe, a stone bridge which carries a *canal* over the Loire, much like one freeway passing over the other at right angles. The canal bridge was begun in 1890. Cross the river again at Châtillon and proceed to

Cosne-sur-Loire (19 m/31 k), an interesting river town and the end of the tour. You may head eastward from here through Burgundy to Dijon to intersect the Taste of Two Wines tour, or go back by train or cycle to Paris.

## ACCOMMODATIONS

*Locations of Youth Hostels*

| | |
|---|---|
| Saumur | Blois |
| Tours | |

*Locations of Principal Campgrounds*

Angers
Saumur
Chinon
Azay-le-Rideau
Tours
Vouvray
Chenonceaux
Blois
Orléans
Sully
Gien
Briare
Cosne

## TOUR #8: A TOWN-AND-COUNTRY TOUR OF HOLLAND

Distance: 225–240 miles / 360–384 kilometers
Time: 5–7 riding days
Degree of Difficulty: Easy
Maps: Michelin map no. 6 (1:200,000) covers the tour route. Available in Holland from the Royal Dutch Automobile Club (A.N.W.B.; see Appendix 7 for address) is a 1:100,000 series that shows bicycle paths.

While Holland is the most densely populated country in the world, with nearly a thousand people per square mile, it is still one of the best cycling countries in the world because of the hundreds of miles of specialized bicycling trails honeycombing the country. This not only makes riding safer but guarantees that, despite the density of the population, you can always find quiet riding. Thus our Town-and-Country tour allows you to visit all the major cities in the west of Holland and to meander across fields,

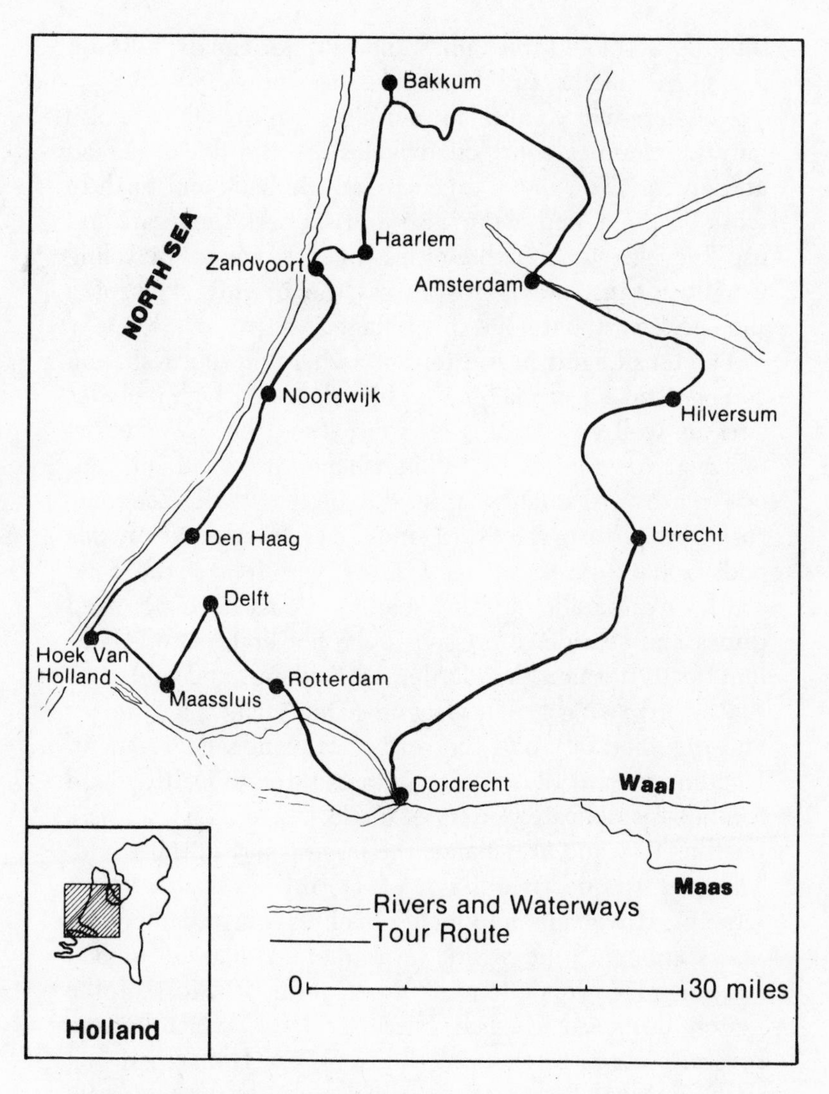


*A Town-and-Country Tour of Holland*

through desolate sand dunes, along quiet canals, by bulb fields, over heaths, and through hushed forests.

Nowhere will you find more fellow cyclists who are also natives. Couples court on bicycles, people deliver bread and groceries on them, executives cycle back and forth to work on them, and many wise tourists park their cars and use bicycles to see the cities—places where bicycling usually means having to possess the driving skills of a Jackie Stewart, but not so in Holland.

The tour begins in Amsterdam, where, if you wish, you can even take a special guided bicycle tour which includes sites as well as cocktails en route (see the VVV tourist office in Amsterdam, 5 Rokin). Then strike off on your own northward along what used to be the Zuyder Zee (now reclaimed), turn westward and head for the North Sea and Holland's seaside resorts. As you follow the road southward paralleling the sea, you pass through sand dunes and seaside resorts, visit the flower town of Haarlem, justly termed the Garden of Holland, and end your southward swing at The Hague (Den Haag), a spacious and dignified city and the seat of Holland's government. Heading toward Rotterdam you pass through Delft, where the famous delicate pottery is made. Rotterdam itself is a bustling city and also claims the largest port in the world. The picturesque river town of Dordrecht is next, then Utrecht, Hilversum, and finally back to Amsterdam again.

If you begin your cycling in England, Holland is a good starting place for a tour of the Continent. Most of the Dutch also speak English. Ferry service is available from several ports in England to the Hoek van Holland. If you wish, you may also make connections in the other direction to France, either cycling there through Belgium or taking the train from Amsterdam to Angers (via Paris), where you may begin the Châteaux of the Loire tour.

ITINERARY

Amsterdam. A city with so many attractions that you will have to limit what you see or you may never leave. The Rembrandt museum, Royal Palace, or just the canals at night will keep you busy enough. Leave via the Schellingwoude Bridge to Durgerdam, passing through Purmerend, Knollendam-West, to Castricum, then north to

Bakkum (37 miles/59 kilometers), a small town on the North Sea. Leave Bakkum passing through the sand dunes to Wijkaan-Zee, Beverwijk, then across the canal locks to Santpoort, and on to

Haarlem (13 m/21 k), in the heart of the bulb fields (best season, April and May), but also interesting in its own right. Medieval architecture, craft shops, and artists' cafés. Swing westward from Haarlem toward the sea to

Zandvoort (18 m/31 k), a popular resort on the North Sea. Leave here toward Aerdenhout, Vogelenzand, then through the dunes to

Den Haag (The Hague) (31 m/50 k), a park-studded city, seat of the government of the Netherlands. A side trip from here to Madurodam is well worthwhile. This is a knee-high replica of a typical Dutch city that stretches out over a two-mile path. Leave The Hague southward through Loosduinen to the

Hoek van Holland (10 m/16 k), a departure point for ferry service across the North Sea. Leave eastward to Maassluis, then turn north to

Delft (18 m/29 k), a city with many canals, small quaint houses, and the home of the world-famous painted Delft pottery. Leave southward to

Rotterdam (8 m/13 k). Completely leveled during World War II, Rotterdam is now a showplace of contemporary city planning. Cycle southward from here to

Dordrecht (14 m/22 k), one of Holland's oldest cities. A busy river town that also possesses many winding streets, niches, gateways, and mansions. Cross the river by ferry and head north toward

Kinderdijk (6 m/10 k). Nearby are numerous working windmills. Leave eastward along the Lek river, through Nieuw Lekkerland, Ameide, Vianen, then cross the Lek to Vreeswijk and head toward

Utrecht (30 m/48 k). The old district is charming, and a climb up the Dom, the tower of Utrecht Cathedral, will give you an excellent view of the countryside. Leave northwesterly through Zuilen, Breukelen, Vreeland to

Hilversum (18 m/29 k). A modern town near Amsterdam, yet set in a countryside of forests and heaths. Leave northward through Bussum, Naarden, and then along the former Zuyder Zee to

Amsterdam (24 m/38 k), the end of the tour.

## ACCOMMODATIONS

*Locations of Youth Hostels*

Amsterdam
Bakkum
Haarlem
Noordweijkerhout (near Noordwijk)

*Locations of Principal Campgrounds*

Amsterdam
Zandvoort
Noordwijk
Den Haag

## TOUR #9: GERMANY'S BLACK FOREST

Distance: 335 kilometers / 201 miles
Time: 4–7 riding days
Degree of Difficulty: Moderate to hard with numerous stiff climbs daily
Map: Michelin map no. 205 (1:200,000), available in this country or in Germany

The Black Forest draws its name from the deep green of its conifers and the seemingly bottomless depths of its dark lakes. It has long been a favorite tourist spot and is perfect for the cyclist because of its numerous small roads and picturesque villages.

Although the hills and mountains of the Black Forest are not high by alpine standards—the tallest cresting somewhere above 4,000 feet—roads tend to rise and fall abruptly, making for hard cycling in many regions. On the other hand, as its name implies, the area is heavily wooded and shady, and most roads take advantage of natural pathways created by numerous rivers and streams.

The tour starts at the north part of the Black Forest, in the town of Baden-Baden, one of the most luxurious resorts in Germany. Its renown as a spa dates from Roman times. From Baden-Baden the cyclist then begins a long ascent, skirting the upper hills overlooking the Rhine, with vistas across the valley to the Vosges in France. You pass through the town of Freudenstadt, which stands on a high plateau amid pine forests. From here you wind slowly southward, mostly on quiet country roads, passing through typical Black Forest towns and villages, to the resort town

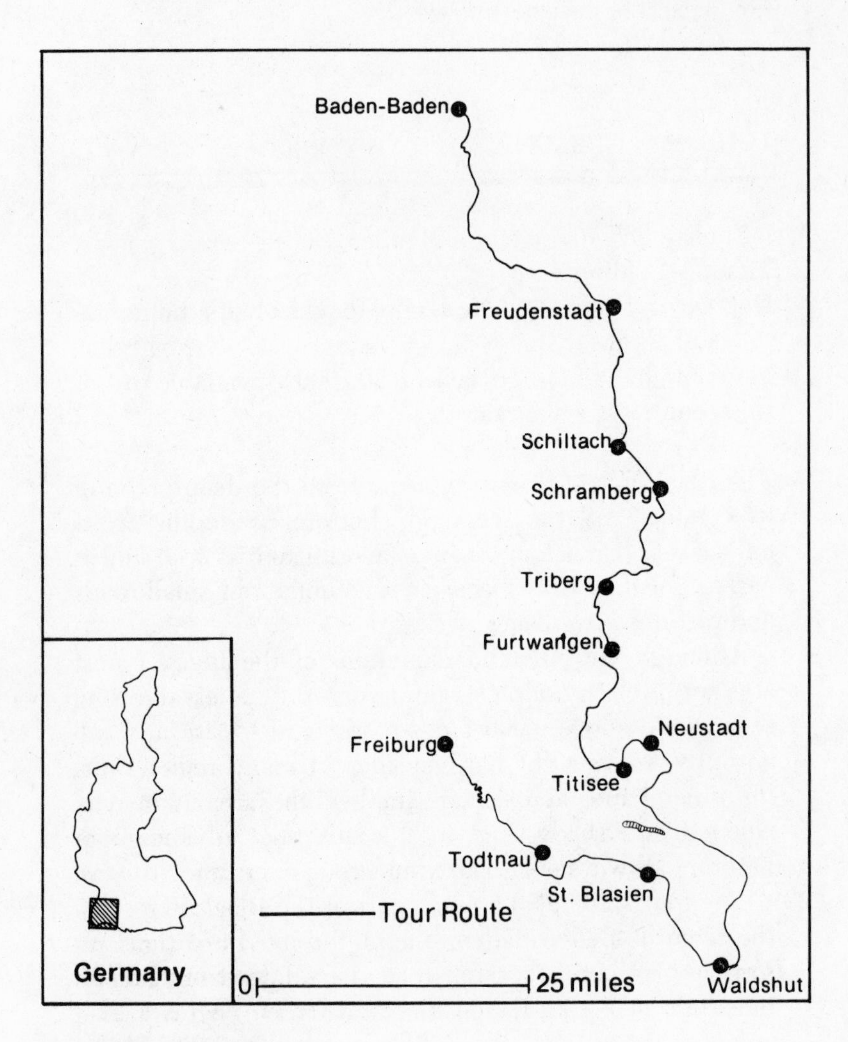


*Germany's Black Forest*

of Titisee, where you can swim in the cool lake, as thousands of Germans do each summer.

Further south you encounter the highest parts of the Black Forest, with its heavily gabled farmhouses, a land of charm and mystery that seems to be a natural place to serve as the center for the manufacture of ornate cuckoo clocks.

At Waldshut, perched on a hill overlooking the Swiss-German border, you reach your most southerly point then swing north to make your way slowly to the pass at Schauinsland, where you may get off your bicycle and climb to an observation tower for a splendid panorama. The road down is used each summer for car rallies, and you will see why as it twists and turns through dense green forests. Fortunately your direction is downward, so you may enjoy the scenery fully. The end of the tour is Freiburg, founded in the twelfth century and today one of the most attractive towns in southern Germany.

The Black Forest tour can be combined with the tour of Burgundy and Alsace. The latter tour ends in Strasbourg, a moderate day's ride from Baden-Baden. Connections are best made by staying on the French side and crossing the Rhine at Drusenheim. Several routes are possible from Drusenheim to Baden-Baden.

### ITINERARY

Baden-Baden. Start of the tour. In addition to the spa and casino, historical attractions for the powerful and well-to-do from all over Europe, don't miss the Lichtentaler Allee, a lovely promenade beside the river Oos. The promenade was planned more than 300 years ago, and at one time or another many of the leaders of western European history have strolled along it, including Napolean III, Bismarck, and

Queen Victoria. Leave Baden-Baden southeast via Lichtental, Mitteltal, and Baiersbronn to

Freudenstadt (59 kilometers/35 miles). A combination of new and old, its church dating from the seventeenth century, its Marktplatz built after the Second World War, Freudenstadt stands as something of a center for tours to the northern Black Forest. Leave south via the small road that goes through the tiny village of Oedenwald and the towns of Schramberg, Tennenbronn, and St. Georgen in Schwarzwald to

Triberg (66 k/40 m), a watch and clockmaking center. The Gutach Falls are nearby, cascading down 531 feet amid dense forest. Leave Triberg south via Schönwald and Furtwangen, to

Titisee (32 k/19 m). Located on a pretty lake, Titisee is popular with Germans for swimming and other water sports. From Titisee take the road east to Neustadt, and on the eastern end of town take the small road up the Gutach river to

Kappel (14 k/8 m), a pretty village with houses clustered around an old domed belfry. There is a view there across terraced hills to the Feldberg tower, atop the highest peak in the Black Forest. Continue on via Lenzkirch and Fischbach to

Schluchsee (13 k/8 m), on a lake of the same name, the largest in the Black Forest. Go to the southeastern end of the lake where the road leads off via Rothaus, Grafenhausen, Birkendorf, and Ühlingen to

Waldshut (41 k/25 m), on the upper Rhine. Across the river is Switzerland. You can make train connections from here to Basel and Freiburg, if you wish. Waldshut is perched on the slopes above the river, and the old town has two fortified gateways. The main street, the Kaiserstrasse, is lined with picturesque houses that have the traditional overhanging gables. Leave

Waldshut via a sharp hill on the road to Waldkirch and Häusern and go to

St. Blasien (28 k/17 m), noted for its unusual domed Church of St. Blaise. From here travel up the Alb river to Bernau, passing a high point some kilometers out of town, after which you descend to Geschwend and Todtnau. Some eight kilometers outside of Todtnau, off on a side road, lies the village of

Todtnauberg (34 k/20 m), the highest resort in the Black Forest (3,300 feet) and one of the prettiest, with its houses of shingle rising along the crest of a hill. Double back to the main road and continue climbing to the pass at

Schauinsland (13 k/8 m), where there is a viewing tower just off the road, and which represents the highest accessible point on your tour. From here you go down a pretty, twisting road, where sports car rallies are held, ending at

Freiburg (19 k/11 m), the end of the tour. Notable is the cathedral, begun in the year 1200 and enlarged periodically since. In addition, there is an Augustine museum, known for its collection of medieval art. In the evenings you may stroll the old streets, cleansed and cooled by small canals that run alongside.

## ACCOMMODATIONS

*Locations of Youth Hostels*

Herrenwies (off the route from Baden-Baden to Freudenstadt)
Freudenstadt
Triberg
Titisee
Schluchsee
Menzenschwand (off the route from St. Blasien to Todtnau)
Freiburg

*Locations of Principal Campgrounds*

Titisee
Neustadt
Schluchsee
Gurtweil
Oberkutterau
Kirchzarten
Freiburg

## TOUR #10: FAINT STRAINS OF MOZART—FROM GRAZ TO SALZBURG IN AUSTRIA

Distance: 440–460 miles / 704–736 kilometers
Time: 10–15 riding days
Degree of Difficulty: Moderate during the first part of the tour over the rolling hills near Graz. Some hard cycling between Siemriach and Mariazell, then moderate between Mariazell and Radstadt. Some hard, stiff climbs to the lakes east of Salzburg, then generally moderate cycling the rest of the tour.
Maps: Michelin map no. 426, *Austria* (1:400,000), is available in this country. Available in bookstores in Austria, *Holzel's* (1:200,000) in four sheets.

Graz and Salzburg are two of Austria's most gracious and charming cities, and this tour takes you to both of them. In between, you can enjoy alternately some of the Old World's most attractive rural scenery and some of its most spectacular mountain views.

The basic tour route is one developed by Dr. Clifford Graves and members of the International Bicycle Touring Society. We have made only minor adjustments of the route. According to Graves, the tour has been "honed to a fine degree [and] it shows you the country in its best possible aspect. Practically all the cycling is on side roads rather than main roads."

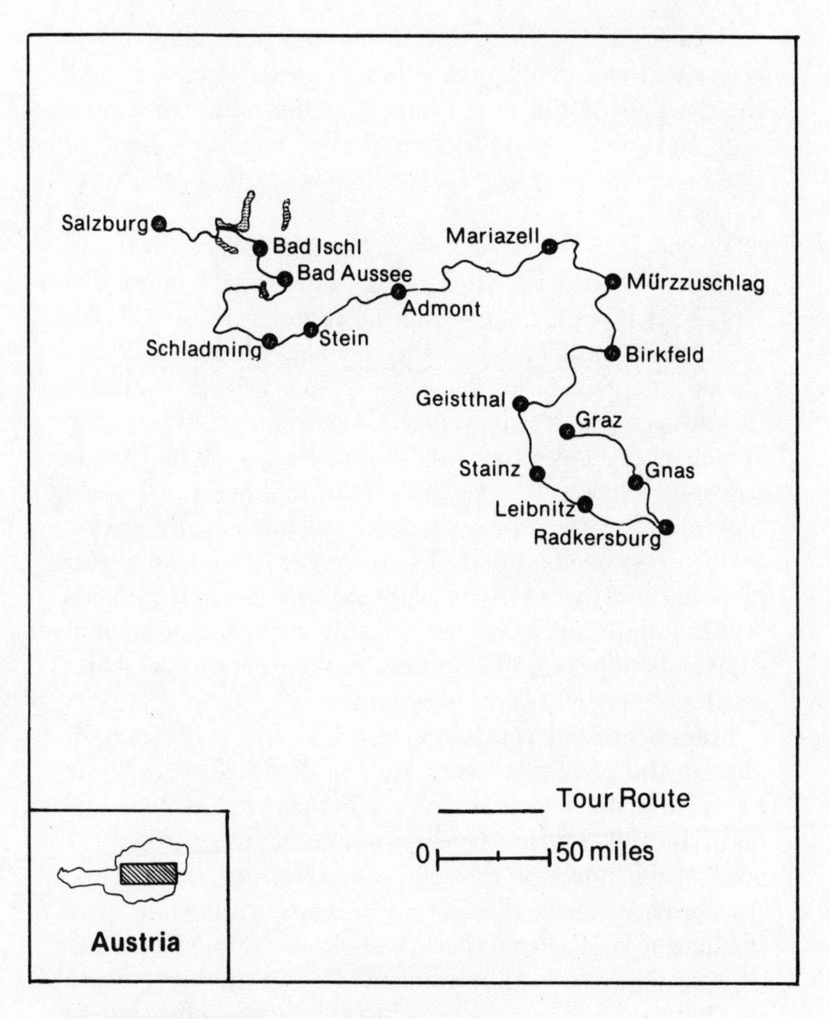


*From Graz to Salzburg in Austria*

Because of this, much of your trip will be highlighted by a series of charming rural villages and quiet scenery. Although part of the tour route is in the mountains, your high elevations are only around 3,000 feet, and much of the route follows river valleys where cycling is easy or moderate.

You begin in the town of Graz, located in the Mur valley near the Steyermark. After enough time to take in some of Graz's famous sites, including the former seat of the Diet of Styria (Landhaus) and the Arsenal, where more than 15,000 weapons dating back more than 300 years are displayed, you make your way via small roads and towns to Gleichenberg, near the Yugoslavian border. A quick side trip into Yugoslavia is possible from this point. The next days are spent in rolling country, making something of a wide sweep back around Graz. You then begin some stiff climbing until you cross a high point of the tour at 3,300 feet at Lahnsattel. Downhill is the ancient pilgrim town of Mariazell, noted for its religious traditions and spectacular setting.

From Mariazell you follow a series of river valleys, including the scenic and sparsely populated Salza, with its basins and steep ravines. In the last part of the tour you find yourself in the Dachstein mountains, certainly a scenic high point of the trip. You then descend to Bad Aussee and Bad Ischl, where side trips are possible to a number of lakes. From there, you wind a serpentine route over easy terrain to the end of the tour at Salzburg, home of Mozart. You can still visit his childhood home, where mementos of the prodigy's life are on display, including the little violin he used as a child. Salzburg offers a number of historic sites as well as the quiet pleasures of exploring its intricate network of streets, where Austria's charm is very much on display.

ITINERARY

Graz. Beginning of the tour. In addition to the Arsenal and the Landhaus, you should make a point to see the Hauptplatz, in the heart of the city, where flower and vegetable markets are held that lend color and life to this ancient setting. Take time out for a funicular to the Schlossberg, a 400-foot hill overlooking the town. In leaving, proceed via a series of small villages—St. Marein, Paldau, and Gnas—to

Gleichenberg (53 kilometers/33 miles), a spa town not far from the Yugoslavian frontier. Gleichenberg is a town of gracious villas, thermal baths and springs, lawns, and shaded parks. The waters are used for the treatment of respiratory and cardiac diseases. Leave via the villages of Kapfenstein and Kloch to

Radkersburg (48 k/30 m), a historic frontier town guarding the left bank of the Mur. Fortifications here date back to the thirteenth century. The town hall (Rathaus) and the parish church (Stadtpfarrkirche) are notable. Leave northwest via Gosdorf, Weinberg, and Leitring to

Leibnitz (47 k/28 m), a pretty provincial town. Proceed via the Stainzbach valley and the towns of Stainz and St. Stephan to Soding. A short side trip is possible here via Highway 70 and side roads to the small town of Piber, where the famous Lippizaner stallions are bred. The mature horses are seen at the famous Spanish Riding School in Vienna. The horses are born bay or black, and do not get their distinctive white coats until they are from 4 to 10 years old. The stud (gestut) may be visited during the summer months. Retrace your route to Soding, then on via Geisthall and Friesach to

Siemriach (96 k/58 m), where you will find both youth hostel and campground, as well as hotels. Get a good night's rest, because the next day marks the transition from the foothills to the mountains. Leave Siemriach north via Rechberg, Sailergroben, and St. Erhard, to the pass at

Strassegg (41 k/25 m), then via Gasen, Birkfeld, Landauer, Krieglach, Murzzuschlag (hostel), Neuburg (hostel), and Murzsteg, to another pass at

Lahnsattel (93 k/56 m), where you crest at 3,300 feet elevation. Continue via Rechengraben to

Mariazell (16 k/10 m). Mariazell is the most popular pilgrim city in Austria. Set amid mountain peaks, it was the site of an early Benedictine priory. In 1377, Louis I of Anjou, who was king of Hungary, won a victory over the Turks which he attributed to the Virgin of Mariazell. From that time on, the place attracted religious pilgrims. The basilica, dating from the fourteenth century, is worth a visit.

From Mariazell you wind downstream through the scenic Salza valley, still wild and sparsely inhabited, passing the small villages of Wildalpen, Erzhalden, Grossreifling, and Gestatterboden to

Admont (103 k/62 m), noted for its Benedictine abbey. The abbey library, with ceiling paintings by Bartolomeo Altomonte, may be seen. The rest of the original structure was destroyed by fire, then rebuilt in 1865. Stay on the south side of the river passing via Selzthal, Versbichl, Dollach, Irdning, Oblarn, Haus, Schladming, and Forstau to

Radstadt (91 k/55 m), a charming village dating from the end of the thirteenth century, its ramparts still intact. The approaches to the town are dotted with country houses built in the Salzburg style, with overhanging roofs, corner turrets, and towers. Leave northwest toward St. Martin, Annaberg, and Lidenthal to

Pass Gschutt, at 3,000 feet (58 k/35 m), then down to

Hallstatt (12 k/7 m). This village clings to the sides of the slopes plunging into Lake Hallstatt. Take some time to stroll through the narrow streets. A number of important excavations of neolithic tombs have been carried out around Hallstatt. The salt mines which brought the earliest residents are still being worked in the Hanging Valley of the Salzberg. Leave Hallstatt east via Obertraun to

Bad Aussee (15 k/9 m), the capital of the Styrian Salzkammergut, surrounded by mountain peaks. Nearby are two picturesque lakes, the Grundisee and the Altausseersee. There is an interesting trail around the latter. Leave northwest to

Bad Ischl (25 k/15 m). A historic watering spot for Austrian royalty, Bad Ischl still retains much of its nineteenth-century elegance and luxury. Its thermal spa is still in use. Leave northeast via Mitterweissenbach, and follow a winding route that touches some of the lakes near Salzburg. Pass via Unterach, Scharfling, Fuschl, Brunn, Feistenau, Hinterwinkel, and Glasenbach to

Salzburg (74 k/44 m). Certainly the gem of the whole trip, Salzburg is worth saving until last. Probably best known as the birthplace of Mozart and for its music festival, it is an old town with narrow streets and historic sites that will take several days to explore thoroughly. Don't miss the Hohensalzburg, the former stronghold of the prince-archbishops, which stands 400 feet above the city on a block of Dolomite rock. The renowned Salzburg Festival is given in August. Mozart's birthplace, at 9 Getreidegasse, is open for tours during the summer months.

### ACCOMMODATIONS

*Locations of Youth Hostels*

Graz
Mureck
Spielfeld
Siemriach
Bruck
Murzzuschlag
Neuberg
Mariazell
Admont
Trautenfels
Pruggererberg
Haus
Schlamding
St. Martin
Gosau
Hallstatt-Lahn
Bad Aussee
Bad Ischl
Salzburg

*Locations of Principal Campgrounds*

Graz
Mureck
Leibnitz
Siemriach
Neuberg
Mariazell
Wildalpen
Grossreifling
Staiach
Schlamding
Hallstatt
Bad Aussee
Unterach
Salzburg

## TOUR #11: THE CHARM AND MAGIC OF BRITTANY

Distance: 522 kilometers/313 miles (including trip to Belle-Île)
Time: 8–10 riding days
Degree of Difficulty: Moderate. The coastal riding involves long, flat rides and some climbing. The interior

is rolling, with some steeper climbs over the head-lands.

Maps: Michelin no. 230 (1:200,000), available both here and in France

Surrounded by the sea and filled with prehistoric traces, Brittany is a land of delicate charm and somber magic. Here a sense of tradition and custom pervade everything from the delicate lace caps to the imposing menhir stones.

Our tour starts with one of the great masterpieces of Western architecture, Mont-St.-Michel. This ancient abbey was started in the eighth century and stands today as a symbol of Brittany and the Breton's ability to live in harmony with the sea. Leaving the abbey you head west and pass through the town of Dol-de-Bretagne, then back up to follow the beautiful Emerald Coast to St.-Malo. This twelfth-century town is full of attractions from the point of view of both pleasure and history. You go south and, following the river Rance, come to the city of Dinan, another picturesque town of ramparts and gardens. Continuing south, you pass through Montauban and into the forest home of Merlin, near Paimpont. Turning east, visit the castle at Josselin before visiting the south coast and the fortified city of Vannes. Turning east, you may visit Saint-Anne-d'Auray before heading down to the sea to the famous menhir beach at Carnac. Here you also have the alternative of riding down the Quiberon peninsula to catch a boat for the Belle-Île, Britany's largest and most beautiful island. From Carnac you skirt the Gulf of Morbihan and ride to La Roche-Bernard, then down to one of the most famous beach resorts in the world, La Baule. St.-Nazaire is the next stop before you conclude your tour in Nantes, the capital of Brittany and gateway to the rest of France.

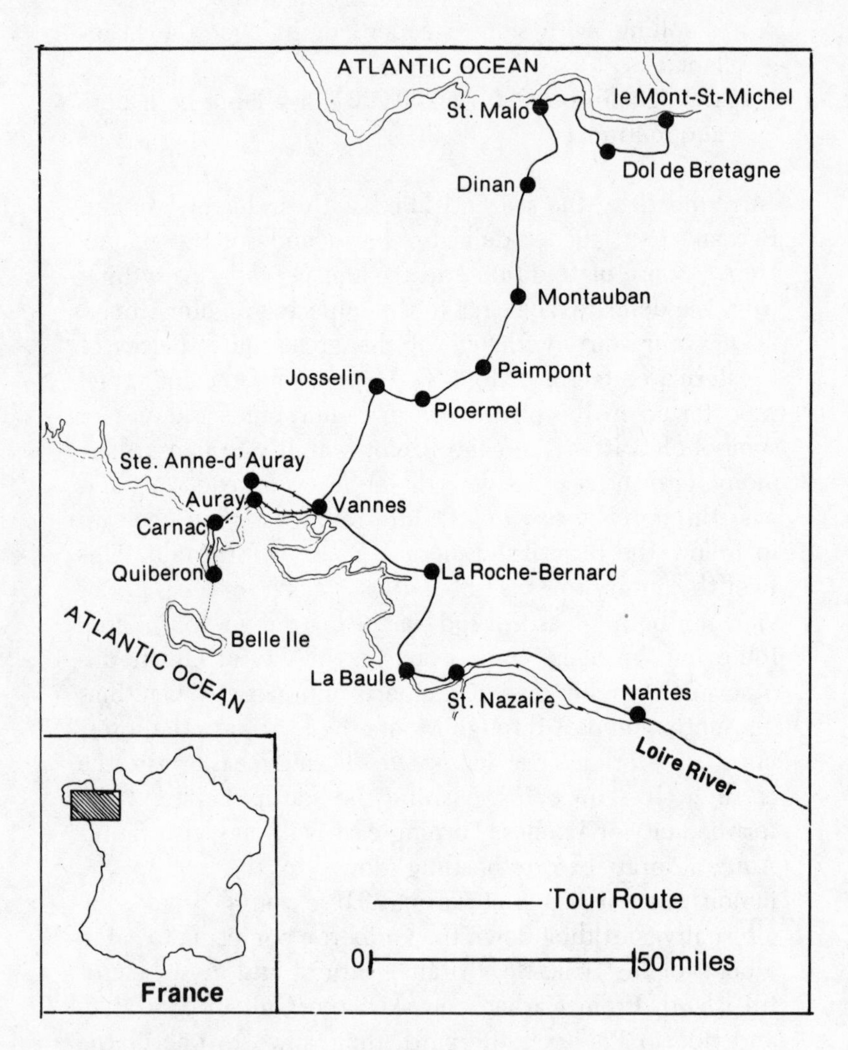


*The Charm and Magic of Brittany*

ITINERARY

Mont-St.-Michel. On this rocky little island stands one of the monuments of the Christian world. The abbey was constructed on its ancient site in the eighth century. All of the granite stones had to be brought across the bay and hauled up the rocky cliffs. Since its beginnings the abbey has undergone many architectural and functional changes. If you can arrange to be there during a new or full moon you'll be able to witness the fantastic force of the Atlantic tides. After visiting the abbey continue west through

Dol-de-Bretagne (28 kilometers/17 miles). Here you can visit the cathedral before continuing north to Mont Dol. This granite mound has yielded the remains of many prehistoric animals and tools. The climb is a stiff one with an average gradient of 1/6 or 16 percent. Continue up to the famous Emerald Coast and around to

St.-Malo (44 k/25 m). The old town of St.-Malo has now merged with the surrounding cities of Paramé and St.-Servan and offers the tourist a number of attractions. St.-Malo is surrounded by ramparts which have been perfectly restored. A walk around them provides many excellent views of the sea and interesting insights into the twelfth-century town. Inside the ramparts you may want to visit the castle and the cathedral. Before leaving you might also consider visiting the Tidal Power Plant that is built on the valley of the river Rance. Leave via St.-Servan and follow the estuary down to Châteauneuf. Cross over the estuary and make your way to

Dinan (30 k/18 m). This is an old town of gardens, winding streets, and beautiful old houses. It is surrounded by ramparts and protected by a castle. A perfect stopover or place to enjoy lunch before continuing on south to

Montauban (40 k/24 m). The château is quite impressive with its tall towers and pepper-pot roof. Continue south into the Forest of Paimpont.

Paimpont (30 k/18 m) is a small village in the heart of the forest. It has a good market and an interesting thirteenth-century church. The surrounding forest once extended from Rennes to Carhaix and was reputed to be the home of the great sorcerer Merlin. Continue through the woods to the southwest to the town of

Ploërmel (24 k/15 m). This was the sixteenth-century seat of the dukes of Brittany. You may visit their house, which, like many of the surrounding houses and the ancient church, is adorned with beautiful woodcarvings. Follow the river Oust to

Josselin (16 k/10 m), the site of the famous Rohan family castle, impressively built on the river Oust. Behind this fortress-mansion is the village, which has many interesting houses and the basilica of Our Lady of the Rosebush. The tour now drops south and crosses the Landes de Lanvaux. For years this area was uninhabited and considered worthless. It is now very fertile and an important agricultural center. You can also see a great many megalithic monuments throughout these moors. Continue south to

Vannes (40 k/24 m). This old town is an important agricultural center. The ramparts and the thirteenth-century cathedral are worth visiting, as well as the Place Henri IV, which has many beautiful fifteenth- and sixteenth-century homes. Leave heading east to

Sainte-Anne-d'Auray (16 k/10 m). This is one of the area's most famous pilgrimages, dating from the early seventeenth century. During the summer many parishes come for the *pardon*, and being present at such a ceremony offers one of the rare opportunities to see the local costumes. From here you can also visit the Carthusian monastery at Charteuse d'Auray before cutting south to

Carnac-Plage (20 k/12 m). Before describing the possibilities at Carnac we propose a side trip down the Quiberon peninsula where you can take a short ferry trip to

Belle-Île, a one-hour boat trip from Quiberon to Le Palais. This lovely little island—only 32 square miles—is full of interesting attractions. It provides the cyclist with some challenging climbing. There are over 140 villages perched above the sea, lush valleys, plateaus, and beautiful beaches. The capital city, Le Palais, is a fortified town with many historical and architectural sites. You can plan a stopover of several days or just go and return in the same day.

Carnac-Plage is perhaps the most famous spot in all of Brittany for the concentration of menhirs. These great monuments were erected between 3500 and 1800 B.C. Little is known about the ancient people who built these monuments, but they must have had a high degree of civilization and technology to plan out and erect these stones. The menhir lines are astronomically perfect and indicate that the people were sun worshipers. The dolmens are thought to be burial chambers. The most outstanding menhirs can be seen in the Menec lines. The other really famous stones can be seen just around the bay at

Locmariaquer (13 k/8 m). Here you visit the Great Menhir and the Merchants Table. The Great Menhir is estimated to weigh over 347 tons and now lies in five pieces. Behind this great stone to the right is the Merchants Table—a massive dolmen that consists of three flat tables with seventeen pointed supports—a tribute to ancient technology. From here you continue up around the Gulf of Morbihan to

Auray (13 k/8 m). An interesting view of this harbor can be seen from the Loc promenade. The old town quarter, St.-Goustan, is also of interest. Continue skirting the gulf; if you haven't already visited Vannes you may do so now.

Vannes (25 k/15 m). For a description of this former capital see page 235 of this tour. Leave for La Roche-Bernard, avoiding, whenever possible, Route N 165.

La Roche-Bernard (45 k/27 m). This town, situated on two rivers, was famous in the seventeenth century for its port. You will want to see the house at 2, Place du Bouffay and those in the Ruicard quarter as well as the famous suspension bridge. Leave for the famous resort

La Baule (35 k/21 m). The jewel of the Atlantic coast is a resort with all the trimmings. If you just want to ride through, it makes a wonderful early morning ride: you will have all the splendor to yourself. Continue along to

St.-Nazaire (28 k/17 m). During the Second World War this was a strategic submarine base. The shipyards and the submarine base may be visited. Leave for Nantes using small roads, as the national is very busy.

Nantes (60 k/36 m). You are now in the capital city of Brittany. It is a city of art as well as an important port at the head of the Loire. The town demands at least one full day to visit. Of outstanding interest are the ducal castle and the cathedral. The cathedral was partially destroyed in 1972, and parts of it may still be closed for restoration. The ducal castle was started in the fifteenth century and is the home of two museums.

This is the end of our Brittany tour. You may now make connections with our tour of the Loire valley and traverse the width of France along one of its most famous rivers.

## ACCOMMODATIONS

*Locations of Youth Hostels*

Cherbourg
St.-Malo
St.-Suliac
Dinan
Quiberon
Saint-Brévin-l'Ocean (near St.-Nazaire)

*Locations of Principal Campgrounds*

Mont-St.-Michel
Dol de Bretagne
Cancale
St.-Malo
Dinan
Paimpont
Ploërmel
Vannes
Quiberon
Le Palais, Port de Goulphar, Port Donnant (Belle-Île)
Locmariaquer
Muzillac
La Roche-Bernard
La Baule
St.-Nazaire
Nantes

## TOUR #12: BLUE WATER PATHWAY TO ATHENS

Distance: 232 kilometers / 139 miles
Time: 3–5 riding days

Degree of Difficulty: Almost all easy, flat riding; some coastal hills on the Saronic Gulf, all of which are only moderately difficult

Maps: Kümmerly+Frey *Greece* (1:1,000,000) is generally available in this country; it is adequate for the tour inasmuch as the route follows the Old National Highway, which is well posted. More detailed maps (Hallwag 1:100,000) are available in Patras, or can be purchased in Athens if the tour is taken in reverse.

The tour of the Old National Highway along the gulfs of Corinth and Saronikos in Greece has a number of attractions for the cyclist. Perhaps most important is the fact that it follows the most accessible route to Athens from the port city of Patras. Cyclists arriving from Italy via either Brindisi or Ancona land at Patras. As Athens is the logical destination for most visitors, the national highway makes the shortest and easiest ride. The route also gives the cyclist a gentle introduction to Greece. Road and town names are indicated in both the Latin and Greek alphabets, making the transition easier for the newcomer. Beyond all that, the route follows along the edge of two lovely bodies of water, the Gulf of Corinth and then the Saronic Gulf. They are quite different: The Gulf of Corinth is calmer, its coastline gentle and scarcely indented, with numerous beaches easily accessible from the road; the Saronic Gulf, on the other hand, is characterized by rocky precipices that plunge down to a deep blue sea. While there are places where beaches and bathing are accessible, they are rarer.

Finally, the route exposes the cyclist to some of the more important archaeological sites in Greece, including the ruins of the ancient city of Corinth, Agamemnon's ancient city of Mycenae, and the striking monastery at Daphni.

In between these important contributions to Western civilization are a multitude of opportunities for bathing in the breathtakingly clear waters, and the first introduction to delicacies such as *souvlaki* and *feta* cheese, not to mention the redoubted resinated Greek wine *retsina.* If the latter is too unusual for the palate, the wine drinker can take comfort in the fact that the tour route also passes through one of Greece's best wine-growing regions, where in autumn loads of grapes can be seen being taken to numerous crushers not far off the road.

The major tour route follows what is known as the Old National Highway. Before the 1960s it was the main road connecting Athens and Patras. Since then, a new toll road has been constructed, which absorbs most of the tourist

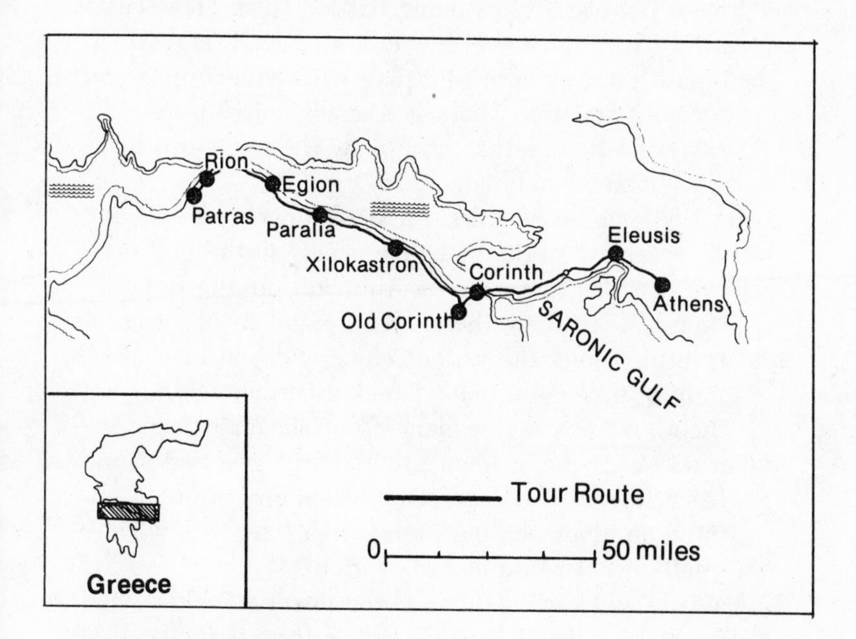


*Blue Water Pathway to Athens*

and much of the local traffic. While the two roads run side by side for much of the way, one never seems to intrude on the other.

Given the popularity of Greece as one of the prime tourist countries in the world, this route is best taken in spring or fall, avoiding the crush of people during July and August. The heat of the Grecian sun also makes touring there very hot during the summer.

We have traveled the road twice in September and have found it quiet; the campgrounds, hostels, and hotels were pleasantly uncrowded.

ITINERARY

Patras. Beginning of the tour. A busy port city, it is also the capitol of a wine-growing region, some of the more popular whites being bottled there. The Turks razed the city in the Revolution of 1821, and it was rebuilt on a modern grid plan with wide streets and spacious squares. There is a small museum and the ruins of a Roman theater. Follow the signs to Athens, staying on the old highway to

Rion (7 kilometers/4 miles), a small town guarding the very narrow straits that give access to the gulf. You can see the twin city of Antirrion on the opposite shore. Near Rion there are a number of pleasant tavernas along the water's edge, and you may catch sight of the first of many Greek fishermen working on their boats as you ride along. Continue on to

Egion (35 k/21 m), a town situated on three tiers rising from the sea. There is a small beach for bathing. Continue on along the old highway passing through the small towns of Krathio and Egira to

Xilokastron (59 k/35 m), one of the towns founded when the exiles from Argos were driven from that city. It is now a popular resort with a good view of the mountains that rise from the other side of the gulf. The beach is good, dotted with pleasantly scented pines. Continue on the road, passing through Kiato. Just before you reach the modern town of Corinth, take the road to your right to the ancient city of

Corinth (34 k/20 m). At one time one of the richest cities in ancient Greece, it is now almost abandoned. Several important ruins remain, including the Temple of Apollo and the Greek-Roman forum. Above the town is an ancient acropolis, whose strategic importance was so great that its control was disputed throughout ancient and most of modern history. Located as it is overlooking the isthmus separating the Peloponnese from the rest of mainland Greece, one can easily see why. Remnants of Turkish, Frankish, and Venetian fortifications can still be seen. The view from the top is one of the finest in all Greece. Double back to the main highway, passing through the new town of Corinth, then on to the high bridge spanning the

Corinthian Canal (11 k/6 m). This narrow waterway, cut through deep cliffs, was a project that preoccupied leaders and military men throughout ancient times. Periander of Corinth, Julius Caesar, and Caligula all had plans to cut such a canal through the narrow isthmus. Nero actually began construction, striking the first blow with a golden pickax, but abandoned efforts due to a rebellion. It was only at the end of the last century, using modern techniques, that the goal was finally accomplished.

You leave the Gulf of Corinth at the bridge and soon see off to your right the Saronic Gulf (the Gulf of Aegina), which you will follow all the way to Athens. Terrain is varied, running from flat delta lands to twisting coastal road. Along the way you skirt the Bay of Salamis, where the Persians were turned back in 480 B.C., changing the course of history. Continue along the bay, through territory increasingly given over to industry and shipbuilding to the ancient site of

Eleusis (61 k/37 m). Little is actually known about the Eleusinian rites that were performed here, although it is believed they had to do with the worship of the goddess Demeter. The performance of the Mysteries was accompanied by torchlight processions, the singing of obscene songs about fertility, and orgiastic dances. As the participants of the rites were sworn to secrecy, their exact nature is lost to us.

From Eleusis continue on the highway to Athens, covering this stretch preferably between 1 and 4 P.M. when traffic will be lighter. Just before reaching Athens stop at the monastery at

Daphni (11 k/6 m), where some of the finest Byzantine mosaics in the world are still remarkably preserved. For campers, there is a campground immediately next to the monastery, and from here there is frequent bus service to downtown Athens. For others, follow the broad, multiple-lane street to the left to

Athens (11 k/6 m). End of the tour. So much has been written about Athens that it would be superfluous to cover it here. The downtown area is exceptionally hectic for bicyclists, and only the most city-hardened riders should try it. We have navigated it during the dead period in the afternoon, alternately riding and walking our bicycles to our destination.

From Piraeus, near Athens, there are ferry connections for all islands in the Aegean, as well as boat service to Turkey, Yugoslavia, Italy, France, and

Spain. Rail connections are available from Athens via Yugoslavia to continental Europe. There is also charter bus service available to London (you must box your bicycle), with stops at a few cities in Italy and France en route.

## ACCOMMODATIONS

*Locations of Youth Hostels*

Mycenae
Athens (reservations recommended)

*Locations of Principal Campgrounds*

Patras
Rion
Egion
Krathio
Daphni
Athens

## TOUR #13: THE SPANISH PYRENEES

Distance: 727 kilometers/436 miles
Time: 10–15 riding days
Degree of Difficulty: While there are some basins and valleys where riding is easy or moderate, much of the tour will involve hard climbs followed by descents into neighboring valleys.
Maps: Michelin maps nos. 42 and 43 (1:400,000), available in this country and in bookstores in Spain

While hundreds of thousands of tourists are drawn each year to the resorts on Spain's Atlantic and Mediterranean coasts, the Spanish Pyrenees remain relatively unvisited.

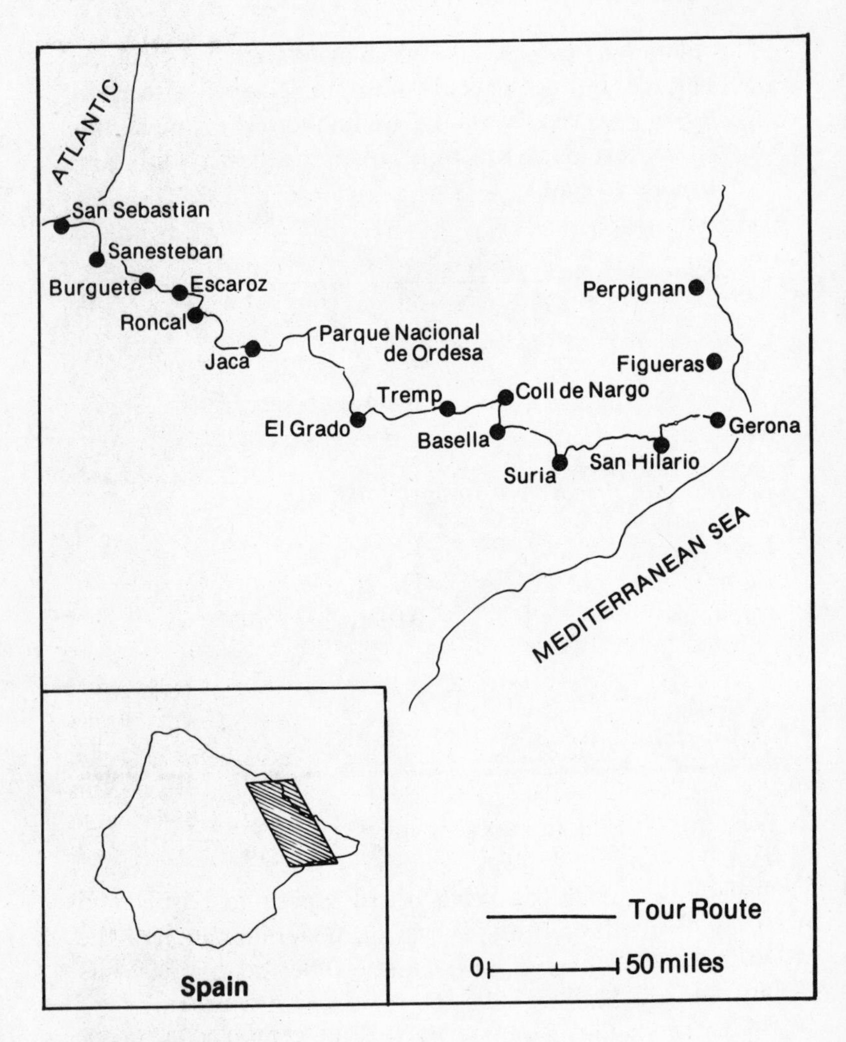


*The Spanish Pyrenees*

This fact alone might make the bicycle tourist perk up his or her ears. But beyond all that, the Pyrenees are as attractive a mountain range as can be found in Europe. The weather is excellent; the scenery is a bit softer than the Alps; and there is a fine mixture of mountain meadows and fields under cultivation, much of the work still done by hand and with animals. In contrast to these pastoral scenes are distant peaks and looming limestone bluffs, clustered in clouds, sunlight playing on hues of green and black.

Add to these attractions a network of small mountain roads uncluttered with automobile traffic (a distinct problem elsewhere in Spain), and you have all the necessary ingredients for a superb bicycle tour.

All that remains are the mountains. The cycling is generally hard. Although no great elevations are reached, most of the route running between 1,000 and 3,000 feet elevation, the Pyrenees drain uniformly southward. As the tour runs basically in a west-to-east direction, the cyclist crosses these streams at right angles, with a series of climbs and descents into river valleys. At times road surfaces will not be up to standards for the rest of Europe. While this may deter the cycle tourist uninterested in mountain travel, the Pyrenees do not require superhuman effort. Anyone in reasonably good condition can make the tour. Moreover, there are a number of long stints down river valleys where cycling is easy, and numerous climbs that are only moderate in difficulty.

The rewards of the tour more than compensate for the energy required. Everywhere you will find a warmth and openness in the people that you will carry with you long after your trip ends.

While most of the people en route speak Spanish, you actually pass through two regions that are the homes of other distinct language groups. The western Pyrenees is the home of the Basques, while the eastern part towards Barcelona is Catalonia (in Spanish, Cataluña), something of a mixture of provincial French and Spanish.

The tour starts in San Sebastián, a city of wide boulevards, spacious parks, a substantial gypsy population, an excellent seaport, fine sandy beaches, and some of the handsomest men and women in Europe. From here you head up into the Pyrenees, scalloping the high ranges, passing your days in mountain valleys where sheep and cow herding are still major occupations, passing through villages that offer a stark simplicity appealing to the person interested in uncovering the still "undiscovered" parts of Europe. Midway in the tour is a transition into Catalonia, where the mountains to the north of you rise more spectacularly, the forest is greener, and the people are a mixture of practicality and warmth. Continuing eastward, you end in the town of Gerona, not far from the Mediterranean, a cathedral city midway between Barcelona and the French border. Rail and road connections are available here either for other parts of Spain or for France.

Persons interested in taking only part of the tour may terminate it at a number of points where rail connections are available (Jaca, Tremp, or Vich), or by taking any of the numerous passes leading into France.

## ITINERARY

San Sebastián. Start of the tour. Set in a beautiful blue inlet, San Sebastián has been known for centuries as the jewel of the Cantabrian Coast. The bay is ringed by two long beaches where shopgirls and office workers come to sun during the long break for lunch. The old town is a place of narrow streets, where the gourmet can spend hours comparing restaurant menus before making a choice for dinner. Two indoor markets within the newer part of the city are crammed with the produce of the sea and fruits and vegetables from all over Europe. Leave southeastward, avoiding the national highway, via Oyarzun, Lesaca, and Ventas de Yanci to

Santesteban (58 kilometers/35 miles), a pleasant city on the Bidassoa River. Leave south via Berroeta, Almandoz, and Ventas de Arraiz to

Olague (30 k/18 m), where you turn east on a small road, passing via Iragui, Zubiri, and Mezquiriz, to the outskirts of

Burguete (39 k/23 m), where you take the road to Escaroz, via Garralda, Garayoa, and Jaurrieta. At Escaroz turn north to Ochagavia, then head east to

Isaba (53 k/32 m), where you are in the picturesque valley of Roncal. A typical isolated valley of the Pyrenees, it clings steadfastly to old traditions. It is known for its sheep raising and the cheese that bears the valley's name. Pass south through the town of Roncal, then turn left 2 kilometers south of town. A stiff climb of about 10 kilometers brings you to a crest where you have a spectacular view of the small town of Ansó lying below you. Wind down to

Ansó (20 k/12 m). From here head down the valley, where at nightfall you may still see cowherds in traditional round, black hats bringing in their herds from pasture. At

Berdun (25 k/15 m) you intersect the river Aragon, which you follow to the town of

Jaca (28 k/17 m). Jaca was a fortified town guarding the Aragon Valley and played an important part in repulsing the Moorish invasion in the eighth century. In the eleventh century it was named the capitol of

Aragon. Its cathedral, dating from that time, is one of the oldest in Spain. A small museum within the cathedral contains Romanesque and Gothic paintings. Leave Jaca east via Guasa to

Sabiñánigo (18 k/11 m), in the valley of the Gállego. Go upstream toward Biescas, where you head east again on a pretty road (and a good climb) to the town of Torla. From here, head north 9 kilometers to the

Parque Nacional de Ordesa (45 k/27 m). Known for its dense forests and outcroppings of limestone cliffs, the park is one of the loveliest natural resources of Spain. A number of footpaths take you into the interior, with views of waterfalls, caves, and canyons plunging below you. A thorough exploration will take most of the day. When leaving, backtrack to Torla, then continue southward via Broto, Fiscal, and Boltana, to

Ainsa (49 k/29 m). Ainsa is an ancient town that was the center of resistance to the Moors. It stands on a cliff overlooking the confluence of the Cinca and Ara rivers. The houses are of rough stone, and the main square is worth a visit with its arcades and Romanesque church. Leave Ainsa south via the road that scallops the hills above the El Grado lakes to El Grado, where you turn east for

Graus (67 k/40 m), a town with an interesting square lined by old houses with painted beams and brick arcades. Graus is at the head of one of the region's many artificial lakes. Leave via the road to Benabarre and Tolva to

Tremp (51 k/31 m), which marks a turning point in the tour. You have passed into the land of Cataluña, where the native language is an offshoot of the ancient language of Oc of southern France. Tremp lies in a great basin from which you leave in an easterly direction and a stiff climb to the pass just beyond Boixols (1,340 meters), the high point of the entire tour. There are fantastic vistas all along the high route around Boixols, shortly after which you descend down a winding, pretty road to

Coll de Nargo (58 k/35 m), in the Segre valley. Follow the road downstream to Basella, where you turn east and head up again to

Solsona (47 k/28 m), a very attractive medieval town that lies below the ruins of an ancient castle. Its cathedral dates from the Romanesque period. The Diocesan Museum has an excellent twelfth-century fresco. Leave southeast on the road to

Cardona (20 k/12 m), where, if you arrive early or are lucky enough, you may stay in the paradore created out of the castle of the Dukes of Cardona. The collegiate church there was consecrated in 1040 and is an excellent example of the Lombard style of architecture. Leave via the road to Suria, then turn northeast to make your way over a headland to the town of Balsareny, then continue on to the town of

Vich (81 k/49 m), a thriving industrial town known for the manufacture of leather and textiles. The cathedral dates from the eleventh century. Leave Vich east through scented pine forests, passing the town of

San Hilario Sacalm (36 k/22 m), a popular resort town known for its fine air. Leave north via the small road to Angles, then follow the river Ter to the end of the tour at

Gerona (43 k/26 m), a bustling modern town with a charming central area which is centuries old. Here the streets are narrow and winding, and above you are balconies fenced by wrought-iron railings. The cathedral is the crowning point of the city, with its

90 steps leading to massive front doors. Within is a treasury with fourteenth- and fifteenth-century gold and silver plate, and a tapestry dating from the twelfth century.

You may make rail connections in Gerona for either France or Barcelona. If you wish to bicycle to Barcelona, don't take the coast road, which, while pretty, is hopelessly crowded with automobile traffic; there are quieter routes inland. Barcelona itself is surrounded by sprawling suburbs, and the town center is best approached by means other than bicycle.

You can bicycle to the French border via a number of small roads. En route are the town of Figueras, where a Salvador Dali museum is being created, and not far away is the ancient Roman settlement at Ampurias, near the sea. You may enter France at either Port-Bou or le Perthus. Avoid the *route nationale* going into Perpignan.

## ACCOMMODATIONS

### *Locations of Youth Hostels*

San Sebastián
Villanua (north of Jaca)
Pueyo de Jaca (north of Biescas)
Gerona

### *Locations of Principal Campgrounds*

San Sebastián
Jaca
Torla
Figueras (near Gerona)

## TOUR #14: THE GRAND TOUR—LONDON TO ATHENS

In the eighteenth and nineteenth centuries it was considered the final polishing for an educated gentleman (and for a woman fortunate enough to come from an enlightened family) to take a year or so off from all ordinary pursuits and tour the Continent. These year-long stays were oriented primarily toward cultural absorption, but there was also an aspect of freedom—of escaping the restraints of home-town America—inherent in the idea of being on one's own for a year.

It is in the spirit of both these concepts that we offer a tour from London to Athens. While you won't take a year to complete it, it can absorb the better part of the cycling season. During this time you will touch base with some important aspects of our cultural heritage, from the neolithic monuments on the Salisbury Plain in England to the cradle of Western thought in Greece. In between you pass remnants of the Roman Empire and see some of the masterpieces of the Renaissance.

All of this tour can be covered by bicycle, with the exceptions of the ferry crossings between England and Spain and Italy and Greece. But we have also indicated stretches that you may wish to cover by train—primarily to avoid traffic build-up on certain well-traveled roads.

In designing the tour, we have taken advantage of some of the itineraries developed in the previous pages. We have made broad connecting links between them, singling out major pathways and some of the important things you will see en route.

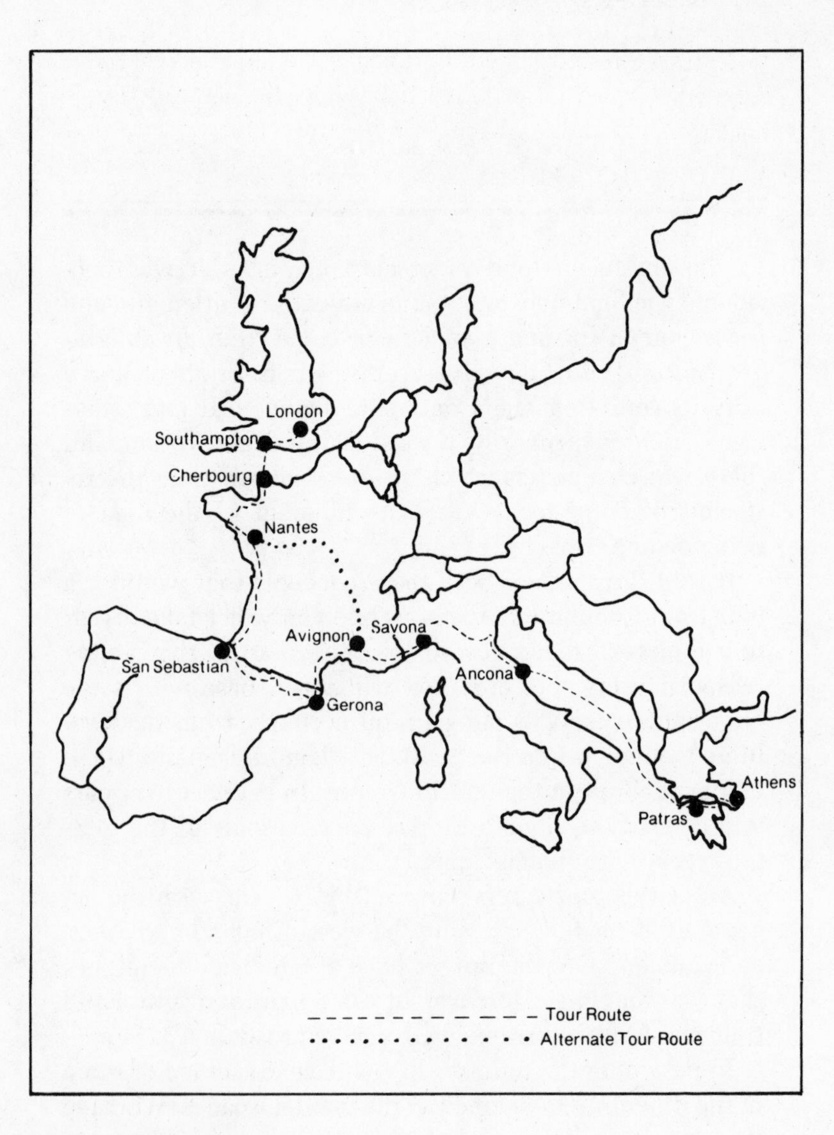


*The Grand Tour*

In addition to the main tour route, we have developed a somewhat easier alternative that omits the Spanish Pyrenees and takes advantage of the natural waterways formed by the Loire and Rhone rivers to get you through France with fewer hills.

Following either tour route will take you at least two months, and an entire summer could easily be spent. If you take circuitous side trips, as we have often done—nestling for three weeks in an orchard in France to pick cherries, or lazing on a beach for several weeks in Greece—time seems to escape into some other dimension entirely.

If you start the tour in England, the month of May is about the earliest you can expect consistently good cycling weather. Even at that, there will be days of rain. Early-season travelers are advised to take the main tour route, as it goes through Spain, which has excellent springtime weather. If you are doing the tour in reverse, you can begin in mid or late April from Athens—but don't expect the weather to be balmy enough for swimming. Northern Italy, through which the tour passes, is also wet in April, so plan accordingly.

### SECTION I: LONDON TO SOUTHAMPTON

Distance: 261 miles/421 kilometers
Maps: Bartholomew GT Series nos. 5 and 2

This section takes advantage of the tour of southern England described earlier, routing you from London (or preferably Canterbury if you want to escape London's heavy traffic) via Battle, Winchester, Salisbury, and Stonehenge. From the famous neolithic monument on the Salisbury Plain you leave the regular tour route and travel a short distance of some 20 miles to the seaport of Southampton, where there are regular ferries during the summer months to Cherbourg, on the French coast. Persons wishing to see more of England than just this small stretch may take the entire tour of southern England, then proceed directly to Southampton from the end of the regular tour route in London.

See the tour of England (Tour # 2) for details of your route.

SECTION II: CHERBOURG TO NANTES

Distance: 742 kilometers/445 miles
Maps: Michelin maps nos. 54 and 230

This section of the tour takes you through the rolling countryside of the Cotentin Peninsula. Cherbourg is the principal port of arrival for the region. During the invasion of Normandy in World War II the town served as the chief supply port for Allied forces. A short side trip to the southeast will take you to the famous landing points of that invasion, Utah and Omaha beaches. In Cherbourg itself is an interesting museum of the war and liberation (Musée de la Guerre et da la Libération). The church of the Trinity and the Hôtel de Ville are also interesting. From Cherbourg head south via Bricquebec, Lessay, and then toward the coast, passing Coutainville and Tourville Montmartin to

Granville (110 kilometers/66 miles). From here you can stay along the coast via Avranches to

Mont-St.-Michel (110 k/66 m). Here you pick up the tour of Brittany (Tour #11) described earlier in this chapter. Should you wish to exclude the Brittany tour, you may head directly south via Rennes and Nort to Nantes, the termination point of that tour. Nantes is also the departure point for the alternate to the Grand Tour which we describe later.

SECTION III: NANTES TO SAN SEBASTIÁN (SPAIN)

Distance: 527 kilometers / 313 miles
Maps: Michelin maps nos. 67, 71, and 78

This part of the tour starts in rolling agricultural country typical of this part of France, scallops along the sea at several points, includes a brief ferry crossing over the Gironde river, then winds down through some of the world's most renowned wine regions in Bordeaux. From Bordeaux south you pass through a densely forested area known as Les Landes, where quiet roads thread through tall alleys of pines. As you exit from Les Landes, you touch briefly at some of France's best-known Atlantic coast resorts, a bit more staid and elegant than the Riviera along the Mediterranean. From Bayonne, you have a choice of covering the last stretch into San Sebastián by train (which we recommend) or by cycling over an exceptionally busy highway.

Nantes. For description, see the tour of Brittany (Tour # 11). Leave to the south, passing via Touvois, Commequiers, and l'Aiguillon-sur-Vie, to

Le Sables-d'Olonne (96 kilometers/58 miles), where you meet the Atlantic again. From Les Sables-d'Olonne, it is possible to trace a variety of routes that take you through an area reclaimed from the sea to

La Rochelle (110 k/66 m), an ancient seaport, once a bastion of the Protestant faith, but finally conquered by the forces of Cardinal Richelieu. La Rochelle remains an important seaport and fishing town. Walk around the old sea walls or treat yourself to some exquisite seafood at any number of restaurants. Leave La Rochelle to the south, avoiding the Route National 137 and passing via Rochefort, then make your way via small roads south to

Royan (85 k/51 m), a town on the estuary of the Gironde river. From Royan there is a ferry service across the Gironde to

Pointe de Grave (about 8 k by ferry). From Pointe de Grave you should keep along the banks of the Gironde. You will pass through a series of towns and villages whose names read like the wine list of an elegant restaurant. Among the famous labels you may recognize will be Châteaux Mouton-Rothschild and Lafite-Rothschild in the commune of Pauillac and Château Margaux in the commune of Margaux. They lie within what is known as the Médoc region of the Bordeaux growing area. As you near Bordeaux, swing westward and circle the town. Should you wish to visit, leave your bicycle at the station in Blanquefort and take the train in. On the other side of Bordeaux you will pass into an absolutely flat, completely forested area known as

Les Landes. Reclaimed from the marshes, the Landes is something of a cyclist's dream. Scented pine forests, a network of quiet roads, and houses that seem to be more Swedish than French combine to make an impression unlike anything else you have experienced so far on the tour. (It was in the Landes that we were treated to the unexpected fireworks display related in Chapter 6.) There are no towns of any size until you are in the southern part of the Landes, but there are excellent camping possibilities, and most of the towns along the route have a number of hotels to choose from. As the road network gives you considerable latitude of route choice, either staying inland or passing near the coast, we have left specific route planning to you. As you leave the southern edge of the Landes, continue south via the coastal road to

Bayonne (about 180 k/108 m from Bordeaux). The road from Bayonne to San Sebastián in Spain was discussed in Chapter 6. If you are up to that kind of traffic, take it. Otherwise, we recommend crossing this section via train. You can also swing away from the coast and proceed to San Sebastián via one of the passes inland from the main road.

San Sebastián (46 k/28 m). The start of the tour of the Spanish Pyrenees (Tour #13). For a description of San Sebastián see that tour.

### SECTION IV: SAN SEBASTIÁN TO GERONA

See our tour of the Spanish Pyrenees (Tour #13) for route and tour itinerary.

### SECTION V: GERONA TO AVIGNON (FRANCE)

Distance: 450 kilometers/276 miles
Maps: Michelin maps nos. 43, 86, and 83

From the termination of the Spanish tour at Gerona, you can make your way via two or three routes into France. The easiest is the low pass at Le Perthus, the route used by invaders from Hannibal's time to that of Napolean. Once across the border, you are in an area of France known as Roussillon, and you commence a long crescent-like route that runs between the sea and the mountains of the Massif Central. The first part of the crescent is one of the greatest wine-producing regions of the world in terms of quantity, although there are few vineyards there of outstanding merit. Later on the route opens up as you pass through the delta regions of the Rhone river. Morning cycling is recommended here, as the winds coming down the Rhone can be exceptionally strong if the mistral is blowing. Whatever you do in crossing the stretch from the Spanish frontier to Arles, avoid the main roads, Routes Nationales 9, 113, and 108. They are exceptionally busy in summer and can be dangerous. There are nearly always plenty of side roads that are more scenic and infinitely quieter. Some will go up into the limestone hills, others will skirt the sea. The Mediterranean along this crescent is noted for its long, sandy beaches, so be certain to avail yourself of the opportunity for a dip or two.

Leave Gerona, passing via Banyoles, Figueras, and Le Perthus to

Céret (80 k/48 m), just inside the French border. At one time the home of Picasso, Braque, and Gris, Céret is a lovely town set in a valley of the Pyrenees. Picasso worked here before the First World War. Some of the first cubist paintings were done in the house he rented at 3, rue des Evadés. Just around the corner is an adjacent square and a home that lacks any distinction whatsoever, except for us, since we used to live there. The enchantment of this Catalan town is still very much a part of our lives. We stayed here for two years. Leave Céret via the Col de Llauro, a 7-kilometer climb, then descend to Thuir, and continue via Tuchan to

Narbonne (135 k/81 m), a pleasant cathedral city. From Narbonne you can make an interesting side trip to the walled medieval city of Carcassonne, which has been completely restored and is one of the most important sites of its kind in Europe. Return to Narbonne, and leave via small roads to

Béziers (30 k/18 m), situated on a high hill overlooking the river Orb. In the twelfth century, hundreds of religious martyrs were thrown from the embankment opposite the main cathedral. As Béziers is situated on a bluff, you may want to view it from afar and continue on, keeping to small roads to

Montpellier (90 k/54 m). A university town and a cultural and educational center for all of France, Montpellier is a bustling city that you may wish to skirt. If so, keep toward the coast and continue on a series of side roads to

Nîmes (65 k/39 m), where you can see some important Roman ruins, primarily a well-preserved temple (Maison Carée) built during the reign of Augustus. Nîmes also has a number of museums, notably the archeological museum and the Musée du Vieux Nîmes. The remains of a Roman gate can be seen at the Porte d'Arles. Leave via Beaucaire, Tarascon, and back roads up the Rhone to

Avignon (50 k/36 m). This was the seat of the papacy in the fourteenth century. The popes built a series of castles in Avignon, of which The Palais des Papes may still be visited. Also at Avignon is the famous bridge, now almost in ruins, that inspired the little song ("On the Bridge at Avignon") that French schoolchildren still memorize and sing. The Calvet Museum houses an important collection of prehistoric stoneware, Greek marbles, and some masterpieces by Brueghel, Manet, Delacroix, Renoir, Cézanne, Dufy, Utrillo, and Toulouse-Lautrec. The cathedral is also worth visiting.

Those who have taken the alternate route along the Loire and Rhône rivers rejoin the tour at Avignon.

SECTION VI: AVIGNON TO NICE

Distance: 323 kilometers / 194 miles
Maps: Michelin map no. 84

Avignon. See preceding section for description. Leave Avignon from the south toward

Arles (40 kilometers/24 miles), the home of Van Gogh for a time. Charming, and thoroughly southern in character, Arles also boasts two important remnants of the Roman Empire, the Theater and the Amphitheater. Both are worth a visit. Leave Arles to the northeast via Fontvielle, Eyguieres, and Salon de Provence, then turn south to

Aix-en-Provence (80 k/48 m). A lovely university town, immortalized by Paul Cézanne, Aix-en-Provence has large shaded streets, a cathedral whose baptistery dates from the fourth and fifth centuries, and a former archbishop's palace, now the Museum of Tapestries. Leave Aix to the north via Peyrolles, then go via Rians, Tavernes, and Salernes to

Draguignan (115 k/69 m), a pretty town with wide boulevards and an interesting old section. Leaving, you climb a steep hill. You have little choice of route here: you will be on a main road connecting Draguignan and Grasse. Traffic is not horrendous, but it can be heavy in August. The road is nonetheless pretty, and you will pass through typical Provençal scenery. We were camping next to an abandoned farmhouse one night and were awakened by a herd of wild pigs snorting through the undergrowth, snapping pine cones open to get the seeds. They strolled leisurely within feet of the tent, where we waited, not so leisurely, for them to disappear into the night. A lone hound bayed somewhere in the distance until dawn. Stay on the main road to

Grasse (56 k/34 m), the perfume capital of the world. Some of the most distinctive names in this industry are located in Grasse. The elegant scents are detectable from some distance away if the wind is right. You will climb to get to Grasse, so you might want to rest and take a free tour of one of the perfumeries. From Grasse, stay on the main road, which is a long downhill run to Villeneuve-Loubet, and then take the road along the coast (busy, but fairly wide at most points) to

Nice (32 k/19 m). For a long time the center of the Côte d'Azur, Nice has maintained its distinctive southern character while accommodating the thousands of summer tourists who flock here. You can swim at any one of a number of beaches (all very pebbly), or stroll along the long Promenade des Anglais, named after the nation (England) which put Nice on the tourist map. When you've had enough of the sea head toward the old town for some narrow streets, birds perched in cages suspended from windows high above you, or take in some good cooking *à la Niçoise*.

### SECTION VII: NICE TO SAVONA (ITALY)

Distance: 129 kilometers/177 miles

Maps: Michelin map no. 84, Touring Club of Italy Grandi Carte no. 10

There is really only one route between these two points—the coastal road that rises and falls along the Mediterranean. It has considerable automobile traffic in summer, but is cyclable if you don't mind traffic. You can avoid all this quite easily by taking the train. Connections between

Nice and Savona are direct, and trains are frequent. If you cycle, leave via the low *corniche* road and keep toward the sea. Leave Nice via Villefranche and Beaulieu to

Monaco (25 kilometers/15 miles). This luxurious resort bears all the trappings of an established playland for the well-to-do. The small casino is open for visits. Also of interest is the port with its yachts from around the world, and of course the palace of the prince and princess of Monaco. Keep on the road toward the sea, passing via Cap-Martin to

Menton (12 k/7 m), a resort town that mixes French and Italian cultures nicely. Continue along the coast to the

Italian frontier (3 k/2 m), where you may secure good detailed maps of Italy from the border post. There are discounts if you are a member of an automobile club. Continue on via the coast road to

San Remo (17 k/10 m), a pretty town on a hill overlooking the sea. It has a number of luxurious resort hotels and some expansive villas on the hills above town. Continue on the coast road, passing a number of towns along the Riviera di Ponente, none of which have any of the splendor or class of their French counterparts to

Savona (72 k/43 m), the beginning of the tour of northern Italy (Tour #4) described earlier in this chapter.

### SECTION VIII: SAVONA TO ANCONA

See the tour of northern Italy (Tour #4) described on pages 197–203.

### SECTION IX: PATRAS TO ATHENS

See the tour of Greece (Tour #12) described on pages 241–247.

## ALTERNATE ROUTE: FROM NANTES TO AVIGNON

The alternate route leaves the main tour at Nantes, on the Loire river in western France. Its principal advantage over the main route is that it uses the natural pathways created by the Loire and Rhône rivers. By following the Loire into its upper reaches, the cyclist has an essentially easy ride. From a point near Roanne on the Loire, you can cross a narrow headland (about 60 kilometers) into the Rhône valley. The Rhône heads directly south to the Mediterranean. The one great disadvantage of the route is that it excludes Spain, which gives the cyclist some beautiful mountain scenery and generally better weather. On the other hand, the Loire route lends itself to some side trips up into Alsace and the German Black Forest (see tours in this chapter).

The alternate route winds up the Loire, through the château country, then touches some pretty river towns, including Nevers, La Charité, and Decize. Finally the Loire passes through some deep gorges, and a small road permits the cyclist to enjoy the route with only one stiff climb out of the valley. Dropping toward the Rhône, you head down the east bank over rolling country. There is a more direct route on the other side of the river if you are hurried and don't mind traffic. The road to avoid here at all costs is the Route National 7 on the east bank. It is impossible, gorged with truck traffic, badly paved on the shoulder, and just plain dangerous to be on, day or night. There are plenty of alternatives, and you should take the rolling route, preferring the hills to the mayhem below. As you make your way down the Rhône, the feeling of the country changes markedly. The farther south you go the drier it gets, the rich soil of the north giving way to a rockier, harsher terrain, where hills have been terraced to give crops a chance for better growth. Still, there are scenic orchards, and on the west bank of the Rhône are the famous Côtes du Rhône, which produce an excellent red wine.

For the first section of this alternate route, from Nantes to Cosne-sur-Loire, see our tour of the Loire valley (Tour # 7, pages 213–218) for details.

The second section of this alternate route takes you from Cosne-sur-Loire to Avignon.

Distance: 532 kilometers/219 miles
Maps: Michelin maps nos. 69, 91, and 93

The route traces the Loire along its upper reaches where the river itself is prettier than down below; it loses its shallow character, the banks closing in more tightly around it. The rolling country along the east bank of the Rhône is agricultural land. As you continue south you encounter numerous remnants of the Roman Empire, once very firmly established in this part of France.

Cosne-sur-Loire. See the Loire tour for description. Leave Cosne on the western side of the river (opposite town), and proceed to

Nevers (66 kilometers/40 miles). En route to Nevers, the town of La Charité, across the river, is worth a visit. Remains of a monastery and the walls that surrounded the town can be visited. Nevers is a busy river city, but if you leave your bicycle below and walk through some of its old streets higher up you will gain a different impression. Its cathedral is worth a visit. Leave Nevers, again crossing to the western side of the river. Keep to that bank as much as possible to

Roanne (172 k/103 m), a pretty stretch of the Loire, with some rising and falling as you make your way over the headlands. After Roanne you head up into the

Gorges of the Loire, breaking out of the valley some miles upstream. At this point you must make a crossing into the Rhône valley. The best point to do so is from Feurs, cutting overland to Vienne, just south of Lyon. Should you wish to visit Lyon, take the train in from Vienne. The road between is busy; Lyon is France's second largest city, bristling with traffic.

Vienne (68 k/41 m) is an important town on the Rhone. It has a number of interesting churches and the ruins of a château overlooking the river. Leave via the road to Beaurepaire, then continue south to Romans-sur-Isère, and continue directly south to

Crest (102 k/61 m). Crest is an interesting town on the Drôme river, which flows directly out of the Alps. The old city has narrow streets, some completely enclosed by the buildings overhead, creating subterranean-like tunnels. High above everything else is an ancient dungeon (*donjon*), which knew its share of misery and death. The rooms may still be visited. Leave south via Grignan, then take any number of small back roads to

Orange (87 k/52 m). This ancient town has the largest Roman theater extant in Europe. Plays are still performed here each summer. There is an even older Roman triumphal arch, the third largest in Europe. It was built to honor the conquering legions of Caesar. Leave south through Châteauneuf-du-Pape to

Avignon (37 k/22 m), where you rejoin the main route from London to Athens. See page 263 for a description of Avignon.

## ACCOMMODATIONS

For the locations of youth hostels and campgrounds in

Sections I, IV, VIII, IX, and Alternate Route Section One, see listings at end of each section or previous tour above.

*Locations of Youth Hostels*

(Section II: Cherbourg to Mont-St.-Michel)

| | |
|---|---|
| Cherbourg | Genêts |

(Section III: Nantes to San Sebastián)

| | |
|---|---|
| La Rochelle | Fuenterrabia |
| Bordeaux | San Sebastián |
| Anglet | |

(Section V: Gerona to Avignon)

| | |
|---|---|
| Gerona | Mèze |
| Perpignan | Nîmes |

(Section VI: Avignon to Nice)

| | |
|---|---|
| Tarascon | Aix-en-Provence |
| Arles | Nice |

(Section VII: Nice to Savona)

| | |
|---|---|
| Menton | Finale Marina |

(Alternate Route Section Two: Cosne to Avignon)

| | |
|---|---|
| Roanne | Rivière |
| Lyon-Venissieux | Valence |

*Locations of Principal Campgrounds*

(Section II: Cherbourg to Mont-St.-Michel)

| | |
|---|---|
| Cherbourg | Avranches |
| Granville | Mont-St.-Michel |

(Section III: Nantes to San Sebastián)

| | |
|---|---|
| Les Sables-d'Olonne | Bayonne |
| La Rochelle | San Sebastián |
| Royan | |

(Section V: Gerona to Avignon)

Céret
Narbonne
Montpellier
Pont du Gard (near route)

(Section VI: Avignon to Nice)

Arles
Aix-en-Provence
Draguignan
Grasse
Nice

(Section VII: Nice to Savona)

Menton
San Remo
Savona

(Alternate Route Section Two: Cosne to Avignon)

Cosne
Nevers
Decize
Roanne
Vienne
Orange

APPENDIX 1

# Estimated weight and expenses

The following is a breakdown of estimated weight and expenses for the three modes of independent travel. Weight estimates are based on lightweight equipment specifically designed for cycling or adapted from lightweight camping equipment. The estimates do not include the weight of the bicycle, packs, or panniers. The minimum and maximum cost per day estimates for restaurants, hotels (based on double occupancy), campgrounds, and hostels were those prevailing throughout Europe in 1978–79. Incidental expenses such as postage and gifts are not included in the estimates.

LIGHTWEIGHT TOURIST

| *Equipment* | *Weight* |
|---|---|
| Personal clothing | 5 |
| Toilet articles | 1 |
| Sleep sheet (optional) | 0.5 |
| Small mess kit (optional) | 1 |
| Miscellaneous | 3 |
| *Total Weight* | 10.5 pounds |

| *Accommodations* | *Cost per person* | |
|---|---|---|
| | *Minimum* | *Maximum* |
| Hotel | $5.00 | $16.00 |

| *Meals* | | |
|---|---|---|
| Breakfast (eaten out) | 1.50 | 1.50 |
| Lunch (self-prepared) | 1.50 | 2.50 |
| Dinner (eaten out)* | 5.00 | 8.00 |
| *Total Daily Food Costs* | $8.00 | $12.00 |

SUMMARY

| | | |
|---|---|---|
| Weight | 10.5 Pounds | |
| Cost—food and lodgings (hotel) | $13.00 | $28.00 |

*Prices include wine.

CAMPER TOURIST

| *Equipment* | *Weight* |
|---|---|
| Personal clothing | 5 |
| Toilet articles | 1 |
| Sleeping bag | 2.5 |
| Sleeping pad | 1 |
| Butane stove and cartridge | 1.5 |
| Cooking kit | 1.5 |
| Food bag (staple food) | 3 |
| Tent | 2 |
| Miscellaneous (camera, tools, etc.) | 3 |
| *Total Weight* | 20.5 pounds |

| *Accommodations* | *Cost per person* | |
|---|---|---|
| | *Minimum* | *Maximum* |
| Campgrounds | $ .50 | $2.50 |

| *Meals* | | |
|---|---|---|
| Breakfast (self-prepared) | .50 | 1.50 |
| Lunch (self-prepared) | 1.50 | 2.50 |
| Dinner (self-prepared) | 1.50 | 3.00 |
| *Total Daily Food Costs* | $3.50 | $7.00 |

SUMMARY

| | | |
|---|---|---|
| Weight | 20.5 pounds | |
| Costs—food and lodging (campgrounds) | $4.00 | $9.50 |

HOSTELER TOURIST

| *Equipment* | *Weight* |
|---|---|
| Personal clothing | 5 |
| Toilet articles | 1 |
| Sleeping bag | 2.5 |
| Sleeping pad | 1 |
| Butane stove and cartridge | 1.5 |
| Mess kit | 1 |
| Sleep sheet (nylon) | 0.5 |
| Miscellaneous (books, tools, etc.) | 3 |
| *Total Weight* | 15.5 pounds |

| *Accommodations* | *Cost per person* | |
|---|---|---|
| | *Minimum* | *Maximum* |
| Hostel | $1.00 | $ 4.00 |
| *Meals* | | |
| Breakfast (self-prepared) | .50 | 1.50 |
| Lunch (self-prepared) | 1.50 | 2.50 |
| Dinner (self-prepared) | 1.50 | 3.50 (eaten in hostel) |
| *Total Daily Food Costs* | $3.50 | $ 7.50 |

SUMMARY

| | | |
|---|---|---|
| Weight | 15.5 pounds | |
| Costs—food and lodgings | $4.50 | $11.50 |

APPENDIX 2

# Average temperature and precipitation in Europe

AUSTRIA

| City | Altitude | May | June | July | Aug. | Sept. |
|---|---|---|---|---|---|---|
| Innsbruck | 1970 | | | | | |
| T | | 55 | 62 | 64 | 63 | 57 |
| P | | 2.7 | 4.0 | 5.0 | 4.5 | 3.4 |
| Vienna | 636 | | | | | |
| T | | 56 | 63 | 66 | 65 | 58 |
| P | | 2.8 | 2.8 | 3.1 | 2.7 | 2.0 |

BELGIUM

| City | Altitude | May | June | July | Aug. | Sept. |
|---|---|---|---|---|---|---|
| Brussels | 328 | | | | | |
| T | | 55 | 61 | 63 | 63 | 59 |
| P | | 2.2 | 2.6 | 2.9 | 2.9 | 2.6 |

BRITISH ISLES

| City | Altitude | May | June | July | Aug. | Sept. |
|---|---|---|---|---|---|---|
| London | 18 | | | | | |
| T | | 54 | 60 | 64 | 63 | 58 |
| P | | 1.8 | 1.7 | 2.4 | 2.2 | 2.0 |

| *City* | *Altitude* | *May* | *June* | *July* | *Aug.* | *Sept.* |
|---|---|---|---|---|---|---|
| Dublin | 153 | | | | | |
| T | | 51 | 56 | 59 | 59 | 55 |
| P | | 2.3 | 2.0 | 2.8 | 3.0 | 2.8 |
| Edinburgh | 441 | | | | | |
| T | | 49 | 55 | 58 | 58 | 54 |
| P | | 2.2 | 1.9 | 3.0 | 3.1 | 2.5 |

FRANCE

| | | | | | | |
|---|---|---|---|---|---|---|
| Brest | 105 | | | | | |
| T | | 55 | 59 | 62 | 63 | 61 |
| P | | 1.8 | 1.7 | 1.8 | 1.9 | 1.7 |
| Bordeaux | 157 | | | | | |
| T | | 60 | 65 | 69 | 69 | 65 |
| P | | 2.8 | 2.8 | 2.0 | 1.9 | 2.3 |
| Paris | 164 | | | | | |
| T | | 55 | 62 | 65 | 64 | 58 |
| P | | 1.9 | 2.2 | 2.0 | 1.9 | 1.9 |
| Biarritz | 112 | | | | | |
| T | | 58 | 64 | 67 | 67 | 64 |
| P | | 4.0 | 2.5 | 3.3 | 3.7 | 5.2 |
| Marseilles | 246 | | | | | |
| T | | 61 | 67 | 72 | 71 | 66 |
| P | | 2.0 | 1.0 | 0.6 | 0.9 | 2.7 |
| Lyons | 643 | | | | | |
| T | | 61 | 66 | 70 | 70 | 63 |
| P | | 3.1 | 3.2 | 2.6 | 3.5 | 3.0 |
| Strasbourg | 456 | | | | | |
| T | | 59 | 64 | 67 | 66 | 61 |
| P | | 2.0 | 2.7 | 2.7 | 2.4 | 2.2 |
| Nice | 39 | | | | | |
| T | | 62 | 69 | 73 | 73 | 69 |
| P | | 2.8 | 1.0 | 0.7 | 1.3 | 3.0 |

GERMANY

| | | | | | | |
|---|---|---|---|---|---|---|
| Hamburg | 66 | | | | | |
| T | | 53 | 60 | 62 | 61 | 57 |
| P | | 2.1 | 2.7 | 3.4 | 3.2 | 2.5 |

| City | Altitude | May | June | July | Aug. | Sept. |
|---|---|---|---|---|---|---|
| Berlin | 187 | | | | | |
| T | | 55 | 60 | 64 | 63 | 57 |
| P | | 1.9 | 2.3 | 3.1 | 2.2 | 1.9 |
| Stuttgart | 876 | | | | | |
| T | | 57 | 63 | 66 | 65 | 59 |
| P | | 2.7 | 3.2 | 3.3 | 2.6 | 2.4 |
| Munich | 1739 | | | | | |
| T | | 54 | 60 | 63 | 62 | 56 |
| P | | 3.7 | 4.6 | 4.7 | 4.2 | 3.2 |

GREECE

| City | Altitude | May | June | July | Aug. | Sept. |
|---|---|---|---|---|---|---|
| Athens | 351 | | | | | |
| T | | 68 | 76 | 81 | 81 | 74 |
| P | | 0.8 | 0.6 | 0.2 | 0.4 | 0.6 |
| Corfu | 89 | | | | | |
| T | | 68 | 74 | 79 | 79 | 75 |
| P | | 1.8 | 0.9 | 0.2 | 0.8 | 3.0 |
| Salonica | 129 | | | | | |
| T | | 67 | 74 | 80 | 78 | 72 |
| P | | 2.3 | 1.7 | 0.9 | 1.2 | 1.6 |

ITALY

| City | Altitude | May | June | July | Aug. | Sept. |
|---|---|---|---|---|---|---|
| Genoa | 177 | | | | | |
| T | | 62 | 70 | 75 | 75 | 70 |
| P | | 3.4 | 2.8 | 1.7 | 2.4 | 4.9 |
| Milan | 482 | | | | | |
| T | | 65 | 71 | 75 | 75 | 67 |
| P | | 3.0 | 3.0 | 2.6 | 2.6 | 2.8 |
| Venice | 69 | | | | | |
| T | | 63 | 70 | 75 | 74 | 67 |
| P | | 2.8 | 2.9 | 1.8 | 2.0 | 2.6 |
| Trieste | 85 | | | | | |
| T | | 63 | 70 | 75 | 74 | 69 |
| P | | 3.6 | 4.0 | 3.1 | 3.5 | 4.6 |
| Rome | 168 | | | | | |
| T | | 64 | 71 | 76 | 76 | 70 |
| P | | 2.3 | 1.9 | 0.9 | 0.9 | 2.9 |

| *City* | *Altitude* | *May* | *June* | *July* | *Aug.* | *Sept.* |
|---|---|---|---|---|---|---|
| Naples | 489 | | | | | |
| T | | 64 | 70 | 75 | 76 | 71 |
| P | | 2.0 | 1.5 | 0.7 | 0.9 | 2.9 |

SCANDINAVIA

| *City* | *Altitude* | *May* | *June* | *July* | *Aug.* | *Sept.* |
|---|---|---|---|---|---|---|
| Stockholm | 146 | | | | | |
| T | | 49 | 57 | 62 | 59 | 54 |
| P | | 1.6 | 1.9 | 2.8 | 3.1 | 2.1 |
| Oslo | 82 | | | | | |
| T | | 51 | 59 | 64 | 60 | 62 |
| P | | 1.8 | 2.0 | 3.0 | 3.6 | 2.4 |
| Copenhagen | 43 | | | | | |
| T | | 52 | 59 | 63 | 61 | 56 |
| P | | 1.7 | 2.1 | 2.2 | 3.2 | 1.9 |

SPAIN AND PORTUGAL

| *City* | *Altitude* | *May* | *June* | *July* | *Aug.* | *Sept.* |
|---|---|---|---|---|---|---|
| Lisbon | 812 | | | | | |
| T | | 62 | 67 | 71 | 72 | 69 |
| P | | 1.7 | 0.7 | 0.2 | 0.2 | 1.4 |
| Madrid | 1965 | | | | | |
| T | | 61 | 69 | 77 | 76 | 68 |
| P | | 1.7 | 1.3 | 0.4 | 0.6 | 1.5 |
| Barcelona | 136 | | | | | |
| T | | 62 | 69 | 74 | 75 | 70 |
| P | | 2.0 | 1.5 | 1.1 | 1.3 | 2.5 |
| Gibraltar | 90 | | | | | |
| T | | 65 | 70 | 75 | 76 | 72 |
| P | | 1.6 | 0.5 | 0.0 | 0.1 | 1.3 |

SWITZERLAND

| *City* | *Altitude* | *May* | *June* | *July* | *Aug.* | *Sept.* |
|---|---|---|---|---|---|---|
| Basel | 1040 | | | | | |
| T | | 56 | 63 | 66 | 64 | 59 |
| P | | 3.1 | 4.1 | 3.3 | 3.3 | 3.1 |

| *City* | *Altitude* | *May* | *June* | *July* | *Aug.* | *Sept.* |
|---|---|---|---|---|---|---|
| Geneva | 1329 | | | | | |
| T | | 58 | 64 | 69 | 68 | 61 |
| P | | 3.0 | 3.0 | 3.3 | 3.3 | 3.6 |
| Lucerne | 1634 | | | | | |
| T | | 55 | 61 | 65 | 63 | 57 |
| P | | 4.8 | 5.7 | 6.5 | 5.6 | 5.3 |

YUGOSLAVIA

| | | | | | | |
|---|---|---|---|---|---|---|
| Belgrade | 453 | | | | | |
| T | | 63 | 68 | 72 | 71 | 65 |
| P | | 2.6 | 2.8 | 1.9 | 2.5 | 1.7 |
| Zagreb | 535 | | | | | |
| T | | 61 | 67 | 71 | 69 | 62 |
| P | | 3.1 | 3.9 | 3.2 | 3.4 | 3.9 |
| Sofia | 1804 | | | | | |
| T | | 59 | 65 | 69 | 68 | 61 |
| P | | 3.3 | 3.2 | 2.7 | 2.1 | 2.2 |

APPENDIX 3

# Guided tours and tour itineraries

## GUIDED TOURS

The following private and nonprofit organizations offer tours with guides or leaders. In the cases of clubs or associations, membership fees or restrictions are noted. All the organizations offering guided tours are discussed in Chapter 3.

American Youth Hostels, Inc.
National Campus
Delaplane, Virginia 22025
MEMBERSHIP: Junior membership (under 18 years of age): $5; senior membership (over 18 years of age): $11; family membership: $12.

Bike Tour France
Box 32814
Charlotte, N.C. 28232

The Biking Expedition
Hall Avenue (P.O. Box 547)
Henniker, N.H. 03242
MEMBERSHIP: Persons between the ages of 13 and 18

Club Tamuré
P.O. Box 1119
Whittier, Calif. 90609

Cyclists Touring Club
68 Meadrow
Godalming
Surrey GU7 3 HS
England
MEMBERSHIP: 21 years and over: £7.00; 18 to 20 years old: £4.20; under 18 years: £2.80; family: £1.80 per person. If joining, send funds via international money order, or check payable to an English bank in sterling, or a

money order in American funds plus 10 percent conversion fee. Add £1.68 to membership fee for airmail return.

Euro-Bike Tours
P.O. Box 40
De Kalb, Ill. 60115

International Bicycle Touring Society
2115 Paseo Dorado
La Jolla, Calif. 92037
MEMBERSHIP: $10 individual or couple

Out-Spokin'
Box 370
Elkhart, Ind. 46515

Rotalis Reisen per Rad
8011 Zorneding bei München
Federal Republic of Germany
(Guided tours with bus throughout Germany)

Welcome Swiss Tours
Avenue Benjamin-Constant 7
1003 Lausanne
Switzerland
(Organizes a tour of Lake Geneva)

## TOUR ITINERARIES

The following organizations provide tour itineraries of different regions within their countries. *Most of them are small, and cannot answer mail inquiries.* The few instances where the organization is able to answer overseas inquiries are indicated with an asterisk. Otherwise, you should contact the organization *in person* upon arrival. When writing, be sure to include an international reply coupon for response via surface mail. For air mail response, include $1.

### AUSTRIA

Österreichischer
Automobil-, Motorrad- und Touring-Club
Schubertring 1-3
1010 Wien

### DENMARK

Danish Tourists' Board/Council
Banegaardspladsen 2
D K 1570
Copenhagen V
(Itineraries throughout Denmark)

### ENGLAND

*British Cycling Federation
Touring Bureau
3 Moor Lane
Lancaster LA1 1QD
(Provides extensive tour itineraries for members)
MEMBERSHIP: £7.25. Send via

international money order or check drawn on an English bank in pounds sterling.

*Cyclists Touring Club
(See previous section for membership details. Provides extensive tour itineraries for members)

Countryside Commission
1, Cambridge Gate
Regent's Park
London
(Itineraries of the Peak District)

*Border Holiday Tours
lla St. John's Hill
Shrewsbury SY11 1JJ
(Cycling tours in Shropshire)

*Cardiff Bicycle Hire and Tours
5 Duke Street Arcade
Cardiff
(3-to-7-day trips in Wales)

*Coombe Cross Hotel
Bovey Tracey
Newton Abbot TZ13 9EY
Devon
(Cycling holiday August 11–18)

*Countryman Leisure Ltd.
Old Council Offices, Main Street
Leiston IP 16 4 ER
Suffolk
(Holidays arranged from Easter to October)

*Enjoy Britain and the World, Ltd.
21 Old Brompton Road
London SW7 3 HZ
(A number of tours, including the Cotswolds)

*Freedom of Ryedale Holiday
8 Bondgate
Helmsley
York YO6 5BT
Yorkshire
(One-week holidays year round)

*G.B. Holidays (Plymouth) Ltd.
88 Vauxhall Street
The Barbican
Plymouth
Devon
(One-week tours in Dartmoor and Cornwall)

*Hobby Holidays (Scotland)
Glencommon, Inchmarlo, Banchory
Kincardineshire
Grampian
(Numerous holidays, including cycling, in Scotland)

*Otterburn Hall Holiday Hotel
Otterburn NE 19 1HE
Otterburn
Northumberland
(Cycling weeks between May and September)

*Paynes Picnics
12 Carisbrooke Road
Gosport
Hampshire

Peak District National Park Study Centre

Losehill Hall
Castleton S30 2WB
Derbyshire
(Cycling holiday in the Peak District July 25–30)

*PGL Young Adventure Ltd.
187 Station Street
Ross-on-Wye
Herfordshire JR9 7AN
(One-week Cotswold tours from April to October)

*Savoy Hotel
Bayshill Road
Cheltenham
(Weekend trips throughout the year)

*Trail Bike Holidays
159 Dartmouth Road
Sydenham
London SE26 4RQ
(Four-day trail bike holidays in Pennines)

*Youth Hostels Association
Trevelyan House
8 St. Stephens Hill
St. Albans
(Week-long tours throughout the country)

FRANCE

Federation de Cyclotourisme
8, rue Jean Marie Jego
Paris 75013

Bicy-Club de France
7, rue Ambroise-Thomas
Paris 75009
MEMBERSHIP: 50 F per year; 10 F initiation fee.

The following regional cycle touring organizations have tours, rallies, and trips within their respective regions of France:

Cyclo-Randonneur Briviste
8, rue Gambetta
Brive 19100

Ligue Régionale de Cyclotourisme
18, rue Gambetta
Toulouse 31000

Fédération de Cyclotourisme
Mr. Jo. Routens
8, Cours Bériat
Grenoble 38000

Tourist Office
11 bis rue des Argentine
La Rochelle 17000

Tourist Office
11, rue Victor Hugo
Poitiers 86000

Comité de Cyclisme des Pyrénées
19, rue d'Aubuisson
Toulouse 31000

Fédération Départmental de Cyclotourisme
14, rue R. Lartigue
Bordeaux 33000

Cyclo-Sport Provençal
4, avenue Victor Hugo
Aix-en-Provence 13100

Association Sportive Marseillaise
358, Promenade de la Corniche
Marseille 13007

Club des Cyclos-Randonneurs Toulonnais
25, rue Victor Clampier
Toulon 83100

Fédération de Cyclotourisme
Mr. Felix Parcillie
22, boulevard du Pape Jean XXIII
Nice 06300

Cyclotourisme Avignonais
Cristal Bar
40, rue des Lices
Avignon 84000

Fédération Française de Cyclotourisme
Mr. Jacques Merville
14, rue Victor Rogelet
Reims 51100

### GERMANY (FEDERAL REPUBLIC OF GERMANY)

*Gebietsgemeinschaft Allgäu-Oberschwaben
D-7988
Wangen im Allgäu

*Verkehrsamt
Berliner Platz 22
D-4400
Münster

*Verkehrsbüro
Markt 13
D–5912
Hilchenbach

### HOLLAND

*Stichting: fiets!
Europaplein 2
1078 gz Amsterdam

*VVV Gelderland
Stationsplein 45
6800 AN Arnhem

*VVV Overijssel
de Werf 1
7607 HH Almelo

### IRELAND

*Raleigh Rent-a-Bike
Irish Raleigh Industries, Ltd.
8 Hanover Quay
Dublin 2
(Cycling itineraries in numerous regions of Ireland. The same information is available in this country from the Irish Tourist Board. See Appendix 4 for address.)

### LUXEMBOURG

Mr. E. Zahlen
16, rue Emile Mayrisch
Soleuvre
(One cycling itinerary covering much of this small country)

### NORWAY

Skiforeningen
Storgaten 2
Oslo 1
(Cycling itinerary using way points along the famous ski trail)

SWEDEN

Cykel- & Mopedfrämjandet
Stora Nygatan 41-43
Box 2085
103-12 Stockholm 2
(Numerous itineraries throughout Sweden)

SWITZERLAND

Schweiz. Rad- und Motorfahrer-Bund
Schaffhauserstrasse 272
8023
Zürich
(Cycle touring organization for German-speaking cantons)

Union Cycliste Suisse
Case postale 30
1211 Geneve 3
(Cycle touring organization for French-speaking contons)

APPENDIX 4

# National tourist offices

AUSTRIA

Austrian National Tourist Office
545 Fifth Avenue
New York, N.Y. 10017

BELGIUM

Belgian National Tourist Office
745 Fifth Avenue
New York, N.Y. 10022

DENMARK

(See *Scandinavia*)

FINLAND

(See *Scandinavia*)

FRANCE

French Government Tourist Office
610 Fifth Avenue
New York, N.Y. 10020

French Government Tourist Office
323 Geary Street
San Francisco, Calif. 94102

GERMANY
(FEDERAL REPUBLIC OF GERMANY)

German National Tourist Office
630 Fifth Avenue
New York, N.Y. 10020

German National Tourist Office
104 Michigan Avenue
Chicago, Ill. 60603

German National Tourist Office
700 S. Flower Street
Los Angeles, Calif. 90017

GREAT BRITAIN
(ENGLAND, SCOTLAND, WALES)

British Tourist Authority
680 Fifth Avenue
New York, N.Y. 10019

British Tourist Authority
612 Flower Street
Los Angeles, Calif. 90017

GREECE

Greek National Tourist Organization
601 Fifth Avenue
New York, N.Y. 10017

Greek National Tourist Organization
627 West Sixth Street
Los Angeles, Calif. 90017

HOLLAND

Netherlands National Tourist Office
576 Fifth Avenue
New York, N.Y. 10036

Netherlands National Tourist Office
681 Market Street, Room 941
San Francisco, Calif. 94105

IRELAND

Irish Tourist Board
590 Fifth Avenue
New York, N.Y. 10036

Irish Tourist Board
230 North Michigan Avenue
Chicago, Ill. 60601

Irish Tourist Board
681 Market Street
San Francisco, Calif. 94105

Irish Tourist Board
510 West Sixth Street, Suite 317
Los Angeles, Calif. 90014

Irish Tourist Board
69 Yonge Street
Toronto M5E 1K3
Canada

ITALY

Italian Government Travel Office
630 Fifth Avenue
New York, N.Y. 10020

Italian Government Travel Office
360 Post Street, Suite 801
San Francisco, Calif. 94108

LUXEMBOURG

Luxembourg National Tourist Office
1 Dag Hammerskjold Plaza
New York, N.Y. 10017

NORWAY

(See *Scandinavia*)

PORTUGAL

Portuguese National Tourist Office
548 Fifth Avenue
New York, N.Y. 10036

Portuguese National Tourist Office
Suite 500, Palmer House
17 East Monroe Street
Chicago, Ill. 60603

Portuguese National Tourist Office
1 Park Plaza, Suite 1305
3250 Wilshire Blvd.
Los Angeles, Calif. 90010

## SCANDINAVIA

Scandinavian National Tourist Office
75 Rockefeller Plaza
New York, N.Y. 10019

Scandinavian National Tourist Office
3600 Wilshire Blvd.
Los Angeles, Calif. 90010

## SPAIN

Spanish National Tourist Office
665 Fifth Avenue
New York, N.Y. 10022

Spanish National Tourist Office
3160 Lion Street
San Francisco, Calif. 94123

Spanish National Tourist Office
Water Tower Place
845 N. Michigan Avenue
Chicago, Ill. 60611

## SWEDEN

(See *Scandinavia*)

## SWITZERLAND

Swiss Center
608 Fifth Avenue
New York, N.Y. 10020

Swiss Center
250 Stockton Street
San Francisco, Calif. 94108

APPENDIX 5

# Bicycle touring organizations

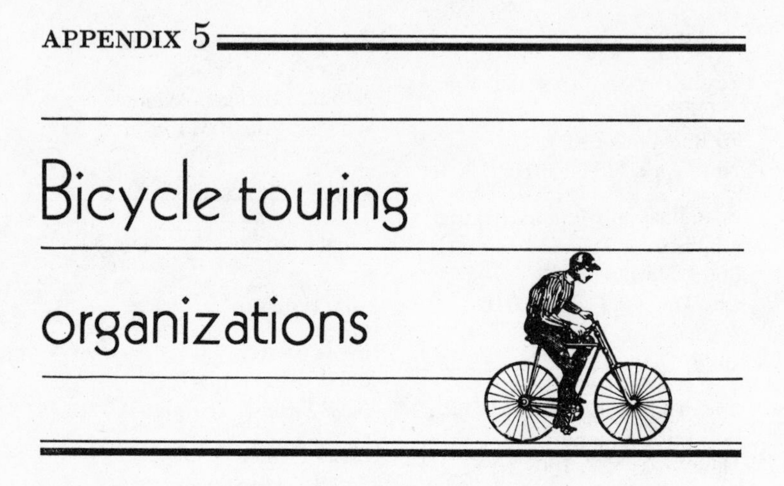

The following organizations promote bicycle touring in their respective countries and throughout Europe in general. Most offer preplanned tours. Many hold bicycling rallies and excursions. Some provide insurance for members, and a few will actually plan trips for individuals. Many of the organizations, particularly those based in Europe, operate on limited budgets. As a courtesy to them—and to insure the quickest possible response—you should include a small sum in the form of a money order if requesting a response by air mail. Air mail rates in Europe are double to triple what it costs to send a letter abroad from the United States.

### BELGIUM

Royale Ligue Velocipedique Belge
49 Avenue du Globe
B-1190 Brussels

### DENMARK

Dansk Cyklist Forbund
Lanskronagade 32
DK-2100 Copenhagen

### ENGLAND

British Cycling Federation
Touring Bureau
3 Moor Lane
Lancaster LA 1 1QD
MEMBERSHIP: £7.25 (18 and over). £5.65 (16 and 17). £3.70 (under 16). Send via international money order or check drawn on an English bank in pounds sterling.

Cyclists Touring Club
68 Meadrow
Godalming
Surrey GU 7 3HS
MEMBERSHIP: 21 years old and over: $7.00; 18–20 years old: $4.20; under 18: $2.80; family membership: $1.80 per person

FRANCE

Fédération Française de Cyclotourisme
8, rue Jean Marie Jego
Paris 75013

GERMANY
(FEDERAL REPUBLIC OF GERMANY)

Bund Deutscher Radfahrer
Westanlage 56
6300 Giessen

HOLLAND

Stichting: fiets!
Europaplein 2
1078 gz Amsterdam

SWEDEN

Cykel-& Mopedfrämjandet
Stora Nygatan 41–43
Box 2085
103 12 Stockholm 2

SWITZERLAND

Schweiz. Rad- und Motorfahrer-Bund (German-speaking cantons)
Schaffhausterstrasse 272
8023 Zürich

Union Cycliste Suisse (French-speaking cantons)
9 rue Pierre-Fatio
CH Genéve

UNITED STATES

Both these organizations devote themselves to cycle touring throughout Europe:

American Youth Hostel, Inc.
National Campus
Delaplane, Virginia 22025
MEMBERSHIP: Junior membership (under 18 years of age): $5; senior membership (over 18 years of age): $11; family membership: $12.

International Bicycle Touring Society
2115 Paseo Dorado
La Jolla, Calif. 92037
MEMBERSHIP: $10 individual or couple

APPENDIX 6

# Where to rent a bicycle

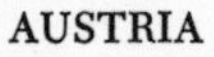

## AUSTRIA

Rental bicycles are available from the following train stations within Austria:

| *Location* | *Telephone* |
|---|---|
| Admont | 03613/22 30 |
| Bad Goisern | 06135/234 |
| Bad Hall | 07258/320 |
| Berndorf Stadt | 02672/22 47 |
| Bruck-Fusch | 06545/220 |
| Feldbach | 03152/24 58 |
| Fürstenfeld | 03382/22 30 |
| Gmunden | 07612/42 07 |
| Hallein | 06245/22 76 |
| Hall in Tirol | 05223/65 10 |
| Hermagor | 04282/20 30 |
| Hofgastein | 06432/206 |
| Hohenems | 05576/23 80 |
| Kammer-Schörfling | 07662/330 |
| Klagenfurt Hbf. | 04222/70 9 11-399 |
| Klaus | 07585/218 |
| Kötschach-Mauthen | 04715/243 |

| | | |
|---|---|---|
| Krems/Donau | 02732/25 36–387 | |
| Leibnitz | 03452/2300-39 | |
| Lienz | 04852/31 66-37 | |
| Lunz am See | 07486/280 | |
| Melk | 02752/23 21 | |
| Mödling | 02236/21 48 | |
| Ossiach-Bodensdorf | 04243/218 | |
| Petronell-Carnuntum | 02163/22 90 | |
| Radkersburg | 03476/22 30 | |
| Reutte in Tirol | 05672/23 13 | |
| Saalfelden | 06582/23 44 | |
| St Johann im Pongau | 06412/226 | |
| Schärding | 07712/30 53 | Tag 37<br>Nacht 34 |
| Seekirchen-Mattsee | 06212/209 | |
| Silz | 05263/6230 | |
| Spitz a. d. Donau | 02713/220 | |
| Tulln | 02272/24 38 | |
| Velden/Wörthersee | 04274/21 15 | |
| Ybbs a. d. Donau | 07412/26 00 | |
| St. Veit a. d. Gölsen | 02763/219 | |

BELGIUM

Rental bicycles are available from the following train stations within Belgium. Bicycles may be returned to nearly any major train station.

| | |
|---|---|
| As | Hasselt |
| Ath | Ieper |
| Bastogne | Knokke |
| Bertrix | Marbehan |
| Braine-l'Alleud | Melreux-Hotton |
| Brugge | Oudenaarde |
| Dinant | Poix-St-Hubert |
| Essen | Puurs |
| Gedinne | Trois-Ponts |
| Geel | Verviers Central |
| Groenendaal | Veurne |

## FRANCE

A number of private establishments in Paris rent good ten-speed touring bicycles. In addition, some 85 train stations throughout France rent serviceable bicycles.

*Paris*

Market Moto
19, place du Marché St-Honoré
Paris 1

Paris Velo Rent-a-Bike
2, rue du Fer à Moulin
Paris 5

Rent a Bike
"Le Cyclobus"
Located near the Hippodrome in the Bois de Boulogne. Rental by hour or day only.

*Train Station Rentals*

The following stations rent bicycles:

Agde
Aix-en-Provence
Alès
Amboise
Annecy
Antibes
Arcachon
Arles
Autun
Avallon
Avignon
Baugency
Baule-Escoublac (La)
Bayeux
Blois
Bordeaux-Saint-Jean
Bourboule (La)
Bourges
Bueil
Caen
Calais-Ville
Cannes
Castres
Chantilly-Gouvieux
Chatelaillon
Colmar
Compiègne
Croisic (Le)
Die
Dieppe
Dinard
Dives-Gabourg
Dourdan
Esbly
Fontainebleau-Avon
Gerardmer
Granville
Gretz-Armainvilliers
Hendaye
Houlgate
Hyères
Juan-les-Pins
La Motte Beuvron
Lorient
Maintenon
Malesherbes
Manosque-Gréoux-les-Bains
Meaux
Millau
Montbuisson

Mont-Dore (Le)
Montfort-l'Amaury-Méré
Montsoult-Maffliers
Mulhouse-Ville
Nemours-Saint-Pierre
Neuilly-Porte-Maillot
Nîmes
Orléans
Pontoise
Pontorson-Mont-Saint-Michel
Pornic
Rambouillet
Rochefort
Rochelle-Ville (La)
Roscoff
Royan
Sables-d'Olonne (Les)
Saint-Amand-les-Eaux
Saint-Brieuc
Saint-Jean-de-Luz-Ciboure
Saint-Malo
Saint-Nazaire
Saint-Raphael-Valescure
Saint-Sulpice-sur-Tarn
Sète
Souillac
Strasbourg
Tours
Tréport-Mers (Le)
Trouville-Deauville
Vannes
Villars-les-Dombes

GERMANY

Bicycles may be rented at any of the following train stations within Germany. Those marked with a bullet are open for rentals year round. Rental stations are categorized by region (in boldface), then specific station within the region.

**Holsteinische Schweiz**
**Lauenburglsche Seenplatte**
**Göhrde**
Eutin
Klanxbüll
Malente-Gremsmühlen
Molln (Lauenburg)
Niebüll
Plon
Preetz
Ratzeburg

**Münsterland**
**Emsland**
**Oldenburger Land**
**Wiehengebirge**
• Ahaus
Ahlhorn
• Borken (Westf)
• Burgsteinfurt
• Capelle (Westf)
• Coesfeld (Westf)
• Davensberg
• Dülmen
• Haltern (Westf)
• Handorf (Westf)
Holzhausen-Heddinghausen
Huntlosen
Lathen
• Lembeck
• Maria Veen
Meppen
• Münster (Westf) Hbf
Norddeich
Norden
• Reken
Rheine
• Werne an der Lippe

**Lüneburger Heide**
**Teufelsmoor-Wümmetal**
**Vorharz**
**Werraland**
**Kurnessen-Waldeck**
Arolsen
Bad Gandersheim
Bennemühlen
Bissendorf
Bodenteich
Bremen-Oberneuland
Bremen-Vegesack
Eschede
Eschwege
Fallingbostel
Hann-Münden
Hodenhagen
Holm-Seppensen
Isenbuttel-Gifhorn
Kassel-Wilhelmshöhe
Mellendorf
Melsungen
Neustadt (Rbge)
Schneverdingen
Soltau (Han)
Unterluß
Visselnovede
Walsrode
Willingen
Wintermoor
Witzenhausen Nord

**Niederrheln**
**Sauerland**
**Bergisches Land**
**Elfel**
Alpen
Attendorn
Blankenheim (Wald)
Gerolstein
Heimbach (Eifel)
Junkerath
Kall
Kleve
Kranenburg
Matienbaum
Matienheide
• Olpe
• Sondern
Xanten

**Rhein-Main**
**Taunus**
**Kinzigtal**
**Fuldatal**
Bad Hersfeld
Bad Homburg
Bad Nauheim
Bad Soden (Taunus)
Bad Vilbel
Büdingen (Oberhess)
Gelnhausen
Goddelau-Erfelden
Groß Gerau
Hofheim (Taunus)
Idstein (Taunus)
Kronberg (Taunus)
Salmünster-Bad Soden
Wachtersbach
Weilburg
Wetzlar

**Mosel**
**Hunsrück**
**Pfalzer Wald und Nahe**
**Rheinhessen**
Alzey
Bundenthal-Rumbach
Ehrang
Guntersblum
Hauenstein
Hermeskeil
Hinterweidenthal

Idar-Oberstein
Kell (Bz Trier)
Landau (Pfalz) Hbf
Mettlach
Munchweiler (Rodalb)
Neustadt (Weinstr) Hbf
Oppenheim
Speyer Hbf
Traben-Trarbach

**Odenwald**
**Bergstraße**
**Neckarland**
**Kraichgau**

- Bad Friedrichshall-Jagstfeld

Bad König (Odenw)
Bad Rappenau
Bad Wimpfen
Bensheim
Besigheim
Eberbach
Erbach (Odenw)
Heidelberg Hbf
Hetzbach (Odenw)

- Lauffen (Neckar)

Mingolsheim-Kronau
Mosbach (Baden)
Neckargemünd
Osterburken
Schwaigern (Württ)
Weinheim (Bergstr)
Weinsberg
Zwingenberg (Bergstr)

**Schwäbischer Wald**
**Hohenlohe**
**Altmühltal**
Backnang

- **Bad Mergentheim**
- **Blaufelden**

Bopfingen
Crailsheim

- **Eichstatt Stadt**

**Ellwangen**
**Gaildorf West**

- **Möckmühl**

Murrhardt
Ohringen
Oppenweiler
Schwäbisch Hall
Sulzbach (Murr)
Tauberbischofsheim

- Treuchtlingen

Weikersheim

**Franken**
**Ostbayern**
Altdorf (b Nürnberg)
Bad Kissingen
Bad Windsheim
Brückenau Stadt
Ebermannstadt
Feucht
Forchheim (Oberfr)
Furth i Wald
Gemünden (Main)
Gerolzhofen
Grafenau
Heigenbrücken
Hersbruck (links Pegnitz)
Hersbruck (rechts Pegnitz)
Kitzingen
Lauf (links Pegnitz)
Marktleuthen
Miltenberg Hbf
Neuhaus (Pegnitz)
Obernburg-Elsenfeld
Rothenburg ob der Tauber
Spiegelau
Wiesau (Oberpf)
Zwiesel (Bay)

**Schwarzwald**
**Bergland Junge Donau**
**Oberrhein**
Alpirsbach
Altglashutten-Falkau
Bad Bellingen
Bad Krozingen
Bayersbronn
Biberach (Baden)
Bleibach
Breisach
Calmbach
Forbach-Gausbach
Freudenstadt Stadt
Gengenbach
Hinterzarten
Höfen (Enz)
Horb
Immendingen
Kirchzarten
Löffingen
Muhlheim (b Tuttlingen)
Oberkirch
Sackingen
St Georgen (Schwarzw)
Schenkenzell
Schluchsee
Schonmunzach
Steinen
Sulz (Neckar)
Tiengen (Oberrhein)
Titisee
Tuttlingen
Waldkirch
Wildbad
Wildberg (Wurll)
Wolfach

**Oberschwaben**
**Schwäblsche Alb**
**Bodensee**
**Allgäu**
• Aulendorf
• Bad Schussenried
Bad Waldsee
Bad Worishofen
• Biberach (Riß)
Ehingen (Donau)
• Füssen
Herbrechtingen
• Immenstadt
• Isny
• Kißlegg
Langenargen
Laupheim West
• Leutkirch
• Lindau Hbf
• Lindenberg (Allgäu)
Ludwigshafen (Bodensee)
• Meckenbeuren
Metzingen
• Nesselwang
• Oberstaufen
Oberuhldingen-Mühlhofen
Oy-Mittelberg
• Pfronten-Ried
Rottenburg (Neckar)
Sigmaringen
• Sonthofen
Tübingen Hbf
• Wangen (Allgäu)
• Wasserburg (Bodensee)

**Oberbayern**

- Bad Aibling
- Bad Reichenhall
- Bad Tölz
- Bayrischzell
- Berchtesgaden
- Bergen (Oberbay)
- Bernau (Oberbay)
- Brannenburg
- Dachau Bf
- Dießen
- Dorfen Bf
- Eisenärzt
- Endorf (Oberbay)
- Erding
- Freilassing
- Freising
- Fürstenfeldbruck
- Garmisch-Partenkirchen
- Geltendorf
- Gmund am Tegernsee
- Grafing Bf
- Grafrath
- Hammerau
- Herrsching
- Holzkirchen
- Ismaning
- Kirchanschoring
- Kochel
- Kreuzstraße
- Laufen (Oberbay)
- Lenggries

Murnau

- Oberammergau
- Oberaudorf
- Oberschleißheim
- Phen
- Rimsting
- Ruhpolding
- Schaftlach
- Schliersee

Seeshaupt

- Siegsdorf
- Starnberg

Tegernsee

- Teisendorf
- Tutzing
- Ubersee
- Waging am See
- Wasserburg (inn) Stadt

Weßling
Weßling (Oberbay)
Wolfratshausen

## GREAT BRITAIN (ENGLAND, SCOTLAND, WALES)

The following establishments rent bicycles within Great Britain. Shops are listed by country, county, and by the name of the shop within each country.

### ENGLAND

*London (Greater London)*

Bell Street Bikes
73 Bell Street, London NW1
T 01–724 0456

Bicycle Revival Rental
28 North End Parade, North End Road, West Kensington, London W14
T 01–602 4499

Hira-Bike Ltd.
Vine House, 11 Balfour Mews, London W1Y 5RJ
T 01–499 3085

The Kensington Bicycle Co.
Rent-a-Bike
Kensington Student Centre, Kensington Church Street, London W8
T 01–937 6089

Savile's Cycle Stores Ltd.
97/99 Battersea Rise, London SW11 1HW
T 01–228 4279

*Avon*

Bath Bike Hire
72/74 Walcott Street, Bath
T Bath 62546

Coastal Concessions
72/74 Walcott Street, Bath
T Bath 62546
R.J. Blunt, Director
"Rent-A-Cycle" at the following sites: Lido Seafront, Minehead, Somerset. Butlins Holiday Camp, Filey, North Yorkshire. Butlins Holiday Camp, Pwllheli, Caernarfon, Gwynedd, Wales. Garage opposite Butlins Holiday Camp, Clacton, Essex. Harbour Master's Office, West Itchenor, Chichester, West Sussex. Old Bus Station, Queen Street, Arundel, West Sussex. Opposite the Tourist Information Centre, Coastguard Road, Littlehampton, West Sussex. For details of sites contact Coastal Concessions. Bicycles can be delivered to any part of the United Kingdom at cost of delivery.

*Cambridgeshire*

Ben Hayward
69 Trumpington Street, Cambridge
T Cambridge 52294

J. Howes
46 Regent Street, Cambridge
T Cambridge 50350

P.H. Allin & Sons
189 Histon Road, Cambridge
T Cambridge 53431

Reids Cycles
68 Victoria Road, Cambridge
T Cambridge 54009

S. Bacon
77 Norwich Street, Cambridge
T Cambridge 54805

University Cycles
59 King Street, Cambridge
T Cambridge 311560

*Cheshire*

Roy Vernon & Sons
208 Stockport Road, Timperley, Altrincham
T 061–980 3069

*Cornwall*

G. Pascoe & Co.
62 Meneage Street, Helston
T Helston 2655

Langdon Cycle Shop
20 St. Mary's Street, Truro
T Truro 2207

Robert Horne
Kemyl Vean, 3 Lariggan Hill, Penzance
T Penzance 2653

Silly Cycles
Wesley Yard, Newquay
T Newquay 2455
June-end of season

*Cumbria*

Ghyll Side Cycle Shop
Bridge Street, Ambleside
T Ambleside 3592

John Peel Garage
Market Place, Cockermouth
T Cockermouth 2113

Keswick Cycle Hire
Pack Horse Court, Keswick

Lake District Cycle Hire
46 Linton Street, Carlisle
T Carlisle 30058

Lake District Cycle Hire
Lakeside Car Park, Keswick
T Keswick 73639

Lakeland Cycles
104 Strickland Gate, Kendal
T Kendal 23552

Rent-A-Bike
Langdale View, 117 Craig Walk, Bowness-on-Windermere
T Windermere 2878

*Derbyshire*

Bicycles for hire at Parsley Hay, site on High Peak Trail

The Peak Park Joint Planning Board
Aldern House, Baslow Road, Bakewell
T Bakewell 2881

*Devon*

Cyril Webber
50 Bear Street, Barnstaple
T Barnstaple 3277

Hirabike
2a Chudleigh Road, Lipson Vale, Plymouth
T Plymouth 28601

Plymouth Camping Hire Centre
107 North Hill, Tavistock Road, Plymouth
T Plymouth 21881

*Dorset*

Cy-Sales
644 Wimbourne Road, Winton, Bournemouth
T Bournemouth 55880

Hirabike At Bournemouth
Action Holidays, 4 Westover Road, Bournemouth
T Bournemouth 28855

*Essex*

Coastal Concessions
See under *Avon*

Lexden Cycles
West Berholt
T Colchester 240474

Oxley Hill Farm
Layer Road, Abberton, Colchester
T Peldon 522

*Gloucestershire*

T.W. Morris
Manor House Antiques, The Square, Stow-on-the-Wold

Williams of Portland Street
8–14 Portland Street, Cheltenham

*Hampshire*

Chesil Cycle Depot
3 Chesil Street, Winchester
T Winchester 63703

Payne's Picnics
12 Carisbrooke Road, Rowner, Gosport PO13 0H8
T Farnham 86499

Peter Hansford
The Cycle Shop, Bridge Road, Park Gate, Southampton
T Locks Heath 3249

*Hereford & Worcester*

Dial-A-Bike
Bosbury, Herefordshire
T Bosbury 676 or Ledbury 2585

Hirabike
89 East Street, Hereford
T Hereford 57431

Little & Hall
Auto and Cycle Engineers, 48 Broad Street, Ross-on-Wye, Herefordshire
T Ross-on-Wye 2639

PGL Holidays
Station Street, Ross-on-Wye, Herefordshire
T Ross-on-Wye 4211

T.L. Kemp (Broadway) Toys and Cycles
Cycle Hire Centre, 39 High Street, Broadway, Worcestershire

*Humberside*

Dale Hire
Froge Garage, St. John's Street, Bridlington
T Bridlington 78031

*Kent*

Andy Cycles
156 London Road, Dover
T Dover 204401

Calor and Tool Hire Centre
7 Portland Road, Hythe
T Hythe 67954

*Lancashire*

Fernlea Hotel
11–17 South Promenade, Lytham St. Annes
T St. Annes 726726

*Lincolnshire*

Ward & Son
36 High Street, Skegness
T Skegness 2936

*Norfolk*

Dodgers
69 Trinity Street, Norwich
T Norwich 22499

Rent-A-Bike
The New Inn, Roughton, Nr. Cromer
T Cromer 389

*Northumberland*

Chappells Cycle Dealers
17a Bridge Street, Berwick-upon-Tweed
T Berwick 6295

*Nottinghamshire*

National Trust East Midlands Regional Office
Clumber Park, Worksop
T Worksop 81341

*Oxfordshire*

Denton Cycles
194 Banbury Road, Oxford
T Oxford 53859

North Oxford Bike Shop
North Parade Avenue, Oxford

Penny Farthing
27 George Street, Oxford

Robinson's Cycles
46 Magdalen Road, Oxford
T Oxford 49289

*Salop (Shropshire)*

Border Holiday Tours
11a St. John's Hill, Shrewsbury SY1 1JJ
T Shrewsbury 65150

Roberts
39 Belle Vue Road, Shrewsbury
T Shrewsbury 50562

*Somerset*

Coastal Concessions
See under *Avon*

Quantock Rent-A-Bike
Rowford Cottage, Cheddon Fitzpaine, Taunton
T Kingston St. Mary 248

Rent-A-Cycle
The Lido, Seafront, Minehead

West Country Rent-A-Bike
Merriott, Crewkerne
T Crewkerne 72401

*Straffordshire*

Roy Swinnerton
69 Victoria Road, Fenton, Stoke-on-Trent
T Stoke-on-Trent 47782

Scotia Road Sports Centre
Scotia Road, Tunstall, Stoke-on-Trent
T Stoke-on-Trent 812008

*Suffolk*

Back to the Bike
Mount Pleasant, Reydon, Southwold
T Southwold 3775

Countryman Leisure Ltd.
Old Council Offices, Main Street, Leiston
T Leiston 830250

Holiday Leisure and Hire Services Ltd.
329 Whapload Road, Lowestoft
T Lowestoft 64759

Ranelagh Road Cycles
Ranelagh Road, Ipswich
T Ipswich 50610

*Surrey*

DBS Garages
High Street, Cranleigh
T Cranleigh 5133

Rentabike (Farnham) Ltd.
Hunters Lodge, 44 Crooksbury Road, Runfold
T Runfold 2532

The Shire
Byworth Road, Farnham
T Farnham 24433

Walton Cycle Shop
Walton-on-Thames
T Walton 21424

*Sussex, East*

A.J. Russell
1 The Strand, Walmer, Nr. Deal
T Deal 4535

Andy Cycles
156 London Road, Dover
T Dover 204401

Calor & Tool Hire Centre
7 Portland Road, Hythe
T Hythe 67954

Cronin's Garage
1 St. John's Road, Hove
T Brighton 732350

2 Elphinstone Road
Hastings

F.C. Couchman
8 Station Approach, Tonbridge
T Tonbridge 353569

Hira-Bike
13 Blatchington Road, Hove
T Brighton 724191

R.J. Search & Sons
97 London Road, Bexhill
T Bexhill 213299

Rentabike
Silverdale Road Garage, Silverdale Road, Eastbourne
T Eastbourne 34549

Smith's
5 Sevenoaks Road, Otford
T Otford 2517

Stubberfield's
12 South Street, Eastbourne
T Eastbourne 30795

Tutt Brothers
Clinton Lane, Seaford
T Seaford 893130

*Sussex, West*

B.C. Floyds Ltd.
31 Surrey Street, Littlehampton
T Littlehampton 3957

Coastal Concessions
See under *Avon*

R.C. Floyds
31 Surrey Street, Littlehampton
T Littlehampton 3957

Rent-A-Cycle
Old Bus Station, Arundel

Rent-A-Cycle
c/o Tourist Information Centre, Windmill Complex, Windmill Road, Littlehampton
T Littlehampton 21681

Rent-A-Cycle
Harbour Master's Office, West Itchenor

Ron Mills Cycles and Prams
118 Chapel Road, Worthing
T Worthing 33125

### *Tyne & Wear*

Sanders Bros. Cycle Corner
6a Brighton Grove, Newcastle upon Tyne
T Newcastle 35045

### *Warwickshire*

Hirabike at Stratford Marine Ltd.
Clopton Bridge, Stratford-upon-Avon
T Stratford 69669

### *Wiltshire*

C.F. Haynes
8–10 Water Lane, Salisbury
T Salisbury 4915

### *Yorkshire, North*

Brian Shannon
171 Boroughbridge Road, Acomb, York
T York 791610

Coastal Concessions
See under *Avon*

Crescent Cycles
5 The Crescent, York
T York 28844

Dale Hire
Forge Garage, St. John's Street, Bridlington
T Bridlington 78031

Dale Hire
5 Gladstone Road, Scarborough
T Scarborough 67575

Dale Hire
Clarence Street Filling Station, York
T York 29838

Freedom of Ryedale
8 Bondgate, Helmsley
T Helmsley 282

Hire-A-Bike
12 West Park, Harrogate HG1 1BL
T Harrogate 60506

ENGLAND/ISLANDS

## Channel Islands

### Alderney

Mr. R. Butler
"Loroma," Longy Road
T Alderney 2184

Mr. J. Gorman
St. Margarets, Ollivier Street
T Alderney 2199

### Guernsey

A.T. Domaille & Sons
16 Bordage. St. Peter Port
T Guernsey 21551

G.L.F. Domaille
The Bridge, St. Sampsons
T Guernsey 44542

H.C. Tostevin
Grande Rue, St. Martins
T Guernsey 37671

Millard & Co.
Victoria Road, St. Peter Port
T Guernsey 20777

Perrio
Chescot, Route Carre, L'Islet, St. Sampsons
T Guernsey 45217

R.J. Le Moignan
Lindale, Rue Maze, St. Martin's
T Guernsey 36815

T.G. Moullin & Co.
St. George's Esplanade, St. Peter Port
T Guernsey 21581

### Jersey

Anne's Bike Hire
Villa Annvern, Douet, St. Peter
T Jersey Central 44379

Boudin's
10 Sand Street, St. Helier
T Jersey Central 32221

Don Road Hire Service
Don Road, St. Helier
T Jersey Central 20181

Doubleday Garage Ltd.
19 Stopford Road, St. Helier
T Jersey Central 31505

Easy-Ride
23 Havre des Pas, St. Helier
T Jersey Central 33876

Hireride
1 St. John's Road, St. Helier
T Jersey Central 31995

Morley's Automatic Stores
80 Halkett Place, St. Helier
T Jersey Central 20135

St. Brelade's Garage
Airport Road, St. Brelade
T Jersey Central 41131

### Sark

Gallery Stores, Sark

Mr. J. Jackson
Cycle Shop, La Rue Lucas
T Sark 102

*Isle of Man*

ABA Cycles
Central Promenade, Douglas
T Douglas 21869

Calwood Sports Cycle Hire
86 Bucks Road, Douglas
T Douglas 5742

*Isles of Scilly*

Cycle Shop
St. Mary's

*Isle of Wight*

Parkes of Ryde
Castle Garage, John Street, Ryde
T Ryde 2752

Pimm Cycle Hire
Pinewood End, Thorley
T Yarmouth 760671

Vectis Products
The Broadway, Totland Bay
T Freshwater 2455

NORTHERN IRELAND

*Co. Antrim*

B.C. Monteith
135 Main Street, Larne

The Cycle Shop
8 Railway Street, Lisburn
T Lisburn 2066

G. Stone
6 Cromac Square, Belfast
T Belfast 30156

Hickland Cycles
Roses Lane Ends, Ballinderry
T Crumlin 52354

J.M. Hanna
Chapel Hill, Lisburn
T Lisburn 79575

James Spence
88 Castle Street, Ballycastle

R.F. Linton & Son
Springwell Street, Ballymena
T Ballymena 2516

Rent-A-Bike
Castle Stores, Castle Street, Ballycastle
T Ballycastle 62487

*Co. Down*

G.P. Marshall & Son
Abbey Street, Bangor
T Bangor 60467

McClure's
17 Dundrum Road, Newcastle
T Newcastle 3262

*Co. Fermanagh*

P. McNulty
22/24 Belmore Street, Enniskillen
T Enniskillen 2423, Enniskillen 2098 (after 6 pm)

Stevenson's Cycle Stores
42/43 Darling Street,
Enniskillen
T Enniskillen 2417

*Co. Londonderry*

Strand Hotel
Portstewart
T Portstewart 3311

William Nutt
4 Newmarket Street, Coleraine
T Coleraine 4776

## SCOTLAND

*Borders*

R.G. Swan
9 Bridge Street, Kelso,
Roxburghshire
T Kelso 2749

*Dumfries and Galloway*

Brandedleys Carafarm
Crocketford, Dumfries
T Crocketford 250

Clyde Centre
Glasgow Street, Dumfries

Crierson & Graham Limited
Church Crescent, Dumfries
T Dumfries 3405

*Fife*

W. Band & Son
Crail Road, Anstruther
T Anstruther 310502

*Grampian*

J. Anderson
46/52 Rosemont Viaduct,
Aberdeen
T Aberdeen 21520

J. Grant & Co.
Castleton Garage, Braemar,
Aberdeenshire
T Bramear 210

Halford's Ltd.
34 High Street, Elgin,
Morayshire
T Elgin 2593

Mr. J. McLean
Gordon Street, Forres,
Morayshire
T Forres 2782

Myrus Caravan Site
Macduff, Banffshire
T Banff 2845

Mr. A. Paterson
Station Square, Ballater,
Aberdeenshire
T Ballater 343

Ross-Hire
Auchattie, Banchory,
Kincardineshire
T Banchory 2839

Wm. Stuart & Son
30 High Street, Forres,
Morayshire
T Forres 2432 (summer only)

*Highland*

Cairdsport
Aviemore, Inverness-shire
T Aviemore 296

Craiglea
Aviemore, Inverness-shire
T Aviemore 210

Craiglynne Hotel
Grantown-on-Spey, Morayshire
T Grantown 2597

D'Ecosse Sports Shop
Aviemore, Inverness-shire
T Aviemore 285

Fairways Guest House
Carrbridge, Inverness-shire
T Carrbridge 240

Highland Guides
Aviemore, Inverness-shire
T Aviemore 729

Hughes Cycles
Princes Street, Thurso, Caithness
T Thurso 2511

Lochbroom Community Association
Ullapool Recreation Park, Ullapool, Ross-shire

Ness Motors
Friar Street, Inverness, Inverness-shire
T Inverness 34367

Mr. Noble
Boat of Garten Caravan Site, Boat of Garten, Inverness-shire
T Boat of Garten 652

Pay-to-Pedal
Brin Estate, Farr, Inverness-shire
T Farr 211

Mr. Trotter
Brin House, Flichity, Inverness-shire
T Flichity 211

Mr. John Urquhart
The Cycle Shop, Main Street, Muir of Ord, Ross-shire
T Muir of Ord 462

*Lothian*

Cycles
12 West Preston Street, Edinburgh
T 031–667 6239

Thingummyjigs
248 Dalry Road, Edinburgh 11
T 031–337 5753

*Strathclyde*

Alexander Bracken (Holiday Hire)
1F Darroch Way, Seafar, Cumbernauld G67 1QA

Dale's Cycles
26/30 Maryhill Road, Glasgow
T 041–332 2705

David Rattray & Co. Ltd.
261 Alexandria Parade, Glasgow
T 041–554 3757

Dialabike
Cressnock, Laurel Crescent, Oban, Argyll
T Oban 3488

Finnies Cycle Centre
40 Newmarket Street, Ayr, Ayrshire
T Ayr 82368

*Tayside*

A. Fender
6 Perth Street, Blairgowrie, Perthshire
T Blairgowrie 2422

McKerchar & MacNaughton Limited
Aberfeldy, Perthshire
T Aberfeldy 567/8

SCOTLAND/ISLANDS

Bremner's Store
17 Cardiff Street, Millport, Isle of Cumbrae
T Millport 521

Messrs. S. Buckeridge & Son
5 Bishop Street, Rothesay, Isle of Bute
T Rothesay 2479

Messrs. Calder Brothers
7 Bridge Street, Rothesay, Isle of Bute

The Cycle Shop
Cromwell Street Pier, Stornoway, Isle of Lewis
T Stornoway 2202

The Cycle Shops
Kyleakin, Isle of Skye
T Kyleakin 332

Eric Brown Cycle Agent
7 Commercial Road, Lerwick, Shetland
T Lerwick 433

F.V.G. Mapes & Sons
4 Guildford Street, Millport, Isle of Cumbrae
T Millport 444

Mrs. Glen
Hillshore, Brodick, Isle of Arran
T Brodick 2444

Mrs. Hislop
Park Cottage, Lamlash, Isle of Arran
T Lamlash 441

A. Howie
Roselyn, Brodick, Isle of Arran
T Brodick 2460

Mr. Hugh Morrison
The Post Office, Castlebay, Isle of Barra
T Castlebay 286

Isle of Barra Hotel
Tangusdale, Isle of Barra
T Castlebay 383

Isle of Eigg Estate
Eigg
T Mallaig 82423 or 82428
Information can be obtained from the Secretary on bicycle and moped hire

Mr. James Young
Heather Cottage, Lochboisdale, Isle of South Uist

Mr. Liddle
Marona, Orphir, Orkney
T Orphir 227

Mr. D.M. Mackenzie
Hairdresser, Pier Road, Tarbert, Isle of Harris
T Harris 2271

Mr. Mason
Corrie Stores, Corrie, Isle of Arran
T Corrie 209

A&T Morton
4 Mount Stuart Street, Millport, Isle of Cumbrae
T Millport 478

Orkney Tourist Organisation
Information Centre, Kirkwall, Orkney KW15 1DE
Will give information on bicycle hire

Mr. Ritchie
Trumland House, Rousay, Orkney
T Rousay 263

H. Rodgers
Glenflorol, Brodick, Isle of Arran
T Brodick 2314

I. Russell
Old Pier Craft Centre, Whiting Bay, Isle of Arran
T Whiting Bay 240

Tourist Information Office
Meall House, Portree, Isle of Skye
T Portree 2137/2317

## WALES

### *Glamorgan, South*

Cardiff Bicycle Hire & Tours
5 Duke Street Arcade, Cardiff
T Cardiff 33445

### *Gwynedd*

Coastal Concessions
See under *England, Avon*

## HOLLAND

There is scarcely a town or village in Holland without a shop that rents bicycles. Below are listed shops located in most of the important towns, cities, and resort areas of Holland. The listing is arranged by region, town within the region, and then specific rental place.

### GRONINGEN

*Groningen (city of)*

Fa. E. Glaudé
Hereweg 1/5

Fa. Jonkman
Eikenlaan 29

J.F.F. Kuis
Zuiderstat

Fa. Laffra
Korreweg 113

Fa. Westerkamp
Moesstraat 44

### FRIESLAND

*Ameland*

Kl. W. Nobel
Camminghastraat 20

Th. Metz
Strandweg 2A

P. Faber
Corn. Bruinpad 5

Fa. Visser
Schoolstraat 22

P.C. de Boer
Strandweg 4

Th. Kieviet
M. Janszenweg 2

*Drachten*

J. Jonkman
Stationsweg 52

B. Koehoorn
Houtlaan 4

H. Numan
Noordkade 115

*Heerenveen*

Fa. Smit
Marktweg 22

T. Veenstra
Station Heerenveen

*Leeuwarden*

R. Elzinga
Hooidollen 530

*Sneek*

F. Postma
Wijde Noorderhorne 8

*Terschelling (island of)*

H.A. Haantjes
Formerum 28

D. Smit (Hoorn)
Dorpsstraat 31

R. Bakker & Zn. (Hoorn)
Lies 8

J. Elslo (Midsland)
Westerburen 7

L. Doeksen (Midsland)
Baaiduinen 36

S. de Groot (Midsland)
Westerburen 20

A.C. de Jong
Burg. Reedekerstrass 15

Tijs Knop
Gorenstrass 10–12

J.A. Vuurer-Heykoop
Parnassiaweg 5

P. Zeeders & Zn.
Torenstraat 49

*Vlieland*

Mevr. S. Dijkstra
Dorpsstraat 8

D. de Jong
Dorpsstraat 79

J.J. Kuipers
Dorpsstraat 71

## DRENTE

*Assen*

E.L. Christian
Stationsrijwielstalling

A. Oosting & Zn.
New Huizen 11

R. van Veen
Ruysdaelstr. 35–37

A. de Vries
Julianastr. 5

C. Watering
Oosterhoutstr. 94

Buitencentrum Witterzomer
Witterzomer 7

*Emmen*

G. Dekker Wzn.
Weerdingerstr. 214–5

M.J. Duinkerken
Noordbargerstr. 5

W.H. Oost/W.J.M. Spruyt
Station Emmen

Joh. Vos
Haagjesweg 283

Joh. Vos
Statenweg 23

Joh. Vos
De Haar 106

*Hoogeveen*

G.W. Danes
Hoofdstraat 192

A. Hartman & Zn.
Schutstraat 98

H. van Holten
Station Hoogeveen

A.S. Sybesma
v. Echtenstr. 10

Velo
Hoofdstraat 22

W. Verhoeven
v. Echtenstr. 10

*Meppel*

H. van Holten
Leliestraat 3

H. van Holten
Stationsstalling

L. Pot
Westerstouwe

*Zweeloo*

J. Huisjes
Mepperstr. 26

J. Seubers
Aelderstr. 1

A. Weerman
Hoofdstr. 17

OVERIJSSEL

*Almelo*

J.R. Bloemendaal
Deldensestr. 125

Fa. Smit
Ootmarsumsestr. 141–3

Jan Wild
Nieuwstraat 151

*Deventer*

J. Evers
Station Deventer

*Enschede*

J.A. Hassing
Brinkstraat 172

J.H. Hassing
Ledeboerstraat 59

A. van 't Slot
Volksparksingel 4

De Wilde B.V.
Haaksbergerstr. 342

B. te Nijenhuis
Kuipersdijk 117–19

H. Verheyen
Stationsplein/Albergenhink 47

*Hengelo*

Fa. G. Elbert
Twekkelerplein 27–28

B. Nijhof
Station Hengelo

*Kampen*

E. Potkamp & Zn.
Oudestraat 152

E. Spruijt
Station Kampen

*Nijverdal*

T. Aanstoot
Rijssensestr. 111

B. Bouwhuis
De Jonckheerelaan 13

J. Konijnenbelt & Zn.
G.H. Kappertstr. 4–4A

H. v. Lindenberg
Stationsstraat 2

L. Overdorp
De Joncheerel. 11–13

*Oldenzaal*

B.J. Siemerink
Berkstraat 9

*Zwolle*

Gait Rigter
Holtenbroekerweg 52

H.J. Scholten
Luttekestr. 7

E. Spruijt
Station Zwolle

GELDERLAND

*Apeldoorn*

Fa. Blakborn
Soerenseweg 3

Fa. Bloemendaal
Hobbemalaan 68

J.A. Doornhein
Schubertlaan 4

F.J. Harleman
Pinksterbloem 10–12

Fa. Hoekman
Zwolseweg 227

F.J. Horst
Hofstraat 41

Gebr. Onderstal
Stationsstr. 3

H.W.H. Rodink
Asselsestr. 214

G. van 't Slot
Groeneweg 4

Fa. Wiegman
Stationsstr. 5

Fa. van Zutfen
Loolaan 14

*Arnhem*

Adr. Bax B.V.
Mariënburgstr. 9

J.H. Bolder
Akkerwindestr. 41–43

H. v.d. Eshof
Station Arnhem

D. Mantel
v. Law. v. Pabststr. 95

H. Matser
Kemperbergerweg 42

H.H.C. Postma
Jacob Cremerstr. 7

W.A. Roelofs
G.A. v. Nispenstr. 1

*Ede*

A. Eikenaar
Parkweg 61

W.F. de Fluiter
Station Ede-Wageningen

Maxstein/J.B. Schut
Slijpkruikweg 30

A. van Riessen
Telefoonweg 104

Ph. van Wijk
Not. Fischerstr. 10

*Eibergen*

W. Grooters & Zn.
Haaksbergseweg 2–4

W. Grooters & Zn.
Rekkenseweg B 184

J. Leussink
Laagte 16

J. Leussink
Kerkstraat 41

A.H.M. Pierik
Grotestraat 66

*Ermelo*

M. Bakker
Groeneweg 17

P. Bijker
Telgterweg 40

Fa. Doggenaar
Stationsstr. 62

L. Ebbers
Stationsstr. 102

J. Elbersen
Horsterweg 131

H.J. Schoeman
Station Ermelo/Dr. v. Dalelaan 4

G. de Bries
Russulalaan 44

*Groenlo*

E.J. Arink
Mattelierstr. 6–8

Camping De Kunne
Lichtenvoortseweg 68

W.N. Elshof
Nieuwestraat 24

Fa. Sprenkelaar
Ruurloseweg 7

*Groesbeek*

H. Th. van Bergen
Burg. Ottenhoffstr. 2

Sjef v. Bergen B.V.
Dorpsstr. 28A.

Gebr. Tielemans
Pannenstr. 31–33

*Nunspeet*

H. Hoegen
Westerlaan 2

B. de Jong
Station Nunspeet

R. Mouw & Zn.
Stationslaan 49

A. Rikkers
Zeeweg 17

E. Spruyt
Station Nunspeet

A. Vis & Zn.
Eperweg 8–10

De Vossenberg
Groenelaantje 25

E. van der Vegt
Stationslaan 79

*Putten*

J. Ceelen
Postweg 35

A. Kleyer
Huinerschoolweg 2

Gebr. Krol
Dorpsstraat 50

H. Pothoven
Dorpsstraat 107

H. Ruiter
Stationsstraat 126

Stationskoffiehuis
Stationsstraat 125

*Winterswijk*

J.B. Bruggers
Gasthuisstr. 56

J.H. Buunk
Torenstraat 2

H.L. Hartjes
Station Winterswijk

J. Hemink
Kotten 69–1

O.H.G. Kwak
Weurden 43

H. Oonk
Misterstraat 47

Joh. ten Pas
Vredenseweg 9–1

*Zutphen*

E. Spruyt
Station Zutphen

K. Siersma
Rozengracht 15

W.M. Weekenstroo & Zn.
Rijkenhage 18

## UTRECHT

*Amersfoort*

E.J. Eckmann
Station Amersfoort

*Doorn*

J. v.d. Berg
Amersfoortseweg

J. Kieboom
Kampweg 45

Th. Schrader
Kampweg 36

*Utrecht*

F. Leeman
B. Bijnkerkhoekl. 413

G.A. Ottevanger
L. Berchmakersstr. 20–24

H.A. Tusveld
Station Utrecht CS

*Zeist*

Fa. Broederlet
Le Dorpsstraat 22

W.F. Brouwer
Oude Arnhemseweg 23

J.M.v. Dijk & Zn.
Panweg 2–4

J.J. Edelman
Slotlaan 246

J.C.v. Gameren
Steynlaan 32

V.V.V.-kantoor
Slotlaan 321

## NOORD-HOLLAND

*Alkmaar*

W. Rumphorst
Station Alkmaar

*Amsterdam*

K.J. van Anholt
Stadioplein 69–71

J. Braad
Schimmelstr. 3

E. Fiesler
Nwe Nieuwstraat 22

Fiets-O-Fietskiosk
Amstelveenseweg 880–900 hk.
v. Nijenrodeweg

M.E. Fikkert
Rokin 71

Fa. Heja/J. Kinsbergen
Bestevaerstr. 39

N. Koenders
Utrechtsedwarsstr. 105

N. Koenders
Buiten Brouwersstr. 20

A. Loozekoot
Centraal Station

A. Loozekoot
Station A'dam-Amstel

A. Loozekoot
Station Muiderpoort

A. Loozekoot
Station Sloterdijk

A. Loozekoot
Voltaplein 35

Fa. Martens
Javastr. 18

R.H.A. Steur
Willemsparkweg 181–179

Fa. Tromm
Europaplein 45

P.C. Vullings & Zn.
Vossiusstr. 2

*Bakkum*

F. Twisk
Bakkummerstr. 105

*Bergen*

W. Busker & Zn.
Kerkstr. 1–5

G. Th. de Goede
Karel de Grootelaan 2

J. der Kinderen
Oosterweg 7–8

A. Hoogeboom
v. Hasseltweg 12

*Bussum*

Fa. Daatzelaar
Landstr. 39–41

"Het Centrum"
Kapelstraat 17

Th. Fakkeldij
Station Naarden-Bussum

J.H. Peters
Herenstraat 24

A. Vijn
Voormeulenweg 64

*Castricum*

C.H. Bennes
Dorpsstraat 98

Fa. Rumphorst
Station Castricum

G.N. Tervoort
Stationsweg 13

J. Zijlstra
Mient 53

J.P.J. Eikel
Dorpsstraat 51–55

P.G. Liefting
Torenstraat 38

*Haarlem*

R. van Bentem
Station Haarlem

H.E.L. Wielders
Rozenstraat 51–59

*Den Helder*

J. Beekman
"De Zandloper"

P.M. Heiligenbrug
Spoorstraat 97–99

Fa. Koning
Marsdiepstr. 301

Fa. Lafeber
Spoorstraat 23

K. Majolé
Beatrixstr. 17–15 & 70

G.M. Derks
Station Den Helder

H. Isendoorn
Brakkevelderweg 48

*Hilversum*

L. Bonhof & Zn.
Eikbosserweg 126

G. Eijsink
Stationsplein Hilversum

W.J.H. Hunting
Neuweg 48

H.W. Kok
Koninginneweg 76–78

A. Muys
Neuweg 347a

W. Vlijm
Wandelpad 42

G.D. de Weerd
Kometenstraat 119

*St. Maartensbrug*

C. Slijkerman
Ruigeweg 43

P. Vis
Ruigeweg 41

Zonnewende
Ruigeweg 61

P. Quak
Belkmerweg 64

H. Rens
Westerduinweg 32

J. Wey
Belkmerweg 73

*Zaandam*

A. Tukker
Station Zaandam

*Zandvoort*

Fa. Versteege
Haltestraat 18

ZUID-HOLLAND

*Delft*

J. Hectors
Nw. Lange Dijk 1

W.v.d. Wel
Station Delft/van Leeuwenhoeksingel 40A

*Dordrecht*

J.B. Isendoorn
Admiraalsplein 401

P.v.d. Sluis
Eddingtonweg 44

H.M. Voorwinde
Station Dordrecht

*Gouda*

W. Buitelaar
V. Hogendorpplein 7

G. Maissan
Station Gouda

*'s-Gravenhage*

J.J. de Beer
Station H.S.

J.J. de Beer
Station C.S.

H.E. de Booij
Thomsonplein 12

P. Ederveen
Billitonstraat 33

L. de Kok
Theresiastraat 396

H. Scheijgrond
Pr. Willemstr. 14

H.J.v. Zijl & Zn.
Kikkerstraat 14

*Leiden*

R. van Walsum
Lekdijk 5

A. Evers
Station Leiden

J. van Zijp
Haarlemmerstraat 295

*Rotterdam*

Fa. Hofele
Paradijslaan 29

N.A. Kollen
Station Rotterdam C.S.

*Schiedam*

A.F.J. Kamphuis
Station Schiedam–Rotterdam-West

ZEELAND

*Goes*

Fr. de Jonge & Co.
Patijnweg 100

L. Jansen
Station Goes

*Middelburg*

Fa. v.d. Driest
Gravenstraat 18

J.F.H. Meerman
Station Middelburg

Fa. de Pree
Zusterstraat 8

*Vlissingen*

D. de Kam
Station Vlissingen

Rijwielcentrale
Koudekerkseweg 53

De Wielerwinkel
Scheldestr. 84–86

L. Wijckhuis
Badhuisstraat 19

NOORD-BRABANT

*Bergen op Zoom*

H. Hopmans
Steenbergsestr. 50

Fa. v. Loon
Piusplein 144

G. Vriens
Stationsstalling

F.M. Demmers
Korte Bosstr. 11

*Breda*

G. de Jong
Stationsplein 2

Fa. Schietekat
Korte Bosstr. 3

*Eindhoven*

A.M. Becht de Brees
Gen. Bothastraat 61

Jac. Ligtvoet-Philippe
Aalsterweg 91–95

De Rijwielcentrale
Nieuwstraat 30

De Rijwielcentrale
Kruisstraat 98

*Helmond*

"Den Drietip"
Drietipstr. 1

Th. Ketelaars
Hoofdstraat 156

J. v.d. Linden
Kromme Steenweg 33

P. Spierings
Stationsplein 2

*'s Hertogenbosch*

H.J. Burgers
Station Den Bosch

*Roosendaal*

W. Heijnen
Station Roosendaal

Fa. Marijnissen
Stationsstraat 49

Fa. de Rooy
Hulsdonkstraat 80

*Tilburg*

H.J. Burgers
Station Tilburg

A. v.d. Klundert
Watertorenplein 4

N.v. Loon
Jac. Oppenheimstr. 19

A. v.d. Put
Besterdring 38

## LIMBURG

*Heerlen*

J. Nettersheim
Rijksweg 62a

C.L.A. Soelmans/Marseal
Benzenraderweg 14a/22

J. Tonneur
Station Heerlen

*Maastricht*

A.G.C. Peeters
Dorpstraat 28

Fa. J. Felix
St. Pieterstr. 32–34

J. Tonnaer
Arkebusruwe 66

J. Tonnaer
Station Maastricht

*Roermond*

J.H. Jansen
Station Roermond

*Venlo*

H. Rouken
Station Venlo

*Weert*

Van Maurik
Stationsplein

## IRELAND

Raleigh bicycle dealers throughout Ireland participate in a rent-a-bike program. In some cases, bicycles may be rented at one shop and returned to another. These arrangements must be made with the local dealer. Shops are listed under the appropriate county, then town within the county.

### CARLOW

*Carlow*

A.E. Coleman
Dublin Street
Tel: 0503–41273

### CAVAN

*Cavan*

Wheels
Farnham St.
Tel: 049–31831

*Killeshandra*

E. Hastie

### CLARE

*Ennis*

Tom Mannion Travel
O'Connell Street
Tel: 065–21985

Also at Rent-A-Cottage, Ballyvaughan, Broadford, Carrigaholt, Corofin, Feakle

*Kilkee*

P. Keller
Circular Road

*Kilrush*

Michael Gleeson
Henry St.
Tel: 127

*Scarriff*

Treacy's Filling Station
Tel: 14

### CORK

*Bantry*

J. O'Mahony
New Street
Tel: 240

*Castletownbere*

Dermot Murphy
Bridge House
Tel: 20

*Charleville*

Moloney's Cycle Depot

*Clonakilty*

J.E. Spiller & Co. Ltd
39/41 Pearse Street
Tel: 023–43321

*Cork City*

Harding & Co. Ltd.
15/17 South Terrace
and Oliver Plunkett Street
Tel: 021–23930

Ross & Co.
Winthrop Street
Tel: 021–22055

*Crosshaven*

Barry Twomey
Whispering Pines
Tel: 021–831448

*Fermoy*

Cavanagh Motor Cycles
Tel: 025–31339

*Goleen*

J.C. Harrington
Tel: 1

*Kilbrittain*

Ocean Breeze Horse Caravans
Tel: 023–49626

*Schull*

S. Barnett

*Skibbereen*

N.W. Roycroft & Sons
Ilen Street (opposite West Cork Hotel)

*Youghal*

Bob Troy
Tel: 024–2509

DONEGAL

*Ardara*

D. Byrne
Tel: 56

*Ballyshannon*

P.B. Stephens & Co. Ltd.
Castle Street
Tel: (072) 65178

*Donegal Town*

C.J. O'Doherty
Main Street (Doherty's Fishing Tackle)

*Dungloe*

Rosses Service Depot
Tel: 17

*Ramelton*

H. Whoriskey
Tel: 22

*Raphoe*

B. Connolly
William Street
Tel: 32

DUBLIN

*Clondalkin*

Clondalkin Service Station
Monastery Road
Tel: 01–592941

*Dean's Grange*

The Bike Shop
Tel: 01–857474

*Dublin City*

Charley's
35 Ballybough Road
Tel: 01–744090

Clonard Cycles
Clonard Road
Tel: 01–909725

Joe Daly
Lower Main Street, Dundrum
Tel: 01–981485

Gem Cycle Service
47/48 Chelmsford Road
Ranelagh
Tel: 01–978438

Thos. Hollingsworth & Son
54 Templeogue Road
Tel: 01–905094

A. MacDonald
38 Wexford Street
Tel: 01–752586

McHugh Himself
38 Talbot Street
Tel: 01–746694

Northside Camping
Northside Shopping Centre
Tel: 01–316090

P.J. Power
Emmet Road, Inchicore
Tel: 01–752647

Rathgar Cycles
99A Rathgar Road
Tel: 01–970268

Ryan's
115 Upper Dorset Street
Tel: 01–305090

P. Walsh
194 Harold's Cross Road
Tel: 01–977671

*Dun Laoghaire*

M. Sleigh
95 Lower George's Street
Tel: 01–803984

*Malahide*

Executive Cycles
Malahide Shopping Centre
Tel: 01–453562

*Rush*

A. Leonard
Millview Garage
Tel: 01–437297

*Sutton Cross*

Sutton Cycle Service
Tel: 01–322270

GALWAY

*Aran Islands*

Aran Hire
Frenchman's Beach, Cill Ronan

*Ballinasloe*

P. Clarke
Dunlo Street
Tel: 0905–2417

*Clifden*

John Mannion
Tel: 13

*Inishbofin*

Day's Hotel
Tel: 103

*Oughterard*

T. Tuck
Tel: 82335

*Renvyle*

P. Coyne
Tullycross
Tel: 4

*Salthill*

Salthill Rentals
Tel: 091–61821 (Day)
091–62341 (Night)

*Tuam*

Murphy's Cycle Stores
Tel: 093–24292

KERRY

*Cahirciveen*

Paddy Casey
New Street
Tel: 164

*Dingle*

J. Moriarty
Main Street
Tel: 66

Michael O'Sullivan
Waterside
Tel: 46

*Kenmare*

J.P. Finnegan
Henry Street
Tel: 94

*Killarney*

O'Callaghan Bros. (Killarney) Ltd.
College Street
Tel: 064–31465 and 31175
Telex: 6821

Kingdom Cycles
1 Fair Hill
Tel: 064–32542

D. O'Neill
Plunkett Street
Tel: 064–31970

*Killorglin*

J. O'Shea
Lower Bridge Street
Tel: 80

*Listowel*

J. McKenna Ltd.
Tel: 12

*Tralee*

E. Caball
15 Ashe Street
Tel: 066–22231

J. Caball & Co. Ltd.
Staughton's Row
Tel: 066–21654

Tralee Gas Supplies
Strand Street
Tel: 066–22018

KILDARE

*Kilcullen*

T.J. Kelly
Naas Road

*Naas*

John Cahill
Sallins Road
Tel: 045–9655

KILKENNY

*Kilkenny*

John Wall
88 Maudlin Street
Tel: 056–21236

LEITRIM

*Carrick-on-Shannon*

Fred Holt
Bridge St.

LAOIS

*Portlaoise*

M. Kavanagh
Railway Street

LIMERICK

*Limerick City*

Limerick Sports Store
10 William Street
Tel: 061–45647

Limerick Travel
Bedford Row
Tel: 061–43844

Noel McMahon & Son
24 Roches Street
Tel: 061–46718

Nestor Bros.
28 O'Connell Street
Tel: 061–44096

*Newcastle West*

Scanlan's Cycle Stores
Maiden Street
Tel: 348

LONGFORD

*Longford*

E. Denniston
Central Cycle Store
Tel: 043–6345

LOUTH

*Drogheda*

P.J. Carolan
77 Trinity Street
Tel: 041–8242

*Dundalk*

George Elliott
Anne Street
Tel: 042–32224

R. O'Neill
6 Earl Street
Tel: 042–34718

## MAYO

### *Ballina*

W.J. Kearney
Abbey Street
Tel: 21249

### *Ballinrobe*

E. Finlay
Glebe Street

### *Ballycastle*

Barretts Stores
Tel: 6

### *Castlebar*

Josie Bourke & Son
Main Ford Dealers
Tel: 6

### *Westport*

J.P. Breheny & Sons
Castlebar Street
Tel: 4

Westport House
Tel: 130

## MONAGHAN

### *Monaghan*

J.J. Clerkin
Market Street
Tel: 550

Patrick McCoy
Dublin Street
Tel: 047–81283

## OFFALY

### *Birr*

P.L. Dolan & Sons
Main Street
Tel: 6

### *Edenderry*

L. Moran
O'Connell Square
Tel: 77

### *Tullamore*

C. McCabe
Church Street
Tel: 0506–21717

## ROSCOMMON

### *Castlerea*

T. Bruen
Main Street
Tel: 73

### *Roscommon*

Vincent McManus
12 Castle Street
Tel: 6409

## SLIGO

### *Enniscrone*

G. Helly
Tel: 101

### *Sligo*

Woods Cycle Co.
7 Castle Street
Tel: 071–2021

## TIPPERARY

### *Carrick-on-Suir*

O'K Garage

### *Clonmel*

Sean Hackett
Westgate
Tel: 052–21869

Bill Purcell
The Mall
Tel: 052–21002

### *Nenagh*

R. Moynan
Central Garage, Pearse Street
Tel: 067–31293

### *Tipperary*

J.J. O'Carroll
10 James's Street
Tel: 062–51229

## WATERFORD

### *Cappoquin*

Bob Troy
Main Street
Tel: 46

### *Dungarvan*

Colum Moloney (Colum's Shop)
O'Connell Street
Tel: 058–41278

Bob Troy
O'Connell Street
Tel: 058–41590

### *Tramore*

P. Murphy
Pickardstown Service Station
Tel: 051–81094

### *Waterford*

Wright's Cycle Depot
Henrietta Street
Tel: 051–4411

## WESTMEATH

### *Athlone*

Hardimans
48 Connaught Street

Michael Hardiman
Irishtown
Tel: 0902–2951

### *Mullingar*

D. O'Callaghan & Son
Tel: 044–8306

## WEXFORD

### *Wexford*

John Murphy
92 North Main St.

Roche Cycle Service
Spawell Road
Tel: 053–23737

## WICKLOW

### *Arklow*

J. Caulfield Motor Cycles
King's Hill

John Owens
Main Street
Tel: 0402–2329

*Bray*

Eric R. Harris
87C Greenpark Road
Tel: 01–863357

*Wicklow*

Brian W. Harris
1 Church Street
Tel: 0404–2247

## LUXEMBOURG

Francis
16, rue Beaumont
Luxembourg
Telephone 296–54

Hotel Beau-Sejour
Esplanade 12
Diekirch

Syndicat d'Iniative et de
Tourisme Reisdorf
Reisdorf

Bastin Remy
rue du Vieux Marché, 25
Vianden

Edm. Poos, Station ARAL
Maison 8
Berdorf

Schmit Georges
rue Ermesinde, 27
Echternach

## SCANDINAVIA

### DENMARK

Bicycles are available for rental in many towns within Denmark. Approach the local tourist agency for addresses of rental shops. In addition, there is an established rental agent in Copenhagen. The address is:

Koebenhavns Cykelboers
Gothersgade 157
DK-1123
Copenhagen K
Telephone: (01) 140717

### NORWAY

N A F Bogstad Camping
Oslo

Gustav Steensland
Løkkeveien 38
Stavanger

## SWEDEN

Bicycles may be rented in most major cities and towns within Sweden. Inquire at the local tourist agencies for addresses. In Stockholm, rental information may be secured from the Swedish bicycling organization, Cykel- & Mopedfrämjandet (see Appendix 5 for address).

## SWITZERLAND

Three-speed bicycles for men and women can be rented from and returned to any station of the Swiss Federal Railways and most stations of private railway companies. In addition, rental bicycles are available from the following Cycle Centers located in different parts of the country:

Cyclo-Center Yens
Garage de la Gare
Yens
Telephone: 021–77–11–06

Fahrrad-Zentrum
Gas station Total
Kallnach
Telephone: 032–82–16–25

Cyclo-Centre Jura
Gas station ESSO
Saignelegier
Telephone: 039–51–12–09

Fahrrad Zentrum
Hans Rebstein
Rebstein
Telephone: 071–77–14–35

Gahrrad-Zentrum
Rothens Cycle Shop
Oberaegeri
Telephone: 042–72–23–17

Fahrrad-Zentrum
Werner Huerlimann's Cycle Shop
Albisstrasse
Mettmenstetten
Telephone: 01–99–03–70

APPENDIX 7

# Mail order map sources

Michelin, Bartholomew, Kummerly+Frey, and other maps of sufficient detail (1:500,000 or better) may be available in a local book or map store. Check first. If unavailable, detailed regional maps covering most western European countries may be ordered by mail from a variety of sources.

Following are a list of useful maps for bicycle touring, the countries covered by the map series, and the places from which they may be ordered. In certain instances, notably the British Cycling Federation and the Cyclists Touring Club of Britain, you must be a member to use their map order services. In all cases when making map orders from overseas sources allow at least two months for the order to be placed and completed. None of the maps listed (except Michelin 1:500,000, Portugal) cover a country in one sheet.

*Map*

Bartholomew GT Series (1:253,440)
Bartholomew National Series (1:100,000)

*Countries covered*

England
Scotland
Wales
Ireland (1:253,440 only)
Ulster (1:253,440 only)

*Sources*

John Bartholomew & Son
Duncan Street
Edinburgh EH9 1TA
Scotland

British Cycling Federation
(See Appendix 5 for address)

Cyclists Touring Club
(See Appendix 5 for address)

---

*Map*

Michelin 1:200,000

*Countries covered*

France
Belgium
Holland
Luxembourg
Switzerland
Germany (western section only)
Italy (north of Milano only)

*Sources*

The French and Spanish Book Corporation
115 Fifth Avenue
New York, N.Y. 10003

Michelin Guides and Maps
P.O. Box 5022
New Hyde Park, N.Y. 11042

British Cycling Federation
(See Appendix 5 for address)

---

*Map*

Michelin 1:400,000

*Countries covered*

Austria
Great Britain
Spain (Pyrenees only)

*Sources*

The French and Spanish Book Corporation
(See above for address)

Michelin Guides and Maps
(See above for address)

British Cycling Federation
(See Appendix 5 for address)

---

*Map*

Michelin 1:500,000

*Country covered*

Portugal

*Sources*

The French and Spanish Book Corporation
(See above for address)

Michelin Guides and Maps
(See above for address)

---

*Map*

A.N.W.B. 1:100,000

*Country covered*

Holland

*Source*

A.N.W.B.
Wassenaarseweg 220

Den Haag
Holland

---

*Map*

Mairs

*Country covered*

Germany

*Source*

British Cycling Federation
(See Appendix 5 for address)

---

*Map*

Cappelin

*Country covered*

Norway

*Source*

British Cycling Federation
(See Appendix 5 for address)

---

*Map*

Touring Club Italiano *Grandi Carte* 1:200,000

*Country covered*

Italy

*Source*

Touring Club Italiano
Corso Italia, 10
20122 Milano
Italy

APPENDIX 8

# Bicycle equipment sources

The following mail order houses provide bicycles, parts, or accessories. Catalogue costs and phone numbers are noted.

Avacado Cycles
647 Morin St.
Ottawa, Ontario K1K 3G8
Canada
Telephone: (613) 745–8604
Catalogue: $1.00

Bikecology Bike Shops
1515 Wilshire Blvd.
Santa Monica, Ca. 90406
Telephone: (800) 421–7153
(toll free outside California)
(213) 829–7681 (within California)
Catalogue: $2.00

Bike Warehouse
215 Main
Middletown, Ohio 44442
Telephone: (1–800) 321–2474
(toll free)
Catalogue: 50¢ (Canada: 75¢)

Cycle Goods Corp.
17701 Leeman Drive
Minnetonka, Minn. 55343
Catalogue: $3.00

Lickton's Cycle City
310 Lake St.
Oak Park, Ill. 60302
Telephone: (312) 383–4433
Catalogue: $1.00

Pedal Pushers, Inc.—Wheels n' Things
1130 Rogero Rd.
Jacksonville, Fla. 32211
Telephone: (1–904) 725–2211

Recreational Equipment, Inc.
Co-op (REI Co-op has four branches)
1526 11th Avenue
Seattle, Wash.

1798 Jantzen Beach
Portland, Ore.

1328 San Pablo Ave.
Berkeley, Calif.

495 West Torrance Blvd.
Los Angeles, Calif.
Telephone: Alaska & Hawaii:
(1–800) 426–4770 (toll free)
Washington:
(1–800) 562–4894 Other
states: (1–800) 423–4840
Membership: $2.00
Catalogue: free with
membership

Touring Cyclist Shop
2639 Spruce St.
Boulder, Colo. 80306
Catalogue: free

APPENDIX 9

# Camping and hosteling information

## CAMPING

National Campers and Hikers Association
7172 Transit Rd.
Buffalo, N.Y. 14221
Membership includes international camping carnet
Fee: $14 per year for entire family

The Camping Club of Great Britain and Ireland, Ltd.
11 Lower Grosvenor Place
London S.W. 1
England
Membership includes international camping carnet and complete camping guide for Great Britain and Ireland.

National Tourist Offices. See Appendix 4 for addresses of individual countries.

## YOUTH HOSTELS

Membership in any Youth Hostel organization provides you with access to all hostels. The American Youth Hostel Handbook is free, but for Youth Hostel locations in Europe you must purchase the International Youth Hostels Handbook (vol. 1 covers Europe). Cost is $4.50 plus 50¢ postage.

American Youth Hostels, Inc.
National Campus
Delaplane, Va. 22025

| Membership: | Under 18 | $ 5.00 |
|---|---|---|
| | 18 and over | $11.00 |
| | Entire family | $12.00 |

Canadian Youth Hostels Association
233 River Rd.
Ottawa, Ontario K12 8B9
Canada

Youth Hostel Association (for England and Wales)
29 John Adam Street
London W.C. 2
England

APPENDIX 10

# Conversion charts

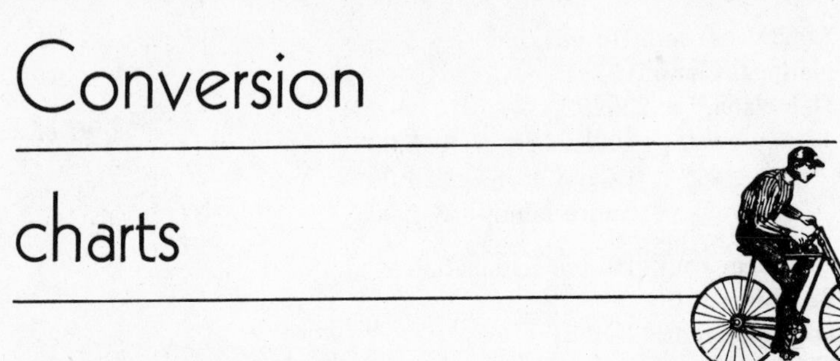

## MEASURES

| | | | |
|---|---|---|---|
| 1 centimeter | 0.39 inches | 4 kilometers | 2.48 miles |
| 1 meter | 3 feet 3¼″ | 5 kilometers | 3.10 miles |
| 1 kilometer | 0.62 miles | 10 kilometers | 6.21 miles |
| 2 kilometers | 1.24 miles | 50 kilometers | 31 miles |
| 3 kilometers | 1.86 miles | 100 kilometers | 61 miles |

## KILOMETERS—MILES CONVERSION TABLE

| *km to miles* | | *miles to km* | |
|---|---|---|---|
| 1 | 0.62 | 1 | 1.609 |
| 2 | 1.24 | 1 | 3.22 |
| 3 | 1.86 | 3 | 4.83 |
| 4 | 2.48 | 4 | 6.44 |
| 5 | 3.10 | 5 | 8.05 |
| 6 | 3.72 | 6 | 9.66 |
| 7 | 4.34 | 7 | 11.27 |
| 8 | 4.96 | 8 | 12.87 |
| 9 | 5.58 | 9 | 14.48 |
| 10 | 6.20 | 10 | 16.09 |
| 15 | 9.30 | 15 | 34.30 |

| | | | |
|---|---|---|---|
| 20 | 12.40 | 20 | 32.30 |
| 25 | 15.50 | 25 | 40.50 |
| 30 | 18.60 | 30 | 48.60 |
| 35 | 21.70 | 35 | 56.70 |
| 40 | 24.80 | 40 | 64.80 |
| 45 | 27.90 | 45 | 72.90 |
| 50 | 31.00 | 50 | 81.00 |
| 55 | 34.10 | 55 | 84.10 |
| 60 | 37.20 | 60 | 97.20 |
| 65 | 40.30 | 65 | 105.30 |
| 70 | 43.40 | 70 | 113.40 |
| 75 | 46.50 | 75 | 121.5 |
| 80 | 49.60 | 80 | 129.60 |
| 85 | 52.70 | 85 | 137.70 |
| 90 | 55.80 | 90 | 145.80 |
| 95 | 58.90 | 95 | 153.90 |
| 100 | 62.00 | 100 | 162.00 |

## CAPACITY

| | | | |
|---|---|---|---|
| 1 liter | 1.06 quarts | 25 liters | 6.62 gallons |
| 5 liters | 1.33 gallons | 50 liters | 13.25 gallons |
| 10 liters | 2.65 gallons | 100 liters | 26.50 gallons |

## EQUIVALENTS

| | | | |
|---|---|---|---|
| 1 kilo | 1 liter | 34 ounces | 4¼ cups |
| ½ kilo | ½ liter | 17 ounces | 2⅛ cups |

| | | | | |
|---|---|---|---|---|
| 50 grams | | 1¾ ounces | 1 ounce | 28 grams |
| 100 grams | | 3½ ounces | 2 ounces | 56 grams |
| 125 grams | | 4¼ ounces | 5 ounces | 146 grams |
| 250 grams | | 8¾ ounces | 8 ounces | 227 grams |
| 500 grams | (½ kilo) | 1 lb. ½ ounce | 12 ounces | 340 grams |
| 1000 grams | ( 1 kilo) | 2 lb. 2 ounces | 16 ounces | 453 grams |

# Bibliography

## PERIODICALS

*Bicycling*. Published monthly March-August, bi-monthly September-February. 33 East Minor Street, Emmaus, PA 18049. Contains information on touring, including European touring, as well as related information on equipment, conditioning, and matters of general interest to the recreational cyclist.

*Bike World*. Published monthly. Box 366, Mountain View, CA 94042. A general-interest publication with occasional articles useful for planning a European tour. Features information on racing, equipment, and bicycle history.

*Cycletouring*. Published by the Cyclists Touring Club, 69 Meadrow, Godalming, Surrey, England. Members of the CTC receive it automatically. Has articles on touring emphasizing the British Isles, but also regular features on European touring in general.

## BOOKS

*Basic Riding Techniques*. Published by the editors of *Bicycling* magazine. Emmaus, Penn.: Rodale Press, 1979. A collection of short and exceptionally helpful articles; valuable even for the experienced cyclist.

Davidson, Sharon and Gary. *Europe with Two Kids and a Van.*

New York: Charles Scribner's Sons, 1973. Though written for car campers, this has a great deal of information useful for the cyclist thinking about a bicycle/camping trip.

DeLong, Fred. *DeLong's Guide to Bicycles and Bicycling.* New York: Chilton Book Co., 1974. DeLong is one of the best technical writers in the field, and his book reflects this expertise. The most complete treatment of its kind.

Europa Camping and Caravaning. Stuttgart: Reise und Verkehrsverlay, 1973. Somewhat dated but still an excellent guide to campgrounds throughout Europe. Lists sites, facilities, opening and closing dates. Too bulky to take on tour, but useful for planning.

Fletcher, Colin. *The New Complete Walker.* Second Edition. New York: Alfred A. Knopf, 1977. An excellent discussion of lightweight backpacking equipment, much of which is useful for a cyclist in search of the best lightweight equipment to take on a tour. The book is also fascinating reading on a general level.

*Fodor's Guides.* Edited by Eugene Fodor. New York: David McKay Co., various dates. Fodor's guides have good general information about countries and excellent discussions of what to see and do in the major cities and tourist centers. These guides, most of which are issued annually, cover the following countries: Belgium and Luxembourg, France, Germany, Great Britain, Greece, Holland, Ireland, Italy, Portugal, Scandinavia, Spain, Switzerland, and Yugoslavia. Each country is covered in a single volume.

Glenn, Harold T., and Clarence W. Coles. *Glenn's Complete Bicycle Manual.* New York: Crown Publishers, 1973. A good general book on the mechanics of bicycle maintenance and repair.

*International Youth Hostel Handbook, Volume 1.* Published by the International Youth Hostel Federation and issued annually, this covers locations, opening and closing dates, and general information about European youth hostels. Essential for the hosteler. May be purchased from the AYH Association, Delaplane, VA 22025.

*Let's Go: The Budget Guide to Europe.* Edited by Eric D. Goldstein. New York: E. P. Dutton, 1979. Published annually by the Harvard Student Agencies, this is an excellent guide for budget travelers, containing a good deal of information useful to bicyclists.

*Michelin Green Guides*. Published by Michelin and Co., Clermont Ferrand, France. The Green Guides are the most useful tour books for the bicyclist; those available in English cover Austria, Germany, Italy, Portugal, Spain, and Switzerland. Individual volumes for France cover the Châteaux of the Loire, Brittany, Pyrenees, Normandy, and Paris. All give geographical descriptions, sample routes, and the most detailed lists of important sites throughout the country as well as in the major cities.

# INDEX


accommodations, *see* camping; hostels; hotels; names of countries
Alliance International du Tourisme, 76
American Youth Hostel Association, 42, 44–45
Austria, 31, 37, 45, 51–53, 292–3; itinerary, 228–34
Austrian Automobile and Motorcycle Touring Club, 52

Belgium, 31, 37, 45, 53–54, 146, 293
Bicy-Club de France, 64
bicycle: adjusting, 85–87; checking, 30; five-speed, 130–1; shipping, 116–17, 147–9; purchasing, 145–7; ten-speed, 131–2; twelve- and fifteen-speed, 132–3
bicycle accessories and equipment, 140–5; kickstands, 141; lights, 140; locks, 141–2; packs, 157–61; sources of, 336–7; tire pumps, 141; toe clips, 140; tool kit, 144–5; trailers, 143–4; water bottles, 142–3
bicycle construction and parts, 133–40; brakes, 139; derailleurs, 138–9; fenders, 139–40; frame, 133–5; gearing, 127–33; handlebars, 136–7; saddle, 137–8; tires, 135–6
bicycle rental, 33, 292–331. *See also* names of countries
bicycle touring: age and, 15–16; diary of, 100–11; fatigue, 12–13; psychology of, 93–94. *See also* training and technique
*Bicycling!*, 16
Bike Tour France, 49
Biking Expedition tours, 46–47
British Cycling Federation, 42, 56
British Isles, 31, 54–62; accommodations, 57, 58, 59, 60–61, 192–3, 212–13; bike rental, 56, 60, 299–311; climate, 57, 58, 61; geography and roads, 54–56, 57–58, 59–60, 61; guided tours, 45, 46–48, 49; maps, 36–37, 56, 60, 188, 193, 208–9, 257; planned itineraries, 41–42, 188–97, 208–13. *See also* England; Ireland; Scotland; Wales

camping, 21, 23–25, 27, 32, 125–6, 142, 273–4, 338; documents, 24, 40–41; equipment, 161–6, 176–80
children, 16–17, 143–4
climate and weather, 31–32, 117–22, 276–80. *See also* names of countries
clothing, 118, 119, 121, 122, 150–5
Club Tamuré tours, 47
costs, 19–27, 37–38, 44, 48, 273–5; bike purchase, 146–7
Cyclists Touring Club, 41–42, 49, 56, 75
Czechoslovakia, 49

Denmark, 31, 76–78, 147, 204–8. *See also* Scandinavia

England, 54–57, 116, 146, 188–93, 256, 257–8. *See also* British Isles
Euro-Bike tours, 47–48

Federation Française de Cyclotourisme, 63–64
first-aid kit, 156–7
food, 15; equipment, 176–80; nutritional, 169–71; recipes, 175–6; schedule, 171–4; shopping for, 167–9
France, 31, 62–65, 116, 146; accommodations, 65, 187–8, 217–18, 241, 270–1; bike rental, 64, 294–5; climate, 65; geography and roads, 62–64; guided tours, 45, 46, 47, 48, 49; itineraries, 183–8, 213–18, 234–41, 258–69; maps, 64–65, 183, 213, 235, 258, 259, 261, 264, 265, 268

Germany, 37, 65–67, 116; accommodations, 25, 67, 227–8; bike rental, 66–67, 295–9; guided tours, 45, 47, 48; itinerary, 223–8

Great Britain, *see* British Isles
Greece, 32, 45, 67–68, 126, 241–7
group travel, 20, 21, 26–27, 94–96; guided tours, 43–49, 56, 281–2
guidebooks, 40
guided tours, *see* group travel

hills and mountains, 31, 111–17, 130–2
Holland, 31, 43, 69–71, 116, 146, 218–22; accommodations, 70, 222; bike rental, 70, 312–23; geography and roads, 69–70; guided tours, 45, 48
hostels, 21, 25–26, 27, 32, 42, 183, 275, 338–9. *See also* names of countries
hotels, 20–21, 22–23, 27, 183, 273–4. *See also* names of countries

International Bicycle Touring Society, 45–46, 52
International Camping Carnet, 24, 40
*International Youth Hostel Handbook*, 32, 40
Ireland, 31, 46, 47, 59–61, 323–30. *See also* British Isles
Italy, 71–73, 116, 126, 146, 198–203, 265–6; accommodations, 73, 203, 270, 271; itineraries, 198–203, 265–6; maps, 72–73, 197, 265
itinerary: daily, 182–3; guided tours, 43–49; prepared, 41–43, 282–6. *See also* names of countries

*Let's Go: Europe*, 40
Luxembourg, 37, 330

maps, 35–40, 332–5; terrain on, 111–12. *See also* names of countries

Netherlands, *see* Holland
National Campers and Hikers Association, 41
national tourist offices, 42, 56, 60, 64, 75, 76–77, 81, 82, 287–9
Norway, 78–79. *See also* Scandinavia

Out Spokin' tours, 48

Portugal, 32, 37, 73–74

rain, 13–14, 117–19
Raleigh Company of Ireland, 60
roads, *see* bicycle touring *and* names of countries

Scandinavia, 74–79, 330–1. *See also* Denmark; Norway; Sweden
Scotland, 46–47, 61–62, 208–13. *See also* British Isles
Spain, 31, 32, 37, 79–80, 116, 126, 146; accommodations, 80, 254, 270, 271; geography and roads, 79–80; itinerary, 247–54; maps, 80, 247, 259
Strichting Fiets!, 43, 69
Sweden, 31, 49, 74–76, 146. *See also* Scandinavia
Swedish Touring Club, 75–76
Swiss Touring Club, 81
Switzerland, 25, 31, 37, 80–82; guided tours, 45, 47, 48

toiletries, 155–6
Touring Club Italiano, 72–73
training and technique, 84–99; ankling, 88–89, 114; cadence, 90, 130; distance, 87–88; gear selection, 90, 114; group travel, 94–96; hills, 31, 111–17, 130–2; pacing, 91; rain, 117–19; riding positions, 90–91; road safety, 14–15, 122–5; shakedown trip, 99; weight, 98–99; women's, 96–98
trains, 20, 116–17

Wales, 57–59, 193–8. *See also* British Isles
weather, *see* climate and weather
weight, 98–99, 273–5
wind, 119–20
women, 96–98; clothing, 154–5

Yugoslavia, 82–83